Bibliotheca Britannica Philosophica

The Works of George Berkeley Bishop of Cloyne

Volume Eight

The Works of George Berkeley
Bishop of Cloyne

Edited by

A A Luce and T E Jessop

Volume Eight

Letters

Edited by

A A Luce DD LittD

Berkeley Professor of Metaphysics
Trinity College, Dublin

NELSON

THOMAS NELSON AND SONS LTD
36 Park Street London W1
Parkside Works Edinburgh 9
117 Latrobe Street Melbourne C1
10 Warehouse Road Apapa Lagos

THOMAS NELSON AND SONS (AFRICA) (Pty) LTD
P.O. Box 9881 Johannesburg

THOMAS NELSON AND SONS (CANADA) LTD
81 Curlew Drive Don Mills Ontario

THOMAS NELSON AND SONS
Copewood and Davis Streets Camden 3, N.J.

SOCIÉTÉ FRANÇAISE D'ÉDITIONS NELSON
97 rue Monge Paris 5

———

First published 1956
Reprinted 1964

PREFACE

THE collection and publication of Berkeley's letters began within thirteen years from his death, and has proceeded by stages. By the end of the eighteenth century some eighty-five letters of his were published, most of them addressed to Thomas Prior. In 1871 A. C. Fraser's *Life and Letters* raised this total to over one hundred and thirty. The present century has seen the total more than doubled, and the quality of the correspondence enriched ; but only now has collection caught up with publication. From the Egmont Papers Rand published the letters to Sir John Percival —a fine collection about equal in size to the Prior collection, and superior in quality and interest. I have found (if that is the word) some fifty new letters by Berkeley in various places, and have published most of them already in various periodicals. But scattered letters and scattered groups of letters are like stooks of corn out in the open field, of very little use to anybody. So now for the harvest home.

The present edition of the *Works* contains (so far as is known to me) a complete collection of the extant letters that Berkeley wrote. I have brought together all the letters previously published by Stock, Monck Berkeley, Fraser, Rand, myself, and others. Some few of them, because of their public character, have already been published in earlier volumes of this edition (see the list on page 18) ; the remaining letters, the great bulk of the collection, to the number of two hundred and seventy, are presented in this volume. I give without comment the text of all these letters, arranged in chronological order and numbered serially. My introduction deals with the history and contents of the letters, the principal correspondents, the autographs and subsidiary matters.

I should mention that Nos. 1, 4, 5, 6, 181, 249, and 250 came to light when the other letters were already in galley proof, and many months after my main editorial work of comment and annotation was done. The consequential task of altering the number series in text and notes has been heavy. I hope I have succeeded in eliminating all traces of the earlier number series ; but I can hardly hope to have detected and smoothed out all rough places in my notes, caused by the eleventh-hour discovery of these four early and important letters to Molyneux.

In Volume IX I have annotated every letter separately. I have begun each note with a brief statement on provenance and bibliographical fact. I have described, where necessary, Berkeley's situation at the time he wrote the letter. I have tried to elucidate obscure passages and phrases. I have sketched historical background, adding biographical notes on public personages and cross references to other letters.

I have not disfigured the text with reference signs. I do not think they are needed. Those who wish to read the text alone are much better without them, and those who are looking for comment, if they will open the two volumes and place them side by side, will find, I believe, that the notes speak for themselves, and do not require reference signs.

As regards the general lay-out I am well aware of the advantage of having text and notes under one cover ; but the large size of this correspondence makes the ideal arrangement here impracticable.

My thanks are due to the Delegates of the Clarendon Press for permission to reproduce letters by Berkeley from A. C. Fraser's *Life and Letters of George Berkeley, D.D.* (1871) ; to the Cambridge University Press for a similar courtesy in respect of B. Rand's *Berkeley and Percival* ; to the editor of *Hermathena* and to the Royal Irish Academy for permission to include those letters that from time to time they have published for me ; to Dr. E. St. John Brooks for drawing my attention to the Molyneux letters, and to the Mayor and Corporation of Southampton for permission to publish them ; and lastly to Mr. H. J. Cadbury of Harvard University Library for telling me of the two letters to Dr. Bearcroft, the Secretary of the Society for the Propagation of the Gospel.

In the micro-film hunt for material I have received invaluable assistance from the National Library, Dublin, and from Dr. Hayes, the learned Librarian.

In compiling my notes I have received help, here gratefully acknowledged, from several of my colleagues, from the late Provost E. H. Alton, Professor J. E. L. Oulton, Professor H. M. O. White, Professor Constantia Maxwell, Professor T. W. Moody, Professor J. A. Coutts, Professor D. A. Webb, Professor H. W. Parke, Professor G. V. Jourdan, Dr. R. B. McDowell, and Dr. A. J. Lventhal.

CONTENTS

LIST OF ABBREVIATIONS

AD   *Alumni Dublinenses*, edd. G. D. Burtchaell and T. U. Sadleir, Dublin 1935

ALS   Autograph letter, signed

Brady   W. M. Brady, *Clerical and parochial Records of Cork, Cloyne and Ross*, 1863

Ball   F. Elrington Ball, *The Correspondence of Jonathan Swift, D.D.*, London, 1910

BM   British Museum

DNB   *Dictionary of National Biography*

EP   The Egmont Papers, now in the Public Record Office, London

Life   A. A. Luce, *The Life of George Berkeley*, Edinburgh 1949

LL   A. C. Fraser, *Life and Letters of George Berkeley, D.D.*, Oxford 1871

Monck Berkeley = George Monck Berkeley, *Literary Relics containing original Letters* . . . 1789

PC   Berkeley's *Philosophical Commentaries* (the references are to the entry numbers in my *editio diplomatica*, 1944)

PRIA   *Proceedings of the Royal Irish Academy*

RBP   B. Rand, *Berkeley and Percival*, Cambridge 1914

SPCK   Society for Promoting Christian Knowledge

SPG   Society for the Propagation of the Gospel

Stock   Stock, *An Account of the Life of George Berkeley* . . ., prefixed to the 1784 edn. of the *Works*, together with extracts from his letters

TCD   Trinity College, Dublin

EDITOR'S INTRODUCTION

BERKELEY'S career was colourful, and he lived in stirring times. His letters reflect the interest both of his life and of the times. In a few of the earlier letters he appears as the philosopher, as also in the two important letters to Johnson published in an earlier volume of this edition[1]; but for the most part he writes as the man of action and affairs, as the traveller who twice crossed the Alps in mid-winter, and as the influential statesman-philanthropist who piloted through Parliament a far-sighted measure for the benefit of the American colonies, and himself crossed the Atlantic to carry it into effect. He lived through days of war with France and Spain, through the days of Marlborough's victories and the Tory Peace. He watched the British Empire expand after Utrecht. Twice he saw the Protestant Succession challenged. Twice he saw Scotland aflame and Ireland ready to catch fire. The 'Fifteen he watched from his London lodgings, the 'Forty-five from his episcopal palace at Cloyne, and of both risings he wrote at the time in his letters.

More than two hundred and eighty letters of his, private and public, survive. They cover most of his mature life with but few gaps, and are distributed fairly evenly over more than forty years. The earliest was written in 1709, when he was a Junior Fellow of Trinity College, Dublin, of two years' standing; the latest in 1752, a few months before his death. Many of the letters are of a purely private character, and their interest is personal and biographical. A few are addressed to the public. A good number deal with public matters, and often there is public interest in what he wrote on private matters; for Berkeley was a public-minded man, a man of wide outlook, concerned for the public weal; he had influential friends in high stations, and he lived and thought in the spirit of his motto: *non sibi, sed toti.*

The problems of the Peace and the Protestant Succession during the years 1713–15 furnish the high-light of the period, and occasioned and provoked a fine series of Berkeley's letters (Nos.

---

[1] VOL. II, pp. 279 ff.

26–59). Queen Anne is sick, is dying, and the Succession is in
doubt ; the parties struggle, politicians trim, and the people's
mood is uncertain. And now King George has succeeded to the
vacant throne ; but can he hold it ? The answer was not given
finally until the Highlands had risen, and their rising had been
crushed. Throughout this anxious period Berkeley corresponded
regularly with his friend, Sir John Percival. Percival was in
Ireland, and he needed reliable news and comment. Berkeley
was in London, and could supply the news and comment. Both
young men were vitally concerned. Percival had Whig sympathies ; he had inherited from his father, who had served in
Ireland under Cromwell, large estates in County Cork, and he
could not hope to keep them if the Jacobite cause prevailed.
Berkeley had Tory sympathies ; his grandfather had suffered for
King Charles I ; in Church matters Berkeley, like Swift, was
definitely a Tory ; but he was a ' Hanoverian Tory ' with the
accent on *Hanoverian* ; that is, he was a loyal Protestant, who
placed first the Protestant Succession and the House of Hanover.

Berkeley had a High-Tory friend, he says, who served him as
' a political weather glass. When his spirits were high I concluded our affairs went wrong, and the contrary when they were
low.' The metaphor well describes his own letters to Percival
of this period ; they form a political barometer ; and in the
autumn of 1715 when the climax came, and suspense was at its
height, and Percival was in Dublin and Berkeley at the hub of
affairs in London, Berkeley's letters are a very sensitive barometer, registering accurately from day to day and week to week
the hopes and fears of Whig and Tory, the rise and the fall of
Jacobite fortunes.

Berkeley left Ireland for the first time early in 1713, and
went to London. He was a social success at once. Presented at
Court, he was admitted into the inner circle of wits and writers,
and of statesmen who had learned recently the political value
of the pen. The excitement of his new surroundings shows in his
letters to Percival, which are full and frequent, lively and des-
criptive. ' Caressed,' like Swift, by both Whigs and Tories, he
had friends in both camps, and he watched intelligently every
turn in the struggle of parties, and reported to Percival. He
dined with Dr. Arbuthnot, author, court physician, and his ' first
proselyte ' to immaterialism, at his lodging in the Queen's Palace.
On the day that the Peace was proclaimed, instead of dining
with the Tories who made the peace, he dined with Whigs at

Dr. Garth's and drank the health of the Duke of Marlborough. Another day he breakfasted at Swift's lodgings, and Addison joined them (what a constellation of talent !) ; and Berkeley draws the inference that a coalition is being mooted. He was particularly intimate with Sir Richard Steele, and wrote twelve essays for him in the *Guardian*, receiving for each ' a guinea and a supper.' The most vivid description in these letters (Nos. 31, 32) is of the memorable ' first night ' of Addison's *Cato* at Drury Lane, on 14 April 1713. Berkeley and two or three friends were in a side box with Addison, and they had a table and two or three flasks of burgundy and champagne, ' with which the author (who is a very sober man) thought it necessary to support his spirits . . .' Harley was in the next box, and clapped as loud as any. There was some hissing at Pope's prologue, but the clap got much the better of the hiss.

Pope, who credited Berkeley with ' every virtue under heaven' ; Bishop Atterbury, who praised his angelic blend of understanding, learning, innocence, and humility ; Bolingbroke, philosopher and statesman who backed the wrong horse ; the Earl of Pembroke, formerly Lord Lieutenant of Ireland, patron of two philosophical classics, Locke's *Essay* and Berkeley's *Principles*—these and many other men of note may be met in Berkeley's letters.

After a summer holiday at Oxford and an eight-month trip to France and Italy as chaplain to the Earl of Peterborough, who had been sent as ambassador to the King of Sicily, Berkeley settled for a while in England, and during the critical summer and autumn of 1715 he wrote letters of outstanding interest. In July he was in Gloucestershire, and saw with his own eyes the shadow of things to come ; he witnessed (or heard of it at first hand) the pulling down of the meeting-houses at Gloucester ; from an eye-witness he heard of the rioting and bloodshed at Birmingham ; twenty thousand men there were ' ready to take arms against the Government.' His somewhat appreciative report of these incidents brought on his head a stern rebuke from Percival, and he took the rebuke to heart, and realised that the public situation was serious, and that sectional interests must be subordinated to the public weal. He published anonymously his *Advice to the Tories who have taken the Oaths* (see Vol. VI, pp. 53–8). He reminded the Tories of the oaths of loyalty they had taken, and told them bluntly that if they were false to those oaths, they would dishonour their Church, encourage her enemies, and give occasion for scandal.

On his return to London he gathered information on the great question of the hour, and during the anxious months of September and October he sent Percival well-informed bulletins regularly, which with the letters already mentioned constitute an exciting record (Nos. 51–59) of the rising as seen from London.

The Earl of Peterborough, his former chief, has left the country on the King's pass. The Duke of Ormonde has fled the country —a painful reflection for Berkeley ; for the Ormonde name and fame dominated his birthplace, Kilkenny, as the Ormonde Castle towers dominated his school, Kilkenny College, at the bend of the River Nore. And Ormonde had been, like his grandfather immediately before him, for more than a quarter of a century Chancellor of Dublin University. Whatever Berkeley's feelings were about it, he hides them ; he was present in the House for the impeachment, and reports the debate dispassionately. He announces the movements of the loyal generals, Argyle, Sutherland, and Roxburgh ; and he has himself seen letters from the French Regent and the young King of France containing assurances of friendship for the House of Hanover. The general uncertainty and the fear of treachery are illustrated by a curious little piece of personal observation ; Berkeley tells Percival how he had himself overheard a suspicious-looking person, a Jacobite agent, discussing hereditary right with a sentry on duty in St. James's Park. The tone of the letters varies from week to week, and swings like a pendulum from optimism to pessimism and back. One week the Government is well-prepared, and is acting with decision. The Dutch troops are coming. Lord Landsdowne and Sir William Wyndham have been arrested ; this suspect and that have been laid by the heels. Next week, No ! The rebels are advancing ; the Dutch troops will be too late. No one knows whom to trust. The general bent of the people is toward Jacobitism ; ' the scene every day opening and discovering new cause to apprehend a popish power, and all the dismal consequences of it.' The best course is to take ship to the Mascarenes (the islands in the Indian Ocean, now Mauritius, Reunion, and Rodriguez) ; ' for I assure you I ever did and ever shall abhor a Popish government.' Thus at the end of October hope has almost fled, and fear prevails ; but early in November the gloom lightens ; ' the enemies of our Constitution hang down their heads,' and with dramatic suddenness on 17 November the skies clear, and Berkeley gives his friends in Ireland joy ' of the victory which his Majesty's forces have gained over the rebels in Preston.'

I have surveyed this early portion of the correspondence at some length ; for no other part is so closely packed with dramatic interest. The Bermuda scheme, however, launched in 1723 with letter No. 85 and closing with No. 152, written in 1731 on the eve of the departure from Rhode Island, contains drama of its own, the drama of empire knit with the central drama of Berkeley's personal life. Here is a slow-moving epic, written around the theme, ' Westward the course of empire takes its way.' The drama is of eight years' duration, and demands a sustained effort on the reader's part, rewarding the effort with an insight into the shaping of Britain's colonial policy in the early days of her empire-building. Here, like alternating currents, are the competing views of shortsighted politicians, blind to all but trade, seeking the profits of empire without its claims and duties, and here are the views of far-seeing statesmen who thought of empire in terms of stewardship, and accepted responsibility for the moral and spiritual welfare of the Plantations.

The story of the Deanery of Derry and the romance of Vanessa's legacy may be read as episodes in this drama. Berkeley at any rate took them as ' providential ' events enabling him to answer the call and fulfil his mission. The business letters to Prior need not detain the reader, but in the others of this period, mark the steps by which Berkeley raised a private missionary venture to the rank of national enterprise, considered and approved by King and Parliament. The letters come from both sides of the Atlantic ; and those from America contain sketches of colonial life, and illustrate the conflict of the sects and the growth of the spirit of tolerance.

Berkeley was a traveller in his young days and in his middle life ; and the charm of his correspondence traces in part to the quick change of scene and viewpoint. He writes now from Dublin, now from London, now from Paris and now from Rome. Here are letters from sunny Naples, and from the Isle of Ischia, and from Sicily. Then the scene changes to Ireland once again, and for some years Berkeley lives a shuttlecock life between Dublin and London. Then he crosses the ocean, and for three years his letters are dated from Rhode Island. This stir and bustle and movement *end* with his appointment to the bishopric of Cloyne ; for eighteen years he remained in Ireland, and only twice or thrice (it seems) during his episcopate did he leave his diocese. The quiet of Cloyne is reflected in the calm of his letters. He is still in touch by post with English bishops and he writes on English politics. He is still concerned about education in distant America and the affairs of Harvard and Yale ; but now his chief secular concerns are his family and friends, the relief of local distress, the promotion of Irish industry, and the prevention and cure of plague and sickness.

Of the letters themselves from the Cloyne period there is little to say. Berkeley kept up with all his old correspondents, Prior and Percival and Johnson, and added new friends, chief of whom was Isaac Gervais, his neighbour at Lismore and, later, Dean of Tuam, whose gay French wit won from his friend several sparkling little letters, light and bright, containing memorable phrases. To this period belongs what, to me, is the gem of Berkeley's letters (No. 258), the note he sent to Bishop Benson telling of the death of his young son, William, ' whose loss at an early age was thought to have stuck too close to his father's heart ' (Stock). As a Christian expression of parental love and longing his words are unsurpassed. May I conclude this survey by quoting them :

I was a man retired from the amusement of politics, visits, and what the world calls pleasure. I had a little friend, educated always under mine own eye, whose painting delighted me, whose music ravished me, and whose lively, gay spirit was a continual feast. It has pleased God to take him hence. God, I say, in mercy hath deprived me of this pretty, gay plaything. His parts and person, his innocence and piety, his particularly uncommon affection for me, had gained too much upon me. Not content to be fond of him, I was vain of him. I had set my heart too much upon him—more perhaps than I ought to have done upon anything in this world.

Thus much suffer me, in the overflowings of my soul, to say to your Lordship, who, though distant in place, are much nearer my heart than any of my neighbours.

The style of the letters hardly calls for comment. Few, if any, of the private letters are studied, or even tidied. Berkeley wrote to his friends, just as he spoke to them, in plain, straightforward English, with occasionally a striking phrase. His epistolary style, if he can be said to have had such a thing, was not distinguished ; you would not, I think, notice it ; yet analyse any of his ordinary sentences ; taste the words, and repeat them sotto voce, and you will notice unconscious felicities, as if Berkeley without bestowing conscious care on what he wrote instinctively selected ' the proper word for the proper place,' and savoured it and listened to its sound. He is sincere with his pen, but rarely is he clever. His correspondents, except Gervais, would not have appreciated cleverness. Prior and Percival were not the sort of men to draw out his powers. The letters to Gervais are witty, and the philosophical letters to Johnson are dignified ; but there is nothing in Berkeley's correspondence to match the epistolary brilliance of some of Swift's letters, such as his letter to Lord Carteret on Berkeley's Bermuda scheme. I should add, as I have made the comparison, that Berkeley's epistolary style, if it never rises to the heights with Swift, never falls to the depths touched in some of Swift's letters.

History of the Letters

When for any length of time Berkeley was absent from either Prior or Percival he wrote to them fairly regularly, and they kept his letters or copies of them. Eighty-eight letters to Prior survive, and ninety-three to Percival, covering a period of about thirty-eight years in both cases. After his return from America Berkeley wrote to Johnson once or twice a year, and twelve letters survive. From Cloyne he wrote often to Gervais, and seventeen of the letters survive. For some years he corresponded at intervals with Pope, with Archdeacon (afterwards Bishop) Benson, and with Bishop Gibson of London, and we have a few of these letters. He wrote to his brothers, but not a single letter to any member of his family survives. He wrote to Swift, and Swift to him, but not a line from the one great Irishman to the other is known to survive. The tragedy of this literary loss is all the more tragic because someone only forty years ago had two autograph letters from Berkeley to Swift, and photographs of the signatures are on a plate in *Dean Swift*, by Sophie Silleto Smith.[1] No doubt the letters are extant still, but I have failed to trace them. After Prior's death Mervyn Archdale, then a young clergyman, took his place, and did Berkeley's Dublin business, and half a dozen letters of small importance from Berkeley to Archdale have come down to us.

The collecting and publication of Berkeley's letters began soon after his death along with the early memoirs. *Life* and *Letters* go together as a rule, and in this case they grew together. The account of Berkeley in the *Biographia Britannica*[2] contains extracts from his letters to Pope (Nos. 46, 50, 67) that had appeared

---

[1] London 1910, facing p. 128.
[2] 1766, VOL. VI, Part ii.

in Pope's published correspondence. Kippis's edition of the *Biographia* (1780) gives longer extracts from the letters to Pope, and adds the letter to Arbuthnot on the eruption of Vesuvius that had been already published in the *Transactions* of the Royal Society.[1] Joseph Stock, a Fellow of Trinity College, Dublin, afterwards Bishop of Killala, in 1776 published a *Life* of Berkeley that is almost identical with the account in Kippis's edition and not so very different from the account in the edition of 1766. Stock was in touch with the Berkeley family, and was probably responsible for all this early biographical work, though he kept in the background. It is morally certain, too, that he was the editor of the quarto edition of the *Works* (1784) to which is prefixed 'An account of his life and several of his letters.'[2] The *Advertisement* thanks 'the Rev. Mervyn Archdall, rector of Attannah, Ossory, and the Rev. Henry Gervais, L.L.D. archdeacon of Cashel, for their obliging communication of the letters to Thomas Prior, Esq., and Dean Gervais, which have added so much to the value of this edition.' Thus was launched the first collection of any size. The edition gives extracts with dates from seventy of the letters to Prior, and a much smaller number of letters to Pope, Arbuthnot, Archdale, and Gervais.

Five years later the Prior collection was given to the public in a much fuller form by George Monck Berkeley, the Bishop's grandson. His *Literary Relics* (London 1789) contains eighty-five letters by Berkeley, dated and printed in full; seventy-nine of them are addressed to Prior, two to Archdale, one each to Pope and Arbuthnot, and two to the public. Monck Berkeley says that he printed from the originals, and that he had them 'from my friend, Mr. Archdale, the learned author of the *Monasticon Hibernicum* etc.,' adding that some extracts from them had been prefixed to the quarto edition of the *Works*.

There for ninety years the publication of Berkeley's letters rested; the next advance came in 1871 with the publication of A. C. Fraser's *Life and Letters*. Fraser reprinted those that had already appeared, with the addition of the letters to Johnson and a few others mostly from America, making a total of about one hundred and thirty-three.[3]

The twentieth century has seen the correspondence greatly

---

[1] The letter is published in Vol. IV of the present edition, p. 247.

[2] For the evidence as to editorship, see my *Life*, pp. 14, 15.

[3] The letter from a George Berkeley printed by Fraser on p. 93 has been proved, I am thankful to say, not to be by our George Berkeley.

increased in size and enriched in quality. The number of letters has been more than doubled, and the new letters are on the whole more interesting than the old. B. Rand's search in the Egmont Papers added eighty-nine letters by Berkeley, and my searches there and elsewhere added another fifty letters or more. The main addition is that of the Percival correspondence, which moves on a higher plane of thought than the Prior correspondence, and in a more interesting *milieu*.

The Egmont Papers, now deposited in the Public Record Office, London, are a large collection of documents, made originally by Sir John Percival as material for the family history he published in 1742, *A genealogical History of the House of Yvery*. The collection includes original letters, copies of letters sent and received, accounts, reports from land agents, occasional papers, such as Percival's memorandum on the question of a national bank for Ireland, autobiographical notes, his Journal, etc. Pictures of local conditions in the south of Ireland can be reconstructed from these documents, and they become of special interest at the time of the Jacobite rebellion of 1745. For us the focus of interest is the Berkeley-Percival correspondence. The Seventh Report of the Royal Commission on Historical Manuscripts, pp. 232-49, and the Report on the Manuscripts of the Earl of Egmont by the Manuscript Commission in 1909, contain an account of the collection and extracts from it. A. C. Fraser had access to part of the collection, and he made some use of it in his *Berkeley* (Blackwood, 1881) and in the Memoir prefixed to his 1901 edition of the *Works*. B. Rand in his invaluable *Berkeley and Percival* (Cambridge 1914) gives most of the letters that passed between the two friends. I found a few that had escaped his notice, and published them in *Hermathena*[1] and in *Proceedings of the Royal Irish Academy*.[2]

AUTOGRAPH LETTERS

Some forty autograph signed letters are known to be extant, and I have given particulars of most of them in T. E. Jessop's *Bibliography of George Berkeley* (1934), pp. 92-3 ; to that list should be added the originals of No. 139, a very interesting and well-preserved autograph that came recently on the London market, and is now in Berkeley College, Yale, and of No. 181, recently found in the Diocesan Office, Dublin. The autographs are widely

[1] VOL. XXIII (1933).　　[2] VOLS. XLI (1932-4), C. 4 and XLII (1934-5), C. 6.

scattered ; some few are in the Berkeley Papers in the British
Museum ; some are in the Library of Trinity College, Dublin ;
some are in the Egmont Papers in the Public Record Office,
London ; some are in America in seats of learning and in private
collections. In my notes on the letters (Vol. IX) the bibliographical particulars about each autograph are prefixed.

The original collections, I think, have been dispersed. In
the Percival collection the great majority of Berkeley's letters are
in copy only. The Prior collection ought to have survived as such,
one would think, but the great majority of the originals have
long been lost to sight. In 1789 Monck Berkeley ' received '
them, he says, from Archdale ; if he gave them back, one would
expect to find them treasured in one of the branches of the
Archdale family. I have made inquiries from several members
of that family, and they know nothing of the letters. If, on the
other hand, Monck Berkeley kept them (as perhaps Mervyn
Archdale meant him to do), they should have passed into his
mother's hands, and so, with the other documentary relics of the
Bishop, into the Berkeley Papers, now in the British Museum.
In point of fact two or three of the autographs to Prior are there,
and the presumption is that the remainder were there, too, at
one time.

BERKELEY'S PRINCIPAL CORRESPONDENTS

THOMAS PRIOR.[1]   Prior was born *c.* 1679 at Rathdowney, and
died 21 October 1751 in Dublin. He was at school and college
with Berkeley, and though not a qualified lawyer he seems to have
acted in some legal capacity in Dublin. He was Berkeley's
Dublin agent, and was almost his *alter ego*. Berkeley wishes to
rent a house in Dublin. Prior makes inquiries and takes it. A
book is to be bought, a manuscript seen through the press ;
Prior attends to it. The complex and lengthy business of the
Vanessa legacy was managed (or mismanaged) by Prior working
on a commission basis. He set the lands of the Deanery, and
collected rents ; he received and made payments on Berkeley's
behalf, was his land-agent, secretary, and banker. Once a year
Prior went south to visit his own estates at Rathvilly, and he
usually went on to Cloyne. ' We think we have an annual right
in you,' wrote Berkeley (No. 197). There is no mention of a
marriage, and Prior seems to have been wedded to his work

---

[1] For a sketch of the life of Prior, see the notice of him in Stock's quarto
edition of the *Works*, VOL. I, p. xxviii.

for the welfare, social and industrial, of his country. He was prominent in the group of Dublin philanthropists who followed the precepts of Molyneux and Swift, and laboured to improve the lot of the Irish people. He was one of the founders of the Dublin Society, and was its first secretary, and through his friend the Earl of Chesterfield, Lord Lieutenant of Ireland, he secured for the Society, now the Royal Dublin Society, a royal charter and a grant of public money.[1] In their endeavours for the benefit of the public health, he and Berkeley were hand-in-glove ; they pool their information ; they exchange notes on remedies, and in the tar-water campaign Prior was Berkeley's lieutenant and chief of staff. Prior advertised for testimony to the value of the remedy in answer to the affidavits from Steevens' Hospital,[2] and published a summary of the results in his *Authentick Narrative of the Success of Tar-water* (Dublin 1746). Another publication of his had considerable vogue and influence, viz. his *List of the Absentees of Ireland* . . . 1729. Thomas Prior has two monuments, the Royal Dublin Society, in its infancy ' his darling child,' and the monument in stone erected by public subscription at the south-west entrance to Christ Church Cathedral, Dublin ; its Latin epitaph was composed by Berkeley,[3] and its terms are a fine and well-deserved tribute to a self-effacing patriot, ' qui, cum prodesse mallet quam conspici . . . rem publicam mirifice auxit et ornavit auspiciis, consiliis, labore indefesso.'

SIR JOHN PERCIVAL.[4] Sir John Percival, created (a) Baron Percival of Burton, 21 April 1715, and (b) Earl of Egmont 1733, was born 12 July 1683. His father served in Ireland under Cromwell, and after acquiring estates in County Cork, died young. *His* elder son Edward died 9 November 1691, and his younger son John succeeded to the title and the estates. Sir John, after two years at Oxford (1699–1701), toured England and the Continent.[5] He came to Ireland in May 1708, intending to spend the next winter in County Cork ; we find him in Dublin on 29 November at a house in Capel Street that he owned. About

---

[1] See No. 223n.
[2] See No. 219n.
[3] See No. 263n.
[4] I have followed Rand's spelling of the name. The eighteenth-century mural tablets of the family in St. Michan's, Dublin, spell it *Perceval*. Berkeley's Dedication spells it *Percivale*. I have met eight or nine variants.
[5] There is an account by him of his life up to 1726 on a loose sheet of paper in the Egmont Papers, VOL. CI ; see also VOL. CXXVII, p. 195.

this time he met Berkeley, and a warm friendship destined to last a lifetime rapidly sprang up. To Percival Berkeley dedicated his first great work, *The New Theory of Vision* (1709), and the Dedication speaks of ' these few months that I have the honour to be known to you,' praising in the fulsome manner of dedications Percival's virtue and good sense, his love of country, his religion and his learning. The regard was mutual, and in one of the earliest passages in the Egmont Papers to mention Berkeley, Percival has written the note, ' Mr. Berkeley, Fellow of Dublin College, now Bishop of Cloyne, 1736. A man of the noblest virtues, best learning I ever knew.'

In the early days of the friendship Percival is something of an Irish patriot, defending the rights of the country of his adoption against British exploitation ; later in life the green strain faded, and he became the absentee landlord, occasionally visiting his estates in County Cork and his house in Dublin, but normally residing at his house in Pall Mall or at his villa Charlton near Greenwich. He thought of Ireland as his country, and for a time he took part in Irish politics, but gradually English affairs took pride of place with him.

The language of the letters on both sides is rather stiff and formal, and almost always unemotional. Yet the two friends were on terms of intimacy, and occasionally the affection shows. They lent money to one another ; they advised on one another's projects, and Percival's houses were Berkeley's homes. Percival subscribed to the Bermuda scheme, and at one time had thoughts of accompanying his friend. Percival received his earldom for his humanitarian work in connection with the debtors' prisons, and the consequential task of providing for released debtors led him and Oglethorpe to plan the Georgia settlement that for a time and in some measure ran in competition with Berkeley's educational scheme.

Lady Percival, daughter of Sir Philip Parker, appears in the early days of the correspondence (Nos. 11 and 21) as a young bride ready to join issue with the philosopher about immaterialism ; she was ever his good friend, and her interest with the Duchess of Grafton helped to make him Dean of Derry.

The Earl's son John, later the second Earl, was elected Member of Parliament for Westminster in 1741. He was heir to the friendship, too, and he and his lady visited Cloyne when they came over to see their Irish estates. Several letters to him from Berkeley survive, and to him Berkeley wrote on 14 May 1748, a fortnight after the first Earl's death (No. 252), congratulating him on succeeding to the earldom, and condoling with him ' on the death of a father who honoured me with his friendship for about forty years, and whose life adorned every part of that private path he chose to walk in.'

SAMUEL JOHNSON. Samuel Johnson (1696–1772) was Berkeley's best friend in America, and a man of some importance in the history of American education and American philosophy. Twelve of Berkeley's letters to him survive ; the first two, with Johnson's letters that evoked them, are of interest to philosophers, and they are printed in Vol. II of the present edition [1] ; the rest are mainly of a personal character, and, on Berkeley's side, were prompted by his desire to foster university education in America, and, especially, to keep in touch with Yale.

Son of a Congregationalist minister at Guildford, Conn., Johnson was educated at Saybrook, and he became a tutor at Yale. At first he served in the Congregationalist Church ; then with Cutler and Brown and Wetmore he joined the Anglican Church. He was ordained in England (1722–23), and was appointed minister at Stratford, Conn. He paid several visits to Berkeley in Rhode Island, and the friendship lasted for life, and was continued in the persons of their sons, Canon George Berkeley and William S. Johnson. Johnson made a name for himself as a scholar and philosopher. Jonathan Edwards was among his pupils. In 1743 Oxford conferred upon him the degree of Doctor of Divinity, and in 1754 he was appointed President of King's College.[2] Nine years later he resigned, and resumed his cure at Stratford. His publications include *Elementa philosophica* (1752), which is dedicated to Berkeley ; his autobiography contains interesting comments on Berkeley's visit to America ; it is published along with his other writings and a full account of his life in the four volumes of *Samuel Johnson* by H. and C. Schneider (New York 1929).

ISAAC GERVAIS. Isaac Gervais (*c.* 1680–1756), born at Montpelier of Huguenot stock, was brought as a child from France on the revocation of the Edict of Nantes 1685. His parents settled in the south of Ireland, He entered Trinity College 1694, and graduated B.A. 1700. He became Vicar-Choral of Lismore 1708,

[1] pp. 271–94.
[2] See No. 254*n*.

Prebendary of Lismore 1723, and Dean of Tuam 1743, His son (who was Archdeacon of Cashel from 1772 to 1790) lent to Stock the letters Berkeley wrote to his father.

Gervais enters the correspondence in 1738, and Berkeley's letters to him soon grow intimate ; they are, many of them, bright and lively, and interspersed with jests on Gervais's Gascon extraction, his ' Castle-hunting,' [1] and his gout and gay life. Gervais appears in Prior's *Authentick Narrative* as a strong supporter of tar-water.

MERVYN ARCHDALE.   Mervyn Archdale (Archdall, 1723–91) author of *Monasticon Hibernicum*, 1786, entered Trinity College, Dublin, 1739, and graduated B.A. 1744.   He was domestic Chaplain to Bishop Pococke, who gave him the living of Attanagh. He enters the correspondence on the death of Prior, with whose family he was connected ; and he attended to Berkeley's Dublin business, as Prior had done.   The original letters to Prior were in his possession, and he is thanked by Stock in 1784, and by Monck Berkeley in 1789 for the loan or gift of them.

The great majority of the letters were first published at various periods from autographs that no longer exist or are no longer accessible.   To restore their original orthography is impossible. To modernise throughout would be pointless, and I have left their spelling and punctuation, for the most part, in the form in which the letters have come down to us.   Nos. 1, 4, 5, 6, 139, 181, 203 being specimens of Berkeley's early style and later style, are here printed exactly as they appear in their autographs.

[1] See No. 269n.

LIST OF BERKELEY'S LETTERS
CONTAINED IN THIS VOLUME

LIST OF BERKELEY'S LETTERS
PRINTED IN OTHER VOLUMES
OF THIS EDITION

Two letters to Samuel Johnson on philosophical topics, dated 25 Nov.
1729 and 24 Mar. 1730 : in VOL. II, pp. 279–83 and 292–4.

A letter to Arbuthnot on the eruption of Vesuvius, dated 17 Apr. 1717,
and published in the *Transactions of the Royal Society* : in VOL. IV, pp.
247 ff.

A letter to Prior on the petrifications of Lough Neagh, dated 20 May
1746, the concluding paragraphs being added from Berkeley's letter
to Dr. John Fothergill dated Dublin, 8 Aug. 1746 : in VOL. IV, pp.
251 ff.

A letter on earthquakes, published in *The Gentleman's Magazine*,
xx (1750), p. 166 ; in VOL. IV, pp. 255 ff.

Several of Berkeley's published writings on tar-water, which are in
letter form, namely, *A Letter to T. P. Esq. from the Author of Siris* (1744),
A Second Letter to Thomas Prior Esq. on the Virtues of Tar-water (1746),
*A Letter from the Author of Siris to Thomas Prior Esq. concerning the Usefulness
of Tar-water in the Plague* (1747), *Two Letters from the Right Reverend
Dr. George Berkeley . . . the one to Thomas Prior Esq. concerning the Usefulness of Tar-water in the Plague, the other to the Rev. Dr. Hales on the benefit
of Tar-water in Fevers . . .* (1747), and a public letter on tar-water
published in the *Dublin Journal*, 8–12 May 1744 : all in VOL. V.

A public letter, addressed to ' A. B. Esq.', on a National Bank, published
in the *Dublin Journal*, March 1737 : in VOL. VI, pp. 185–7.

Two letters on the occasion of the Jacobite Rebellion, 1745, one to the
clergy, the other to the Roman Catholics, of his diocese, both published
in the *Dublin Journal*, 15–19 Oct. 1745 : in VOL. VI, pp. 227–30.

A letter to Sir John James, dated 7 June 1741, on the Roman Controversy : in VOL. VII, pp. 143–55.

Burton Augt. 1. 1709

Dr. Molyneux.

Had any thing happend in this place that I could have thought worth imparting to You, You should have heard from Me before now.   But nothing of that Moment occurd.   My Business here has been little else than eating drinking sleeping discoursing & variously sporting to pass away the Time.   My Curiosity has not led Me to make any diligent Search after the Antiquities or other Observables that may possibly be here aboutt tho I believe there are not many, So that You must not expec. any thing from Me, that may lead to the Illustration of Naturall History.   T'other day Mr Clerk & I viewd the Monastery of Buttefont, which is reported to have been formerly a place of great Note, tho now I could perceive nothing remarkable in it except some Remains of painting in Fresco which gives Me but a low Idea of the skill of the antient Irish in that Art.   There are also a great Number of Skulls & dead mens Bones pild up in a very regular Manner, which for the Odness of it gave Me some surprise.   The Building is in all Respects as large and magnificent as could be expected from the Irish before they were civilizd.   There is likewise upon Sir John's Estate a Castle named Liscarol, which in the War of 41 was greatly distinguished : it has a large oblong Court consisting of a High & Thick Wall with four regular Turrets.   But what is most remarkable is, That at some Fields Distance from the Castle a Countrey Man shewd Us the Entrance into a Cave which seems to be the Work of Nature ; He told Us it reachd all the Way to the Castle, and was usd as a Sally Port by the beseigd in 41.   I had not the Courage to go into it for Fear of a Damp.   If You have any News any Objections or Thoughts relating to the Essay of Vision or can give Me an Acct of what others You converse with, think of it, or any thing else You'l please to inform Me of.   I shall gladly hear from You.   Remember me to all Friends.

I am. Your affect. Frd & Servt,

GEOR: BERKELEY.

Enclose Your Letter in a Cover to Sir John at Burton near Charleville.

2 TO PERCIVAL

Trinity College, Dublin, 22nd Sept. 1709

Dear Sir,

I am sorry to hear from Dan Dering that you have lost your statues, medals, &c. that you had coming from Italy ; though on second thoughts I almost doubt whether it may be reckoned a loss. Nobody purchases a cabinet of rarities to please himself with the continual light of them, nothing in it being of any farther use to the owner than as it entertains his friends ; but I question if your neighbours in the county of Cork would relish that sort of entertainment. To feed their eyes with the sight of rusty medals and antique statues would (if I mistake not) seem to them something odd and insipid. The finest collection is not worth a groat where there is no one to admire and set a value on it, and our country seems to me the place in the world which is least furnished with virtuosi.

I have Sir, all the engagements in the world to think myself concerned in anything that in my apprehension may promote your interest. This it is that makes me pretend to advise you, how ill soever that office may become me. There is a person whose acquaintance and conversation I do earnestly recommend unto you as a thing of the greatest advantage : you will be surprised when I tell you it is yourself. Believe me, I am convinced there is nothing else wanting to complete your happiness, so much as a little more satisfaction in your own company, which might provoke you to spend regularly and constantly two or three hours of the morning in study and retirement. I do not take upon me to prescribe what you shall employ yourself about. I only propose the passing two or three hours of the twenty-four in private ; and as for the subject of your reading or meditation I leave that to your own judgment. I have observed in you that you seem to prefer the improving ones self by conversation before private study. This proceeds either from an over modest opinion of your own parts (which fault I know is very incident to you) or else from a belief that the latter is not so profitable and pleasant as is pretended. For my part I am of a different opinion ; and if you will shew that regard for my judgment as to follow it in these two points, you will both do me a great honour and lay a new obligation on me, the most acceptable of all other.

I would not be thought to question your inclination for reading. Whoever has the happiness of any degree of your acquaintance cannot but know you are conversant in books far above the ordinary rate of gentlemen of your rank, but this is what I am earnest with you for, viz. a fixt and settled method of study. And I press it the more earnestly at this time, because if you do not enter upon it before you marry it will be less practicable afterwards. Then to begin a habit of rising early and retirement may be ill interpreted by your lady, whereas if she knows you were used to it before, she can take no umbrage at it. Some there be who think the least reflection unbecoming men of business and action in the world. This notion may if I mistake not be easily impugned by a great number both of reasons and examples which I shall omit at this time. If you have any tincture of that notion, viz. the inconsistency of study with business, I shall take it as a favour if you will be pleased to communicate to me in a line or two your sentiments on that point, with your reasons for them. In the meanwhile I must desire you to pardon the long trouble I have given you in this letter, and am

Sir,

Yr most humle & affect. Servt,

GEO. BERKELEY.

3   TO PERCIVAL

Trinity College, Dublin, 21st Oct. 1709

Dear Sir,

I return you my hearty thanks for the favour you did me in putting me on the perusal of a book, which is (I think) written with great solidity, and which I had not seen before. Mr. Higden has in my mind clearly shewn that the swearing allegiance to the king *de facto* (whether right or wrong) is conformable as well to the laws of the land as to Scripture and reason, and the practice of nations. That it is agreeable to reason is so evident from the very nature and design of government, as one may justly wonder it was ever made a question, and particularly what Mr. Higden relates to have passed in Henry the Seventh's reign, viz. the acknowledging the laws passed by Richard the Third, the methods used in reversing his acts of attainder, and the statute made for the future security of all that should adhere to the king *de facto*, which he shews not to have been repeal'd since ; all this I say demonstrates it to suit with our Constitution. Besides what he says of ancient custom, viz. that during the reigns of thirteen kings who came to the throne without hereditary titles, he does not know of any non-jurors, makes it seem surprising that those men should start up in our days. The reason I take to be that men having felt not long before the great mischief there was in forsaking the king, they now (as is usual to go from one extreme to another) thought they could not adhere too closely to his person, even when he was divested of all government, and utterly unable to protect them. For my part, when I consider what the differ-ence is between a king *de jure* and a king *de facto* I cannot easily find it. As for the right of inheritance, to me it seems a kingdom is not a property, but a charge ; it is not therefore necessary that it go by the same rule as an estate or goods and chattels. But grant it be the property of a single person, and that the crown of right descend by inheritance, yet sure it is that no person who inherits can have by inheritance a better title to the thing inherited than he had to whom he succeeds as heir. Now do but trace the present Royal line and you will end in William the Conquerour, who by conquest had the same title to the crown that a highway-man has to your purse. So that after all, we are forced to place the right of kings in the consent and acquiescence of the people : whence it follows, that whoever has the crown in possession, and the people or their representatives, i.e. Lords and Commons con-curring with him the same is rightful king. If therefore Cromwell had taken the title of king, and got it confirmed to his posterity in a free Parliament, and they remained in possession of it, and the laws ran in their usual channel down to this time, it should seem to be wickedness in anyone to attempt to disturb the public peace, by introducing the family of the Stewarts. Because you desire my sentiments I speak freely what comes uppermost in my thoughts.

But to return to our author, two things there are that I scruple in his book : the first, is his retaining the distinction of kings *de jure* and kings *de facto* without giving any mark whereby we shall know the one from the other. I would ask him for example, how upon his principles it is possible to distinguish between the posterity of the usurper Cromwell (in case they had obtained and continued on the throne) and the posterity of the Conquerour, which is but a more specious name for an usurper. In the two first chapters he proves the legislative authority of the king for the time being and his two Houses of Parliament, to be acknowledged both by the common and statute law ; and at the latter end of the sixth chapter he expressly says the right of the crown is under the direction of the legislative authority, i.e. of the king *de facto* and his Parliament. Whence it plainly follows that every king *de facto* is king *de jure*, and so the distinction becomes useless. The second thing I cannot approve of in Mr. Higden is, that he seems to be against all resistance whatsover to the king *de facto* as is evident from chapter seven. Now by this it appears his principles do not favour the late Revolution, though indeed he is now for submission to the government established.

By this time I may reasonably suppose you are well nigh tired. I must nevertheless ask leave to add that nothing in my mind can be more becoming a gentleman and man of sense, than the resolution you are taking to know the measure of your obedience, and the bounds of their power who rule. As to the latter, I believe you may find some satisfaction in the last part of Mr. Locke's *Treatise on Government*, if you have not yet perused that piece. And with relation to the former, there is a dialogue of Plato's entitled ' Crito,' wherein it is debated how far we are bound to the observance of the laws of our country, of which I would gladly know your opinion. It contains only about five or six leaves in 8° in the 2d vol. of Plato's works translated into English from the French of Mr. Dacier. I believe Mr. Clerke has the book.

You are undoubtedly wise in resolving to have a beautiful lady. I wish she may be healthy too, so that you may be the father of a hardy race, for ever free from colds and toothaches.

Dr. Lambert has lately published a defence of his letter. It has the character of being smooth and trifling. The same person is said to have offended Mr. Tennison's friends, because in his funeral sermon he charged him with ignorance in being against the money bill.

I shall not add that the throwing away half an hour now and then on a correspondence with me is the greatest addition imaginable to the obligations you have already laid on.

Dear Sir,

Yr most humle & affect. Servt,

GEO. BERKELEY.

4 TO MOLYNEUX

Trin: Coll: Novemb. 26. 1709

Dr. Molyneux

I am lately enterd into my Citadell in a disconsolate Mood, after having passd the better part of a sharp & bitter day in the Damps & mustly [*sic*] solitudes of the Library without either Fire or any thing else to protect Me from the Injuries of the Snow that was constantly driving at the Windows & forceing it's Entrance into that wretched Mansion, to the keeping of which I was this day sennight elect'd under an inauspiciary Planet. What adds to my Vexation is that the Senior Fellows have this Evening naild up my Lord Pembrook's Books in Boxes; and so deprivd Me of the only Entertainment I could propose to my self in that place. But for my Comfort Preferment comes on a pace. Yesterday I was advancd a step higher by Dr Edward's being made Senior Fellow, upon a Vacancy occasiond by Dr Lloyd's being made Dean of Connor. And I expect to be promoted two or three steps more in a little Time For the Bishop of Cork dyed t'other day of a purple Fevr in this Town, the Dean of Cork also is dead, and as some say the Bishop of Kilmore. It seems by the Letter I had the Honour to receive from You, that your Expectations are not answered with relation to the Magnificence of Kilkenny; believe me Child that antient & delightfull City is not so remarkable for a splendid Outside as for intrisic [*sic*] Worth the rich Marble that covers the Houses and even the streets not being distinguishable by the Eye from the vilest stone untill by Tryall You have discoverd'd it's Hardness and the Pollish & Lustre it is capable of receiving. As for the peice of my drawing which You sought in the Dutchess's Closet, I am inclin'd to be of your Mind, That it was translated with the rest of the most precious Moveables to adorn the Duke's House in St James's Square. The Cave of Dunmore if I was to see it now, I know not whether it would strike Me with the like Horrour & Surprise, and fill my Mind with the same Images that it did when I saw it about Ten Years agone I need not tell You A Child is easier surprizd and his little Mind sooner filld with Wonder & Amazement than that of a Man so well read in the History of Nature, and of such a daring Spirit as You are. Hoever [*sic*] I should gladly be informd in your next how You were affected with the sight of that Place, or what Adventures You might have had in it.   I am

   Dr. Molyneux.

Your affect. Friend & Servt,

GEOR: BERKELEY.

T'other day I had a Letter from Tom Prior containing some Objections or Difficulties with Respect to the Theory of Vision, wherein he gives his Service to You.

5   TO MOLYNEUX

Trin. Coll. Decem. 8. 1709.

Dr. Molyneux

You desire to know my Thoughts, first, whether the Ideas laid up in the Imagination are all Images of what they represent, and Secondly whether We can reason without Ideas, and if not how comes it that We can reason about a Chiliagen [*sic*] whereof We cannot frame an Idea ?   This if I take You right is the substance of what You propose.   To The first I answer, That the Ideas laid up in the Imagination need not be Images, strictly speaking of what they represent, for Example, in demonstrating the Proposition which says, that the Sum of the Angles of any Polygon is equall to twice as many right Ones, as there be Sides in the Figure, bating four, You may make use of any one Polygon, e.g. a pentogon [*sic*] to represent all the infinite Variety of regular and irregular Polygons that may possibly exist.   Again when You recollect in your Thoughts the Idea of any House or City, for Instance 'tis certain that Idea do's very rudely resemble the Thing it represents, and not in each Circumstance accurately correspond with it.   And yet it may serve to most Interests and purposes as well as if it did.   To the Second, I answer, that We may very well, and in my Opinion often do, reason without Ideas but only the Words us'd, being usd for the most parts as Letters in Algebra, which tho they denote particular Quantities, Yet every step do not suggest them to our Thoughts, and for all that We may reason or perform Operations intirly about them. Numbers We can frame no Notion of beyond a certain Degree, and yet We can reason as well about a Thousand as about five, the Truth on't is Numbers are nothing but Names.   Hence You

3

may reason about a Chiliagon with regard to the Number of it's Sides and Angles, tho the Idea You have of it be not different from that of a Figure of 999 Sides. I am of your Opinion that Descartes flounders often in his Meditations and is not always consistent with himself. In Med. 2. He says the Notion of this particular Wax is less clear than that of Wax in generall, and in the same Med. a little before, he forbears to consider Bodies in generall because (says he) these generall Conceptions are usually confusd. In Med. 3 and in the Answer to the 3 : Objection of Hobbes he plainly distinguisheth betwixt himself & Cogitation, betwixt an extended Substance & Extension, and nevertheless throughout his Principles he confounds those Things as do likewise his Followers. But it would take up too much Time to observe to You all the like Blunders that appeard to Me when I formerly read that Treatise. I know not whether I have hit your Mind, if You explain Me your Thoughts more at Large perhaps I may say something more pertinent. Last Saturday Caldwell went along with I. Bligh for London, where they intend to stay till a peace, and then proceed to make the Tour of Europe.

I am Dr. Molyneux, Yo⟨u⟩rs most affectionately

G: Berkeley

I have lately had much Talk with Dr. Elwood about my Notion, I have communicated my Design & papers to him & am glad I have done so, for I find he is a Man of very good sense

6   TO MOLYNEUX

Trin. Coll. Dec. 19. 1709

Dr. Molyneux.

You desire to know what a Geometer thinks of when he demonstrates Properties of a Curve formd by a Ray of Light as it passes through the Air. His Imagination or Memory (say You) I can affoard him no Idea of it, and as for the rude Idea of this or that Curve which may be suggested to him by Fancy that has no Connexion with his Theorems & Reasonings. I answer first, That in my Opinion he thinks of the Various Density of the Atmosphere the Obliquity of the Incidence and the Nature of Refraction in Air by which the Ray is bent into a Curve, 'tis on these he meditates and from these principles he proceeds to investigate the Nature of the Curve. Secondly. It appears to Me That in Geometricall Reasonings We do not make any Discovery by contemplating the Ideas of the Lines whose Properties are investigated. For Example, In order to discover the Method of drawing Tangents to a Parabola, 'tis true a Figure is drawn on paper & so suggested to your Fancy, but no Matter whether it be of a Parabolic Line or no, the Demonstration proceeds as well tho it be an Hyperbole or the Portion of an Ellipsis, provided that I have regard to the Equation expressing the Nature of a Parabola wherein the Squares of the Ordinates are every where equall to the Rectangles under the Abscissae & Parameters, it being this Equation or the Nature of the Curve thus expressed and not the Idea of it that leads to the Solution Again You tell Me that if, as I think, Words do not at every Turn suggest the respective Ideas they are supposd to stand for it is purely by Chance Our Discourse hangs together, and is found after 2 or 3 hours jingling & permutation of Sounds to agree with our Thoughts. As for what I said of Algebra, You are of Opinion the Illustration will not hold good because there are no Set rules except those of the Syllogisms whereby to range & permute o⟨u⟩r Words like to the Algebraic Process. In Answer to all which I observe first, That if We put Our Words together any how and at Random then indeed there may be some Grounds for what You say, but if people lay their Words together with Design and according to Rule then there can be no Pretence so far as I can see for your Inference. Secondly. I cannot but dissent from what You say, of there being no Set Rules for the Ranging and Disposition of Words but only the Syllogistic, for to Me it appears That all Grammar & every part Logic contain little else than Rules for Discourse & Ratiocination by Words. And those who do not expresly [*sic*] set themselves to study those Arts do nevertheless learn them insensibly by Custom. I am very sleepy & can say no more but that I am

Yo⟨u⟩rs &c.

G. BERKELEY.

Trinity Coll., Dec. 27th, 1709

I was glad to find the small piece I recommended to your perusal entertained you so well. I did indeed believe that anything of that excellent philosopher, whose divine sentiments are preserved to us by Plato and Xenophon, could not fail of being agreeable to a man of sense and virtue. Your reflections on Socrates' behaviour gave me a great deal of pleasure, though not without some concern, in making me more sensible of the loss I sustain in being deprived of the conversation of one who has a taste of those things which (though formerly the chiefest heads of discourse among the politer heathen) are now almost grown out of fashion, and banished the conversation of well bred Christians. Socrates spent his time in reasoning on the most noble and important subjects, the nature of the gods, the dignity and duration of the soul, and the duties of a rational creature. He was always exposing the vanity of Sophists, painting vice and virtue in their proper colours, deliberating on the public good, enflaming the most noble and ungenerous tempers with the love of great actions. In short his whole employment was the turning men aside from vice, impertinence, and trifling speculations to the study of solid wisdom, temperance, justice, and piety, which is the true business of a philosopher. And this great man died as he lived ; he went out of the world with the same indifference that a man rises from an ill play. He spent his last minutes in his usual exercise. In the morning of the last day of his life, you know he made that excellent discourse concerning the obligation that men have to obey the laws of their country, and Plato's dialogue entitled ' Phaedon ' contains an account of his discourse and behaviour during the rest of the day wherein he drank the poison prepared him by the executioner. It is now some years since I read this dialogue, but I remember it entertained me very agreeably, as I believe it will you if you can find leisure to peruse it. It is in the same volume with ' Crito,' and it would be a great favour to let me know your opinion of it. I must own it looks something impertinent to be still troubling you with one amusement or other ; but when I call to mind how unmercifully you suffered me to devour your time when here, I flatter myself that I have a sort of right to the disposal of some few of your

minutes even at this distance. But here is a particular reason
why I could wish you would give yourself the trouble of looking
over the ' Phaedon ' ; for (besides that you will there find the
thoughts of the wisest heathen on that subject which the most
deserves our consideration, I mean the immortality of the soul)
Socrates does therein explain his opinion of self-murder, which
is a point I remember to have heard you discourse on more than
once, and you appeared something fond of discussing it. But if
you need any motive to peruse a discourse of Socrates, I know
none more apposite than the authority of Squire Bickerstaff, a
man I think of excellent sense and whom you may have observed
on all occasions to express a very high esteem of that philosopher.
For my own part, so far as I can judge by what notions of his
I have seen, I cannot forbear thinking him the best and most
admirable man that the heathen world produced.

It was with great concern I read that part of your letter which
relates to Mr. Whiston. He has been (as appears by his writings)
a man of great industry and parts ; but I must own myself very
much surprised to find him espouse such an odd paradox, as
adoration and prayer are not due to the Son and Holy Ghost,
though he acknowledges their divinity. You tell me he says 'tis
none of our business to draw consequences from Scripture, whereas
in my opinion several parts of Scripture would be of little or no
use, if we were not allowed to apply them and draw consequences
from them. Whatever has an evident connexion with any part
of revelation seems to me equally binding with it, otherwise all
use of reason in points of the Christian religion must be quite laid
aside. I agree with you entirely that we have express warrant in
Scripture for praying to our Saviour ; and if we had not, yet
it is so clearly deducible from thence as sufficiently justifies the
conduct of our Church in that point. This notion of Mr. Whiston's
is, I believe, of a new sort, for the Socinians allow our Saviour may
be prayed to, though according to them he is not God. But
though I look on this thought of Mr. Whiston's as an error in
point of judgment, yet I must confess the account you gave me
of it, noways lessened but rather increased my opinion of the
man ; inasmuch as it is easier to find those who conform in the
externals of worship and agree to the tenets of our Church, than
to meet with one that has attained in so eminent a degree, that
great perfection and badge of Christianity, the generous contempt
of the things of this life, which as it is the most severe and least
practised duty of our religion, so it is the surest mark of a true

Christian, being the very root of all the heroical virtues recommended in the gospel.

The large family of Mr. Whiston which you mention (for before I did not know he was married) are indeed to be pitied, but as for Mr. Whiston himself I do not think him any object of pity on account of the temporal misfortunes he is threatened with. There is a secret pleasure in suffering for conscience sake, which I doubt not is sufficient to overbalance whatever calamities may be inflicted on him on that score.

This obscure corner of the world furnishes no occurrences worth your notice. All things are in a dull state of mediocrity. Only the other day there came out a pamphlet in answer to Mr. Stoughton's sermon. It was written by a young clergyman of my acquaintance that was formerly a member of our college. The thing seems to me to have some sense and pleasantry in it. You have here enclosed part of it and the remaining part I defer sending till next post.

Pray remember me to Mr. Clerke.

> I am, Dr Sr,
>
> Yr affect. humble Servt,
>
> G. Berkely.[1]

8 TO PERCIVAL

Trin. Coll., March 1st, 1709/10

Dr Sr,

I take this opportunity of Mr. Molyneux's departure to give you the trouble of a letter, though I must own this corner furnishes scarce any that deserves to be communicated. We are a nation as it were in its nonage, put under the guardianship of a people who do everything for us, and leave us the liberty of transacting nothing material ourselves or having any part in the affairs of Europe, yet for all that we are not free from faction and discord any more than our neighbours. The feast at the Tholsel on the Queen's Birthday has occasioned much talk in this city and given offence to many on account of certain whiggish healths which was there proposed, one whereof I am informed was the bringing in of Presbytery, and another that Dr. Sachervell and his friends may meet with Greg's fate. The said Dr. is entirely

[1] *Sic*, in copy.

the subject of discourse, and everyone is engaged either for or against him. His sermon has been printed here, as well as some pamphlets of our own growth against it. I send you one which is thought to come from Mr. Daniel a famous whigg-clergyman and pretender to poetry in this town. I would not have you think by my sending it that I set any great value on it, for it seems to me writ with an affectation of more wit than in truth it has. The controversy occasioned by Mr. Boyle's sermon against episcopacy is not yet ended. I hear he has a large volume of above three-score sheets ready for the press. Archdeacon Percival's answer to Dr. Lambert is likewise suddenly expected. I know not whether my last came to your hands, it was directed under cover to Mr. Southwell and enclosed a piece of controversy with Mr. Stoughton on the subject of his sermon. Sir Richard Bulkeley and one Whitterow an imposter whom he brought over along with him are lately gone from hence. They distributed a great deal of money and victuals to the poor while they were here, and set a stranger free who had been arrested for forty pounds which sum they paid. In short Sir Richard was resolved to sell his estate and give all to the poor. But I am told the Chancery opposed him as *non compos*. Whitterow is said to have run away with a young woman. Some clergymen would fain have discoursed him on his mission but he carefully avoided it.

The bookseller who printed the *Essay on Vision*, imagining he had printed too few, retarded the publication of it on that side the water till he had finished this second edition whereof be pleased to accept one which I have sent you by Mr. Molyneux. I have made some alterations and additions in the body of the Treatise, and in an appendix have endeavoured to answer the objections of the Archbishop of Dublin. There still remains one objection with regard to the uselessness of that book : but in a little time I hope to make what is there laid down appear subservient to the ends of morality and religion in a treatise I have now in the press, the design of which is to demonstrate the existence and attributes of God, the immortality of the soul, the reconciliation of God's foreknowledge with freedom of men, and by shewing the emptiness and falseness of several parts of the speculative sciences, to reduce men to the study of religion and things useful. How far my endeavour will prove successful, and whether I have been all this time in a dream or no, time will manifest.

Pray if Mr. Clarke be alive give my humble service to him.

I am in pain for him having not heard from him this long time. I met with some who supporting themselves on the authority of the Archbishop of Dublin's sermon concerning the prescience of God, denied there was any more wisdom, goodness or understanding in God than there were feet or hands, but that all are to be taken in a figurative sense; whereupon I consulted the sermon and to my surprise found his Grace asserting that strange doctrine. 'Tis true he holds there is something in the divine nature analogous or equivalent to those attributes. But upon such principles I must confess I do not see how it is possible to demonstrate the being of God : there being no argument that I know of for his existence, which does not prove him at the same time to be an understanding, wise and benevolent Being, in the strict, literal, and proper meaning of those words. About the same time I wrote to Mr. Clarke and desired he would favour me with his thoughts on the subject of God's existence, and the proofs he thought most conclusive of it, which I imagined would prove a grateful entertainment while his sore eyes prevented his reading. But never since have I heard one word from him, either on that or any other subject. I am often inquired of about his character, and I would fain add the love of letters and study to the rest of his good qualities.

All friends here are well. The other night Archdeacon Percival, Dan Dering and myself were drinking your and Dr. Sachervell's healths at your brother's.

I am,

Yr most obliged humble Servt,

G. BERKELEY.

P.S.

This was to have gone by Mr. Molyneux who, sometime since, was in full haste setting about his journey to the Congress, but now finding he is not likely to continue his resolution I chose rather to resume the letter out of his hands and send it by post than that you should escape the trouble of reading it, which trespass I depend upon your good nature to forgive. My Lady Roydon is just giving up the ghost, her goods are all seized and the bailiffs lodging in her house won't suffer her to die in peace.

Trin. Coll. April 18, 1710

May it please yr Grace,

It was with great concern & surprise that I understood my being fallen so far into the displeasure of yr grace, as that you shou'd order me to be prosecuted in your grace's court, especially without any fault of mine that I know of. For I do assure your grace, that if the manner of my ordination was in me a fault, it was a fault of ignorance, as will appear from the following account which I humbly submit to yr grace's consideration. The time drawing nigh at which I was oblig'd by the Statutes of the College to take on priest's orders, I resolved to make use of the first opportunity that shou'd offer, & being informed that a gentleman of my acquaintance had apply'd to the Bishop of Clogher to be ordain'd by him, I thought it proper for me likewise to address his lordship in my own behalf, & the rather for that his relation (as vice-chancellor) to our society entitled me in a particular manner to expect that favour from him. But, my lord, as I was a stranger to the nature & intent of yr grace's jurisdiction, I did not apprehend it was my business to examine how far your grace's licence may be necessary to his lordship's holding an ordination. Whether the B'p of Clogher wou'd ordain me or no, or what licence he had to do it, I left entirely to his lordship's . . . to determine not thinking it became me to intermeddle in . . . of that nature, since I was [ignorant?] & his lordship might be presum'd best to know on [what?] grounds he proceeded. But least of all did it enter into my thoughts that in case there had been any irregular act of his, it wou'd bring me under the resentment of your grace, or be interpreted in me an encroaching on yr grace's authority, which I never meant to lessen or dispute. This, my lord, is the true state of the matter, which I presume to lay before your grace, in hopes it may (if not justifie me altogether) at least make my error appear the more pardonable. I have already engaged to the Dean of St Patrick's (who has been pleased to suspend the prosecution), as I do now to yr grace, that I shall not exercise any ecclesiastical function in yr diocese untill I have first obtain'd licence from yr grace. I am, my Lord, yr grace's most dutifull & most obedient servant,

GEO. BERKELEY.

Trin. Coll., June 29th, 1710

Dr Sr,

Suffer me to interrupt your joys by a short congratulation. I am heartily glad to find you are married to a lady who, by all the accounts I can hear, is just such a one as (had it been at my choice) I should have chosen to be your wife. The first lines of your letter to your brother persuade me that I cannot make you a more agreeable wish than that you and my Lady Percival may spend together a long life in pleasure equal to that you have enjoyed this week past, that as the fury of love abates, the sweetness and tenderness of conjugal affection may increase, together with that unknown delight which springs up in the soul of a parent from the thought of a happy and well educated offspring.

This Sir is the hearty prayer of

Yr most humble and obliged Servt,
GEO. BERKELEY.

P.S.

How unmannerly soever it may be to give you any trouble at this time, yet my affairs so fall out that I cannot possibly avoid it. I have sometime since published a book which is dedicated to my Lord Pembroke. It is necessary that one of them be forthwith presented to his Lordship, and I know not one that is capable of doing me that service but yourself. The book I have delivered to Mr. Conderon who has promised me that it shall be left at your lodging in London by a gentleman who is going thither. By the next opportunity I will send you one for yourself; though I cannot flatter myself you will find time to read it. If I ask an absurd or unreasonable thing, I beg you will excuse one who has good intentions but not the best judge of decorum.

Trin. Coll., Dub., July 29th, 1710

Dr Sr,

The readiness you express to serve me in my affair with the Lord Pembroke has drawn on you this second trouble, viz. that you will do me the favour to let me know if the book I sent to be presented to him, be not yet come to your hands. Mr. Conderon gave it one Mr. Hoar, a parliament man of this kingdom, about a month since, he then went for England and promised to take care of it. I have likewise directed one to be left at your lodging in Pall-Mall for yourself. It goes with some more of the same sort, which my bookseller sends to London. From the conversation I have had with you on that subject, I flatter myself you will not be adverse to the notions contained in it, and if when you receive it you can procure me the opinion of some of your ingenious acquaintances who are thinking men and addicted to the study of rational philosophy and mathematics, I shall be extremely obliged to you.

You could not have conferred a more sensible obligation on me, than was the favour you did in imparting what gave me some idea of the reasonable and sweet rapture you taste in your new state. I have often heard that men are apt to set the best outside on their condition of life, particularly in what relates to matrimony ; but there appears such an unaffected air of truth and passion in what you say, that it will not suffer me to entertain the least doubt of your being in earnest. You must give me leave to tell you, you are mistaken in that part of your letter, where you insinuate it to be your thought that I lie under a prejudice (as I am a bachelour) against marriage ; for whatever reasons I may have to think that state not eligible to one in my own present circumstances, humour, and manner of life ; yet I assure you I cannot easily imagine a more happy condition than that of man and wife, who abide in mutual love and harmony of temper. As for what commonly shocks young men, the being confined only to one and that for life, I am so far from thinking the worse of matrimony on this account that on any other conditions I am convinced it could never be happy. The impossibility I have heard some men say there was in finding a woman accomplished in all those perfections that are necessary to making a happy husband (and which you have so well enumerated in your letter) is what gave me greatest prejudice against matrimony. However I still thought there was such a one somewhere to be found, and I sincerely rejoice with you that you have lit on her. Pray give my service to Mr. Clerke.

I am, Dr Sr,

Yr most affect. and most humble Servt,

GEO. BERKELEY.

Trin. Coll., Sep. 6th, 1710

Dr Sr,

   I am extremely obliged to you for the favourable repre-
sentation you made of me and my opinions to your friends and
the account you have given me of their judgments thereupon ;
and am not at all surprised to find that the name of my book
should be entertained with ridicule and contempt by those who
never examined what was in it, and want that common justice
of trying before they condemn.   But my comfort is that they who
have entered deepest into the merits of the cause, and employed
most time and exactness in reading what I have written, speak
more advantageously of it.   If the raillery and scorn of those
that critique what they will not be at the pains to understand
had been sufficient to deter men from making any attempts
towards curing the ignorance and errors of mankind, we should
have been troubled with very few improvements in knowledge.
The common crys being against any opinion seems to me so far
from proving it false that it may with as good reason pass for
an agreement of its truth.   However I imagine whatever doctrine
contradicts vulgar and settled opinion had need been introduced
with great caution into the world.   For this reason it was I omitted
all mention of the non-existence of matter in the title-page, dedication, preface, and introduction, that so the notion might steal
unawares on the reader, who possibly would never have meddled
with a book that he had known contained such paradoxes.   If,
therefore, it shall at any time lie in your way to discourse with
your friends on the subject of my book, I entreat you not to take
notice to them I deny the being of matter in it, but only that
it is a treatise of the *Principles of Human Knowledge* designed to
promote true knowledge and religion, particularly in opposition
to those philosophers who vent dangerous notions with regard to
the existence of God and the natural immortality of the soul, both
which I have endeavoured to demonstrate in a way not hitherto
made use of.

   Two imputations there are which (how unjust soever) I
apprehended would be charged on me by censorious men, and
I find it has happened accordingly.   The first, that I was not
myself convinced of the truth of what I writ, but from a vain
affectation of novelty designed imposing on the world :—whereas

there is nothing I esteem more mean and miserable, I may add more wicked, than an intention to cheat men into a belief of lies and sophisms merely for the sake of a little reputation with fools. God is my witness that I was, and do still remain, entirely persuaded of the non-existence of matter, and the other tenets published along with it. How desirous soever I may be to be thought well of, yet I hardly think that anyone in his wits can be touched with a vanity to distinguish himself among wise men for a mad man. This methinks should satisfy others of my sincerity at least, and that nothing less than a full conviction not only of the truth of my notions but also of their usefulness in the most important points, could have engaged me to make them public. I may add that the opinion of matter I have entertained some years ; if therefore a motive of vanity could have induced me to obtrude falsehoods on the world, I had long since done it when the conceit was warm in my imagination, and not have staid to examine and revise it both with my own judgment and that of my ingenious friends. The second imputation I was afraid of is, that men rash in their censures, and that never considered my book would be apt to confound me with the sceptics, who doubt of the existence of sensible things and are not positive as to any one truth, no not so much as their own being (which I find by your letter is the case of some wild visionists now in London), but whoever reads my book with due attention will plainly see that there is a direct opposition betwixt the principles contained in it and those of the sceptics, and that I question not the existence of anything that we perceive by our senses.

As to your Lady's objection, I am extremely honoured by it, and as I shall reckon it a great misfortune, in case any prejudice against my notions should lessen the good thoughts, you say, she is pleased to entertain of me, so I am not a little careful to satisfy her in point of the creation's consistency with the doctrine in my book. In order to which I must beg you will inform her Ladyship that I do not deny the existence of any of those sensible things which Moses says were created by God. They existed from all eternity in the Divine intellect, and then became perceptible (*i.e.* were created) in the same manner and order as is described in Genesis. For I take creation to belong to things only as they respect finite spirits, there being nothing new to God. Hence it follows that the act of creation consists in God's willing that those things should be perceptible to other spirits, which before were known only to Himself. Now both reason and scripture assure us there are other spirits (as angels of different orders, &c.) besides man, who, 'tis possible might have perceived this visible world according as it was succesively exhibited to their view before man's creation. Besides, for to agree with the Mosaic account of the creation it is sufficient if we suppose that a man, in case he was then created and existing at the time of the chaos, might have perceived all things formed out of it in the very order set down in Scripture, which is no ways repugnant to our principles. I know not whether I express myself so clearly as to be understood by a lady that has not read my book. Much more I might say to her objection, if I had the opportunity of discoursing with her, which I am sorry to hear we may not expect before next summer. I have a strong presumption that I either should make a proselyte of her Ladyship, or she convince me that I am in error. My reason is, because she is the only person of those you mentioned my book to, who opposed it with reason and argument.

As for the physician I assure him there are (besides several others) two ingenious men in his own profession in this town, who are not ashamed to own themselves every whit as mad as myself, if their subscribing to the notions contained in my book can make them so. I may add that the greatest Tory and greatest Whig of my acquaintance agree in an entire assent to them, though at this time our party men seem more enflamed and stand at a wider distance than ever.

This puts me in mind to tell you a pleasant accident that befel me about ten days since. I was just come into the coffee-house when a drunken gentleman I had never seen before comes up to me and asks me whether I would pledge him in Dr. Sacheverell's health ; to be brief he obliged me whether I would or no to drink the Dr.'s health in a glass of brandy in the middle of the coffee-house and when I had done he fell on his knees and swore and prayed for the Dr. and the Church. Then getting up he swore that all the coffee-house round should drink the same health, and upon a gentleman's refusing it drew his sword, whereupon I made what haste I could out of the house. I understood afterwards that one or two more were obliged to drink it, the one of whom was a Parliament man. This occasioned Mr. Caulfield to complain of it as a breach of privilege next day in Parliament ; but all the effect his complaint had was that it set the whole house a laughing. I am told this involuntary act of mine is like to gain me the reputation of being a great admirer of Dr. Sacheverell's, which is a character I am not at all fond of. I like indeed very well the events which his preaching may have brought about ; for (if I may judge of such things) it seems to me the Government had been much too long in the hands of a party. But for the sermons or conduct of the Dr., I confess I have a very moderate esteem of either.

The book for my Lord Pembroke is delivered to Mr. Hoffman, Mr. Southwell's gentleman, who will give it you as soon as he comes to London.

I am,

Yr most humble and affect. Servt,

G. BERKELEY.

13   TO PERCIVAL

Trin. Coll., 8ber, 1710

Dr Sr,

I find by the last you favoured me with, that there is talk of my Lord Pembroke's being employed in the new ministry. I know not whether upon the delivery of the book you will think it proper to intimate to his Lordship that it was printed off (as indeed it was) the beginning of May, but that I wanted opportunity to present it sooner ; by this it will appear that I meant to address him in his retirement, and not upon any prospect of his returning into favour at Court which I could not foresee. You are, I know, too public spirited not to have your thoughts and conversation taken up with the occurrences of this busy time, which makes me that I can scarce tell how to desire you should lay out any part of them on the perusal of my book. Though I am sure there is no one whose free and deliberate opinion I should be more desirous of than yours.

It is the observation of a wise man (Sir Will Temple) that solitude and leisure are the greatest advantages that riches can give those who possess them above all other men ; and yet these are what rich men least of all make use of. He that is equally fitted for thought and meditation in his closet, or for business and conversation in the world is certainly the best able to serve his country, and can pass with the greatest evenness through all scenes of life. 'Tis thought which governs the world, and all the states in it, and produces whatever is great and glorious in them. Stirring and action is but the handmaid of thought, without which the former can do no good, but may a great deal of harm. Whatever therefore improves the thinking faculty surely ought to be practised. Now, thought is to the mind what motion is to the body ; both are equally improved by exercise and impaired by disuse. In order therefore to obtain health and strength of mind it is useful that we employ our thoughts, though it should be even on useless subjects. How much rather ought we then to exercise them on the grounds and certainty of knowledge, the being and attributes of God, and the nature of our own soul. I mean not by this to persuade you that what I have written deserves much heed, but only to shew you that the subjects I have chosen are worth thinking on.

I am, Sr,

Yr most humble and affect. Servt,
GEO. BERKELEY.

14   TO PERCIVAL

Trin. Coll. 27th Nov. 1710

Dr Sr,

Your last (which came to hand after having been stopped for several posts by contrary winds) obliged me with the account that my ' Treatise of the Principles,' &c., had been perused by Dr. Clarke and Mr. Whiston. As truth is my aim, there is nothing I more desire than being helped forward in the search of it, by the concurring studies of thoughtful and impartial men : on both which accounts no less than for their uncommon learning and penetration those gentlemen are very deservedly much esteemed. This makes me very solicitous to know particularly what fault they find in the principles I proceed upon ; which at this time cannot but be of great advantage to me that it will either convince me of an error, and so prevent my wasting any more time and pains that way, or else it will prove no small confirmation of the truth of my opinions, in case nothing solid can be objected to them by those great men. This makes me trouble you with the two enclosed letters to be sealed and sent by you to those gentlemen respectively, if you shall think it convenient, or if not I must entreat you to get your friend to obtain from them the particulars which they object, and that you will transmit them to me ; which will in truth be a deed of charity, much greater than that of guiding a mistaken traveller into the right way, and I think either good office may be with like reason claimed by one man from another.

As to what is said of ranking me with Father Malebranche and Mr. Norris, whose writings are thought too fine spun to be of any great use to mankind, I have this to answer : that I think the notions I embrace are not in the least coincident with, or agreeing with, theirs, but indeed plainly inconsistent with them in the main points, insomuch that I know few writers whom I take myself at bottom to differ more from than them. Fine spun metaphysics are what I on all occasions declare against, and if anyone shall shew me anything of that sort in my ' Treatise ' I will willingly correct it.

I am sorry that I am not yet favoured with your own free thoughts on this subject. Would you but think away a few leisure hours in the morning on it, I dare say no one would understand it better. And, whether I am in a mistake or no, I doubt not but your own thoughts will sufficiently recompence your labour.

I am, Dear Sir,
Yr most obliged humble Servt,
G. Berkeley.

15   TO PERCIVAL

Rathmore, 20 December, 1710

Dr Sr,

The last post brought me your letter of the fourth instant which informs me what obligations I have to you on account of your care in providing that my book should be delivered to my Lord Pembroke, for which I return you my hearty thanks, and I shall reckon myself farther obliged to you if you will please to let me know whether my Lord has returned it (which you say is customary with him), or if by any other means his approbation or dislike of it shall come to your notice.

I am now at Mr. Blithe's house in the County of Meath. It is a large and fair building and has very fine improvements about it. The young gentleman lives very well and since his father's death has behaved himself so in all respects as to have gained the reputation of a very hopeful and prudent man. He is now building a poor house for the maintenance of the poor of his estate, and intends to assign for that purpose a hundred pounds per annum. I tell you this because I know such news can be to no one more agreeable than to yourself.

The day before I left Dublin (which was something more than a week agone I chanced to meet at the Provost's house with one Mr. Langton a curate in the County of West-Meath, who had formerly been a Dominican friar. He came to complain of one of our College who together with several other of his Whig-parishioners had most grossly abused him during the time of Divine Service for preaching Passive Obedience. The sermon Mr. Langton saith was one of Dr. Scot's which he had transcribed. The said Mr. Langton hath likewise given information upon oath to the government concerning an association or conspiracy on foot amongst the Whig-inhabitants of the County of West-Meath in order to oblige the Queen to restore the late ministry. The Council hath thought fit to take notice of it, and sent up for some persons whose testimony Mr. Langton made use of, but what has since been done in it I know not. I was acquainted with this Langton when I went to school in Kilkenny, and thought him to be somewhat silly. This mighty undertaking of the Whigs of West-Meath is certainly very ridiculous ; but there are some who imagine the project extends farther than that county.

I purposed to have sent by Mr. Percival half a dozen of my books to you, to be presented to such of your friends as are most conversant in those studies, but it happened that his things were then packed up and on shipboard. By that means I hoped the book would become public and known. I must therefore beg the favour of you that you will let any that are curious that way know that both my books are to be sold by Mr. Churchil in Pater-Noster Row. I should not have given you this trouble but that Mr. Churchil (who is my bookseller's correspondent) has neglected to publish them in the usual forms. Mr. Pepyat suspects the ground of this backwardness in Mr. Churchil to be his apprehending that the encouragement of a printing trade in this kingdom would interfere with his interest ; since there are yearly exported great sums of money to him and other booksellers in London for books, which if that trade were encouraged might be printed cheaper in Dublin because there is not here so great an impost on paper. Besides the trial of Dr. Sacheverell and several other things that have been lately printed in Dublin there are now in the press twenty thousand prayer-books and an edition of Erasmus's Colloquies, which for print, paper, and correctness will I believe match any of the Dutch editions. This flourishing of the printing trade, more than ever was known in this kingdom, will I hope bring some benefit to poor Ireland, which consideration will I doubt not prove with you sufficient apology for my troubling you with this narrative of it.

It remains that I acknowledge the favour you do me in sending your thoughts of my Introduction. It would greatly rejoice me to find you thought the whole worth your careful perusal. As for anything requisite to the understanding of it, I am sure to the making it I found little else useful than the plain common sense God hath given me together with an application and eagerness to discover the truth. And if you will take my word for it, I assure you there are not those great flights and difficulties in it that you seem to imagine, nothing more being necessary to a thorough comprehending and judging of it than a little exercise of your native faculties, which I am persuaded the author of nature never intended should be wholly employed in the little bustling affairs of this spot of earth.

I am, Sir,
Your most humble & affect. Servt,
G. BERKELEY.

16 TO PERCIVAL

Trin. Coll., Jan. 19th, 1710/11

Dr Sr,
Being just returned from the County of Meath I received not so soon as otherwise I should have done your last wherein I am informed of my Lord's favourable acceptance of my book. I am very sensible of the obligations I have to Mr. Southwell for the trouble he has given himself in that affair, but since I have not the honour to be known by him, I doubt whether it be proper to return him thanks for the same. I leave it to you (who can best tell) whether it is or no, and if it be must beg the favour of you to do it for me. Dr. Clarke's conduct seems a little surprising. That an ingenious and candid person (as I take him to be) should declare I am in an error, and at the same time, out of modesty, refuse to shew me where it lies, is something unaccountable. For my own part, as I shall not be backward to recede from the opinion I

embrace when I see good reason against it, so on the other hand, I hope to be excused if I am confirmed in it, the more upon meeting with nothing but positive and general assertions to the contrary. I never expected that a gentleman otherwise so well employed should think it worth his while to enter into a dispute with me concerning any notions of mine. But being it was so clear to him that I went on false principles, I hoped he would vouchsafe in a line or two to point them out to me that so I may more closely review and examine them. If he but once did me this favour he need not apprehend I would give him any further trouble, or offer any the least occasion for drawing him into a dispute with me. If you should happen to meet with his friend by chance (for I have already given you too much trouble in this matter) I shall be obliged to you in case you will let him know this was all my ambition. I am very thankful to you for endeavouring to inform me more particular in Mr. Whiston's opinion. For there is nothing I more desire than to know thoroughly all that can be said against what I take for truth.

I am, Dr Sr,

Yr most obliged humble Servt,

G. BERKELEY.

17   TO PERCIVAL

Trin. Coll., Feb. 13th, 1710/11

Dr Sr,

Having so often troubled you with my impertinencies I know not what else to say, but that I leave it to your own good nature to apologise for my repeating the trespass in making this new request to you, viz. that you will take care the enclosed letter be delivered to my Lord Pembroke, either by yourself or by the hands of some friend, or if you shall not think fitting to use one of these methods in the delivery of it, that you will send a servant who will be sure to leave it at my Lord's. I send it unsealed so that if you or your friend please to deliver it you may see what it contains ; but you will remember to seal it if [. . .] upon reading it you think there is anything improper in it (which you are best judge of) as I would not have it delivered at all.

Of late we have been alarmed at several reports of the plague being landed in this kingdom, but they have proved to have nothing in them. Dr. Synge has put forth an answer to Archdeacon Percival's reply to Dr. Lambert's vindication of the letter, I mean to such part of it as concerns himself. I hear too that the Bishop of Cork is about an answer in his own behalf, so that the paper war is likely to prove violent and of long continuance. The new Lord Chancellor is much liked and well spoken of by all parties without seeming to interest himself in any. Your friends here are well, but we all long to see you and my Lady Percival, together with your little son (for such I hope it will prove), arrived safe on this side the water.

I am, Dr Sr,

Yr most obliged hum. Servt,

G. BERKELEY.

P.S. The ends that I propose in writing to my Lord are first to thank him for his acceptance of my book, and secondly to give him to understand by the most gentle and couched intimation possible that I should gladly know the particular grounds of his dissent from me in the point of matter's existence, or the faults he finds in the arguments on that head. But I have conceived a great scruple and suspicion that it is not proper for me to address his Lordship in a letter. It would therefore be a great satisfaction to me if those ends could be obtained by word of mouth from some friend especially yourself (if you are yet introduced into the acquaintance of my Lord). But whether this can be done or not, I beg the favour of you to suppress the letter if you think there is anything in it in the least presumptuous, unmannerly, or apt to give offence, and to let me know your thoughts in a line or two.

18   TO PERCIVAL

Trin. Coll., March 6th, 1710/11

Dr Sr,

This moment yours of the 27th of Feb. came to my hands. I heartily congratulate you upon your being blessed with a new sort of pleasure which bachelors cannot form a just notion of: something its reported there is in the tender passion of a father to his child so different from all other enjoyments. And this I doubt not is considerably heightened by the circumstances that attend it, as first the safe condition of my Lady Percival (which though you mention not, yet your letter assures me of it), and secondly the infant's proving of the nobler sex. It is true, your son and heir comes into the world at a factious and turbulent time, but I am not without hopes that he may spend the greater part of his life in the millennium, since from some modern interpretations we may expect it will be far gone before he comes to age. May he inherit your good qualities as well as your estate in order to which I entreat you will read Mr. Locke's book of 'Education' that abounds with excellent maxims. And, believe me, the foundations of a useful and healthy man cannot be laid too early.

I am, Sir,

Yr most humble and affec. Servt,

G. BERKELEY.

19   TO PERCIVAL

Trin. Coll., April 14, 1711

Dr Sir

The very day I received the favour of your last, I returned you my thanks for the same in a letter of congratulation on that happy circumstance of yr life, you were pleased to impart to me. Whether my letter came to your hands or no, I know not. I shall at present trouble you only with the perusal of the enclosed relation the facts it contains are attested in several letters from very good hands that were present at the Tryal. Some of which I have seen. Particularly Dr. Coghil Judge of the Perogative [*sic*] Court has received an account of the whole sent him by Dr. Tisdal a very ingenious divine who was in Court while the evidence upon oath of several credible persons were given in. So that you may depend upon it this paper tho' but sorrily writ has nothing in it which was not sworn to and after the nicest examination thought true by the Court. The letters mention some other circumstances which still make the story more surprising, and are not to be accounted for without some preternatural power. This is certain that the eight women are condemned. The judges were Upton & Macartney, of whom the former is said to be greatly prejudiced against all belief of witches, and Dr. Tisdal (who had been a Fellow of our College) seems to me the most unlikely man in the world to be imposed on in an affair of that nature, into which he has strictly inquired. I know not what credit this is likely to meet with in London. for my own part as I do not believe one in a thousand of these stories to be true, so neither on the other hand do I see sufficient grounds to conclude peremtorily against plain matter of fact well attested.

I am etc
G. BERKELEY.

20   TO PERCIVAL

Trin. Coll., June 3rd, 1711

Dr Sr,

I was given to expect that before this I should have had an opportunity of returning you my thanks here by word of mouth, but missing of that I cannot forbear any longer troubling you with a letter to express my acknowledgments for the care you were pleased to take of that I sent to my Lord Pembroke. I am very glad that your generous endeavours in behalf of our country have succeeded. Your friends here are well pleased upon their first finding by the printed notes that you stood up in opposition to the bill for a further impost on Irish yarn. I need not mention their sentiments on that occasion being persuaded that you think the inward satisfaction of having served your country a sufficient recompence for whatever trouble you were at on that account. This affair confirms me in a thought I formerly had, viz. that if some Irish gentlemen of good fortunes and generous inclinations would constantly reside in England, there to watch for the interest of their own country, they may at such conjunctures bring it far greater advantage than they would by spending their incomes at home.

Dan. Dering presents his humble service to you. He would be well in all respects if he held an employment suitable to his merit. Since the late ministry did not I hope the new will do something for him. They cannot place their favours on a more deserving young gentleman.

Pray give my service to your brother and to Mr. Clerke.

Sr,
Yr most humble and affect. Servt,
G. BERKELEY.

48

[1711]

Eruditissime Domine

Tractatum de Principiis Cognitionis Humanae Anglico idiomate conscriptum quem anno proxime elapso in lucem emisi Bibliopolae ut ad te transmittendum curaret in mandatis dedi. Unaque litteras ad te exarassem, nisi veritus essem obscurus homuncio celeberrimum virum rebus literariis undequaque occupatissimum ultro interpellare. Quod vero jam hoc facere sustineam, id tuae humanitati ingenuoque veritatis studio quod scripta tua luculenter prae se ferunt acceptum referri debet.

Quippe te cum ejus modi dotibus [?] inclarescas liberamque praeterea philosophandi rationem multum excolueris, si opem tuam sive ad castigandas meditationes nostras sive ad eas uberiori luce donandas rogarem, haud aegre laturum existimavi.

Hoc igitur abs te peto, vir clarissime, ut libro nostro praedicto locum (modo non indignus videatur) in bibliotheca tua selecta concedas, simulque sententiam tuam de doctrina inibi tradita aperte declarare ne detrectes.

Vel si hoc minus placuerit epistola privatim ad me missa errores meos si qui ubi deprehensi fuerint patefacere digneris. Cur vero id impensius optem in causa est quod tractatus iste (uti nec alter cui titulus An Essay etc qui anno 1709 typis mandatus erat) vix cuiquam extra hanc insulam quantum intelligo hactenus innotuit, etsi plurima exemplaria ad dominum Churchil transmissa fuerant.

Unde fit ut doctorum de scriptis meis judicia exceptis solummodo amici squibusdam hoc loco degentibus (qui opiniones nostras amplectuntur) ad me hactenus non pervenerint, id quod magno mihi studiorum impedimento est quippe qui primam tractatus nostri partem eruditorum examini seorsim subjectam voluerim eo fine ut vel ipsorum suffragiis confirmatus me alacrius ad consentanea inde deducenda partemque secundam praetexendam accingerem, vel si quid erratum esset tempestive corrigerem, vel denique falsis principiis dogmata nostra inniti monitus ea prorsus relinquerem meque in istis adornandis haud ultra incassum fatigarem.

$[c.\ 1711]$

Clarissime Vir,

Nuper ad hasce oras appulit Bibliothecae tuae Selectae Tomus vicesimus secundus, cui insertam reperio epitomen Tentaminis mei de Visione anno 1709 editi. Porro te veritatis amantem ratus adeo qui scripta tua quam emendatissima velis prodire, haud inique laturum spero, si errores unum alterumne indicavero, quos vel typographo vel etiam tibi, vir doctissime, festinanti scilicet et multiplici librorum [? laborum] genere occupato, excidisse non est quod admirandum.

Alios si qui sint minoris notae lapsus facile praetermiserim, isti autem quos memoravi, cum sensum a vero nimis quam dissentaneum lectori exhibeant et proinde cogitata nostra apud eos qui anglice non intelligunt, erroris immerito possint arguere, necessarium habui ut ad te scriberem eo utique fine, ut Bibliothecae tuae parte illa, quam proxime typis mandaturus es, corrigantur, quod quin tu libenter feceris, nullus [?] dubito.

P. 59, l. 19, B.S. (Bib. Sel.), pro *plus convergens* legere oportet *minus divergens* v. S.6 Tentaminis de visione.

P. 60, l. 5, B.S. pro his verbis ce qui fait que nous appercevons la distance, est premierement l'etressissement ou l'elargissement de la prunelle selon l'eloignement ou la proximité des objets lege ce qui fait nous appercevons la distance, est premierement la sensation qui accompagne l'etressissement ou l'elargissemment de l'interval, qui est entre les deux prunelles selon la proximité ou l'eloignement des objects ; v. S.15 (? 16) Tentaminis.

P. 52 (? 62), l. 4 pro l'objet lege un point visible ; v. S.34 Tentaminis

P. 62 (63) B.S. legitur convergens et convergence pro divergens et divergence et vice versa.

Animadversionibus utique tuis quae extensionis et figurarum ideas abstractas spectant quod sequitur duxi reponendum.

Primum igitur ad id quod invenio p. 81 me utique efformaturum istius modi ideas ope intellectus puri, si modo eum caute disjunxerim ab imaginatione, respondeo me nullo modo posse effingere ideam abstractam trianguli aut aliuscujuscunque figurae. Nec quidem capio qua ratione id exsequi queam distinguendo intellectum purum (ut metaphysici vulgo solent) ab imaginatione, quod adhibita omni mentis meae, qualiscunque tandem sit aut quocunque nomine insigniatur, vi et facultate, frustra saepe conatus fuerim.

Secundo, etiamsi admittatur distinctio illa, tamen intellectus purus mihi videtur versari tantum circa res spirituales, quae cognoscuntur per reflexionem in ipsam animam, ideas vero ex sensatione ortas, qualis est extensio, nullatenus [?] attingere.

Tertio, illud praeterea animadvertendum est quod aliud sit attendere solummodo ad unam qualitatem, aliud ejus ideam exclusa omni alia re aut qualitate in animo formare ; v.g. possum ego in motuum natura et legibus inquirendis animum tantum ad ipsum motum praecipue advertere atque intendere, nequeo tamen illius ideam efformare, nisi simul mente comprehendatur etiam res mota. Id sane pro certissimo habeo me non alias posse concipere rem aut qualitatem sensibilem adeoque nec ipsam extensionem quam sub imagine rei sensibilis, uti nec ulla mentis vi ideas earum rerum sensibilium disjungere distinctasque animo exhibere. Quae plane impossibile et repugnans sit ut sensum discretae ac invicem feriant atque ingrediantur.

Quod reliquum est, ad ea quae p. 76 habes de objecto geometriae, notandum quod vox *tangibilis* duplicem admittat sensum. Vel enim sumitur stricte pro eo solummodo quod palpari aut manibus attrectari possit vel laxiori significatu ita ut complectatur non modo res quae per tactum actumque [? situmque] percipi possint, ut quies et inane, quae nequeunt palpari, verum etiam ideas a mente ad similitudinem tactu perceptarum fictas. Cum igitur assero objectum geometriae esse extensionem tangibilem, id posteriori sensu accipiendum est. Nimirum figura, angulus, linea, punctum, quae mente contemplatur geometria, etsi ipsa sub sensum non cadant, tamen ad tactum referuntur, unde originem aliquo modo habent, quum per operationem mentis formentur ad speciem idearum tactui primitus impressarum.

Porro haec uberius tractare supervacaneum faciunt quae disseruimus in introductione, in sect 126 etc libri de Principiis Cognitionis Humanae, qui haud ita pridem luce donatus est.

Vale, Vir Clarissime, quodque te intempestive forsan solicitavimus, aequi et bone consule.

Trin. Coll., 17th May 1712

Dr Sr,

Your friends here are beholden to Mrs. Parker for letting us know by her letter to Mrs. Donnellan that you are all arrived safe at your journey's end. And I am very glad that the worst accident we have to condole with you upon, is your being obliged to make a meal at the barracks on cold meat. Burton I find pleases beyond expectation ; and I imagine it myself at this time one of the finest places in the world. And indeed the month of May, with the much more enlivening circumstance of good company, would make a more indifferent place delicious. Dunckarney, however, is not without its beauties ; and as I believe no news can be more agreeable to you than that which brings some account of its lonely inhabitants, I shall give a narrative of a visit I made them this evening.

I took a solitary walk that way, and upon my coming was informed that the little Lady and Esquire were withdrawn to their apartment. Miss indeed was in her deshabille, but for all that I was admitted to visit her, and she entertained me with a familiarity and frankness greater than I had observed before. Both her complexion and carriage are altered for the better, the one being very fair, and the other free from those stately and affected airs which methought she had in Capel Street. In a word she is grown a very charming and conversible Lady, and seemed not at all displeased at my visit. But good manners obliged me to shorten it, so after a little discourse about her absent friends I left her, and my entertainment fell to the Esquire's share who acquitted himself very obligingly. We took a turn in the gallery and then walked in the gardens and avenue. You must not now imagine a child held up by leading strings that has not a word to say, but a brisk young gentleman who walks alone and bears his part in conversation. I told him what news I had heard of my Lady, Mrs. Parker and yourself, with which he was very much pleased. But I observed his discourse ran chiefly on my Lady, whom he often mentioned, and seemed to long for her company to that degree, that if you still think of making the same stay you intended, I don't know but that he may send you a letter to desire you to hasten your return. He shall not want an amanuensis to write what he dictates in case he cannot do it himself.

I must not forget to tell you the following instance of his sagacity. As we were walking in the avenue Mr. Percival being taken with the sight of a fine silver holly must needs touch it, but as soon as he felt the prickles drew back his hand. And upon my insulting him and asking whether he would venture to touch it again, he very orderly borrowed my handkerchief and putting it about his hand touched the holly two or three times, to let me see he had wit enough to find a way of doing what I dared him to, without any inconvenience to his fingers.

He kisses still with open mouth, and has the same comical sneer with his nose. A child that shows such early and pregnant signs of good nature and good sense 'tis impossible I should not have a fondness for, even though he had not been your son. Yesterday I heard of a flaming beauty lately come from England who in Mrs. Parker's absence attracts the eyes of our gentleman, but I foresee her reign is not to last longer than four months at fartherest, and it is in the power of some at Burton to make it as much shorter as they please. But I forget myself, you are a grave married man, and I a sort of monk or recluse in a college ; it doth not therefore become me to talk to you of gallantry. So I conclude.

Pray give my humble service to my Lady, and Mrs. Parker. All friends are as well here as you can suppose them to be in the absence of so much good company.

Sr,

Yr most affect. humble Servt,

GEO. BERKELEY.

24   TO PERCIVAL

Trin. Coll., June 5th, 1712

Dr Sr,

You are grown so distrustful that I doubt you won't believe me, if I should tell you that I no sooner informed your son of the caution you gave him against women, but he fell a laughing, said it was all banter, and swore he would never make his father a liar (alluding, you may suppose, to the predictions you used to make of him in Capel Street), and upon that fell to kissing his sister and nurses with all the eagerness imaginable. That he kissed them heartily is literally true. But what more pretty things he said and did, how he called himself ' brave boy,' and played on the fiddle &c. you shall know nothing of from me, since you gave so little to the adventure of the handkerchief, which was really as I reported it. Miss has two teeth in sight, and is every day so much altered for the better, both in features and complexion, that I am sure she will appear a perfect little stranger to all of you when you see her next. Both she and her brother, being very pretty, hearty, give their duty to you, their mother, and their aunt.

Dan. Dering and I design to visit your paradise, and are sure of finding angels there, notwithstanding what you say of their vanity. In plain English we are agreed to go down to Burton together, and rejoice with the good company there. I give you this timely warning that you may hang up two hammocks in the barn against our coming. I never lie in a feather bed in the college, and before now have made a very comfortable shift with a hammock. I conclude in haste.

Last night a servant of one Mr. Alcock over the water hanged himself for the love of a coachman's daughter.
Sr,

Yr most humble and affect. Servt,

GEO. BERKELEY.

25   TO PERCIVAL

Trin. Coll., 18th Aug. 1712

Dr Sr,

On Saturday night we came safe to town. I know not whether it is worth while to tell you, that the day I set out, being already half dead with the thoughts of leaving so much good company, it seemed as if the weather would have given the finishing stroke to my life ; but the two following days were more favourable. Last night's pacquets have brought nothing remarkable that I can find, though at my first coming I met with a hot rumour in everybody's mouth of an action between the Dutch and French, whereof the event was uncertain. It is believed by some of our college-politicians that the Duke of Ormond stays in Flanders with a design to compel the Dutch to a peace in case they obstinately stand out. His Duchess, I hear, has been complimented by the Queen and Ministers upon his grace's conduct in securing Ghent &c. There is some talk of a triple alliance between Britain, France and Sweden. I am informed by a gentlemen of my acquaintance just come from London that the account of my Lord Albemarle's defeat was publicly cried about the streets by the title of good and joyful news. God grant that we have not a war with the Dutch.

I should have sent you the 4th part of *John Bull* but that Dan. Dering told me he sent it you by last Tuesday's post. My Lord Bolingbroke is expected suddenly from France, whither I suppose you know he lately went along with Mr. Prior. The other day two malefactors were publicly pilloried and afterwards burnt alive in Felster's shop for having offered some affront to the memory of King William, which for ever ought to be held (at least by all Protestants of these nations) glorious and immortal as are his actions.

My best news I keep for the last. The two children are both very well. Master was ill indeed but is at present very easy, and his eye teeth are in sight which makes us think him past all danger. I gave your and my Lady's blessing to him ; told him you were all well and designed to see him soon. He has made a new sort of a language for himself which I am not acquainted with, and as he is neither yet a perfect master of the English tongue, it is impossible for us exactly to understand one another. However, what with words and what with other signs and tokens he let me see his meaning. I am afraid to tell you the secret, but if I do, be sure do not let my Lady know it, lest it might prevent her ever spending another summer at Burton. To be plain the child seems not to care a farthing for you both. Long absence seems to have produced in him a perfect indifference for his parents. And a little longer stay will probably make him forget you quite. In all respects he is the same (with improvement) that he was before ; the same pleasant, sensible, good natured boy. Miss Kitty at first sight methought was grown unwieldily fat, but upon examination I found it to be a plump and firm flesh, which in a very sufficient quantity covers her cheeks and arms, betokening much nourishment and good digestion. She is as brisk and lively as you could wish, and is without dispute the most agreeable young lady that I have seen on this side Burton. Nevertheless if I may be allowed to be a judge of beauty I should give it master for features and miss for complection.

Robin stays impatiently for my letter which makes me conclude in haste with my most humble service to my Lady and Mrs. Parker. My humble service to Mr. Brererton. I delivered his letter, his wife and family are all well. I have made his excuses for not coming up.

> Dr Sr,
>> Yr most humble and most affect. Servt,
>> G. BERKELEY.

26   TO AN ENGLISHMAN   [*c.* 1712]

Sir,

I do not at all wonder that you or any true Englishman should be no less jealous for the honour than the safety of his country, and offended at anything which hath the face of baseness or treachery, however advantageous it may be thought to the public ; nor, by consequence, that you should scrupulously inquire into the justice of a separate peace, as being apprehensive the necessity of our affairs, together with the backwardness of the allies, may possibly oblige our Ministry to enter upon some such measures. But I was surprised that you should write to me to know my thoughts concerning an affair of that nature since you cannot be ignorant how foreign it must needs be as well to my retired way of life, as that particular sort of employment I have always chosen. And as I am an utter stranger to the treatys and engagements between Her Majesty and the high allies and but little skilled in the interests of the several states of Europe ; so I am persuaded there is nothing more misbecoming and unworthy a wise man than to pretend to give a judgment on things he is not acquainted with. Nevertheless since I hold myself obliged to show a particular regard to your commands, I shall give them all the satisfaction I am able ; by laying down some general theoremes and reasonings upon the sacredness of treatys and alliances between nations ; and considering upon or on what accounts they may be broken without guilt. The application of which to the present juncture of affairs I leave to yourself who having an exact knowledge of the engagements and interests of yr country and want nothing requisite to the forming a fine and impartial judgment on the point you are pleased to consult me upon, when you have inquired into the moral part of the question and considered in . . . the obligations by reason and religion on those engaged in an alliance for the prosecution of a war. Therefore with all the brevity and plainness I can, I lay it down in the first place for a fundamental axiom, that no Law of . . .

ought to be violated either for the obtaining any advantage or [escaping any] inconvenience whatever. . . . [Three defective lines.]

From these principles it clearly follows that Public Faith ought not to be sacrificed to private regards, nor even to the most pressing wants of a whole People. The violation therefore of a compact with foreign states can never be justified upon any pretext of that kind. Hence one nation having solemnly entered into articles of alliance with another, in case they afterwards perceive it highly for their advantage to break these articles ; yet a breach upon that score must certainly be looked upon as unjust and dishonourable. Nor doth it alter the case that the Alliance having been made under a former Ministry is disliked and condemned by the succeeding. For though the administration of affairs pass through several hands, yet the Prince and nation continue still the same ; every Ministry therefore is in duty bound to preserve sacred and intire the faith and honour of their Prince or country by standing firm to all alliances contracted under former Ministrys But with this difference, that in case the evils attending such an alliance shall appear to be fortuitous, or such as, at the making of it, could not have been foreseen, then the conditions of that disadvantageous alliance ought to be fulfilled at the public charge ; whereas if the Treaty shall appear originally and in itself prejudicial to the Public, then the fortunes of those ministers who made it ought to go towards defraying the expenses which, through rashness or treachery, they had engaged their country in.

Hitherto I have proceeded upon supposition that the foundation of the Alliance was just, or included nothing contrary to the laws of nature and religion. But in case several States enter into an agreement for commencing and carrying on the war upon unjust motives, [no sooner] shall any of those States be satisfied of the injustice of the cause on which the alliance is grounded, but they may with honour look upon themselves as disengaged from it. For example, suppose a parcel of Popish Potentates should, out of a pretence of doing right to the Pretender, engage in a war for placing him upon the throne of Great Britain, and some one of them was afterwards convinced. . . . [Here the MS. is defective for eight lines.]

It is also to be esteemed an unwarrantable procedure in case divers Potentates enter into a confederate war against an adjacent State for no other reason but because they apprehended it may otherwise become too powerful, and consequently too formidable a neighbour. For example, suppose the Dutch, jealous of that accession of strength to the British nation which will follow upon its union with Hannover, should engage themselves and friends in a war in order to force us to alter our succession ; we would, I presume, think this unlawful, and that it was the duty of any one of the confederates, so soon as he became sensible of the injustice of his cause, to cease from all hostilities, and (in case his allies were for continuing them) to enter into a separate peace with us. The truth of these positions is plain from the two principles at first laid down.

Further, it cannot be denied that one party may, without consent of the rest, break off from an alliance in war originally founded upon just and honourable motives, upon conviction that the ends for which the war was begun and in consideration whereof it was esteemed just are sufficiently answered ; although his allies, whether blinded by passion or finding their advantage in carrying on the war, or by what principle soever actuated, should not concur with him in the same judgment. For it is no excuse for a man's acting against his conscience that he made a bargain to do so. But here you'll demand what must be thought in case it was a fundamental article of the alliance, that no one party should hearken to proposals of peace without consent of the rest. I answer that any such engagement is in itself absolutely void, forasmuch as it is sinful, and what no Prince or State can lawfully enter into, it being in effect no less than binding themselves to the commission of murder, rapine, sacrilege, and of violence, so long as it shall seem good to their . . . what else I beseech you is war abstracted from the necessity . . . but a complication of all these. [MS. defective for three or four lines.]

P.S. Another obvious indisputable case there is which absolves a party from fulfilling the conditions of any contract, namely, when those with whom the contract was made fail to perform their part of it. Lastly, in case two or more States, for their mutual security, enter into a league to deprive a neighbouring Prince of some part of his possessions and add them unto those of another in order to constitute a ballance of Power. Allowing the grounds whereon the war is founded to be just, yet if, during the progress of it, the Prince whose territories were to be enlarged shall, by some unexpected turn, grow far more great and powerful than he was at the making of the treaty, it should seem the afforesaid States are disengaged from their contract to each other, which, having

been originally by all parties introduced and understood only as
a means to obtain a ballance of Power, can never be of force to
oblige them to act for a direct contrary purpose.

27   TO PERCIVAL

London, Jan. 26th, 1712/13

Dear Sir John,

In a fortnight after I left Dublin I arrived here having
made easy journeys and staid some time at Chester. The road
from Coventry to London was very bad, the rest of the way
tolerable enough. I was surprised to find the country in the depth
of winter look incomparably pleasanter than most parts of Ireland
in midsummer. But if the country outdid my expectation, the
towns fell short of it, even London itself seems to exceed Dublin
not so much in the stateliness or beauty of its buildings as in extent.
I wrote from Holyhead to an acquaintance of mine to provide me
a lodging, which he did in the same house with the provost and
Mr. Molyneux. We generally see one another in the morning, but
for the rest of the day are dispersed about the town, and I loving
early hours am gone to bed before either of them come home at
night. Upon my first coming I was confined for some days, till
my portmanteaux came by carriage from Chester. In the meantime Mr. Clerke hearing I was in town came to see me, and next
day engaged Charles Dering and me to dine at his house with
him, which is very neat and convenient. He is as I always found
him very obliging and good natured, and seems in as good health
as ever I knew him. He went with me to Mr. Southwell, who
received me very civilly, and with great willingness introduced
me two days since to my Lord Pembroke, who is a man perfectly
good natured as well as very learned, and with whom I have the
prospect of passing some part of my time as much to my satisfaction as anything can be in the absence of my friends in Ireland.
As I troubled you to ask this favour of Mr. Southwell, so I must
again trouble you to thank him for it the first time you write to
him. There is lately published a very bold and pernicious book
entitled a *Discourse on Free Thinking*. I hear the printer of it
is put into Newgate, as is likewise a woman for selling a ballad
on the Duke D'Aumont as being a wine-merchant.

For want of other news you must give me leave to tell you

a very remarkable story I heard the other morning from the Provost and Mr. Molyneux. Mr. Tickel, fellow of Oxford, an ingenious, credible and sober person, author of the poem on the approaching peace, gave them the following account. That there is in a forest in Hampshire an oak which buds and shoots forth leaves every Christmas day. A year or two ago he went himself to make the experiment. He saw it in a light night about two hours before day, at which time it had not the least appearance of bud or leaf, but when day came was covered with both : several of the leaves about as large as sixpence he plucked and carried to Oxford, where about forty persons saw them. A gentleman, who was present when the Provost and Mr. Molyneux were telling this fact, added he had seen some of the leaves gathered by another.

The first news I heard upon coming to town was that Mr. Steele did me the honour to desire to be acquainted with me : upon which I have been to see him. He is confined with the gout, and is, as I am informed, writing a play since he gave over the *Spectators.* This gentleman is extremely civil and obliging, and I propose no small satisfaction on the conversation of him and his ingenious friends, which as an encouragement he tells me are to be met with at his house. The Bishop of Dromore is dead : yesterday in the afternoon the French Ambassador's house was burnt down to the ground by the carelessness of his servants. They say fine pictures and other moveables of the Duke of Powis's are likewise burnt in it, being locked up in the garrets to the value of forty thousand pounds. The other day dining at a tavern with two or three Irish clergymen, I found it a very difficult matter to persuade them you were no Whig : I venture however to send you the enclosed *Examiners,* as well knowing you are no enemy to wit and humour, though in a Tory. Of late they are written by some new hand, and much better than formerly ; I speak not with regard to the party debates, but to the style and spirit, which is all we moderate sort of men mind in those sort of papers.

Your most affect. & most obliged humble Servt,

GEO. BERKELEY.

This day I dined again at Mr. Clerke's where we drank your health. He talks of seeing you in Ireland this summer, and says Dublin is the finest city in the world.

My letters are directed to the Pall Mall Coffee-House in the Pall Mall.

Dear Sir John,   London, Feb. 23rd, 1712/13

This night Mr. Bligh is to have a ball at the late Duke
Hamilton's house in St James's Square. The Marlborough family
and one Mrs. Warburton and Mrs. Duncomb make part of his
company. Sir Philip is at length come to town. I find in him
that frank good humour and other good qualities which might
be expected in my Lady's and Mrs. Parker's brother : he is
very obliging.

Mr. Addison and Mr. Steele (and so far as I can find, the rest
of that party) seem entirely persuaded there is a design for bringing over the Pretender ; they think everything looks that way,
and particularly three of the best Papist officers, Lieutenant
General Mackoni, Major General Laules, and Brigadier Skelton,
being now all in London. Laules, Mr. Addison assured me, was
discovered by an officer at the Queen's birthnight, the other two
came over, one on pretence of sueing for his wife's or sister's fortune,
the other of being in love with a lady here. All these are Irishmen,
that have followed the fortunes of King James. I have heard
another general officer of the same gang mentioned as being here,
but forgot his name ; and that the Duke of Berwick's aunt was
known to say, her nephew would soon be in London. Some
Jacobite Tories whom I have happened to converse with seem full
of the same expectations. I must desire you will not quote me for
this, not caring to be thought the spreader of such news. But I
tell this to my Lady, Mrs. Parker, and yourself, that you may take
proper measures against that time.

The value you always shewed for the *Spectator* makes me
think it neither impertinent nor unwelcome news to tell you that
by his mother-in-law's death he is come into an estate of five
hundred pounds a year ; the same day his wife was brought to
bed of a son. Before she laid down the poor man told me he was
in great pain and put to a thousand little shifts to conceal her
mother's desperate illness from her. The tender concern he
shewed on that occasion, and what I have observed in another
good friend of mine, makes me imagine the best men are always
the best husbands. I told Mr. Steele if he neglects to resume his
writings, the world will look on it as the effects of his growing rich.
But he says this addition to his fortune will rather encourage him
to exert himself more than ever ; and I am the apter to believe

him, because there appears in his natural temper something very generous and a great benevolence to mankind. One instance of it is his kind and friendly behaviour to me (even though he has heard I am a Tory). I have dined frequently at his house in Bloomsbury Square, which is handsome and neatly furnished. His table, servants, coach and everything is very genteel, and in appearance above his fortune before this new acquisition. His conversation is very cheerful and abounds with wit and good sense. Somebody (I know not who) had given him my treatise of the *Principles of Human Knowledge* and that was the ground of his inclination to my acquaintance. For my part I should reckon it a sufficient recompence of my pains in writing it, that it gave me some share in the friendship of so worthy a man. But though conversation of him and other new friends is very agreeable, yet I assure you it all falls short of Capel Street.

I hear a sudden and general rumour that the peace has passed the seals and will be proclaimed next week. News from your fireside (would you but oblige me so far) would be infinitely more acceptable than from any court in Europe. My most humble service to my Lady and Mrs. Parker.

Your most affect. and obliged Servt,
G. BERKELEY.

29   TO PERCIVAL

Dr Sr John,   London, March 7th, 1712/13

I know not by what accident yours of the 11 Feby came not to my hands till the last post. Your presages of my good fortune I look on rather as kind wishes that deserve my thanks, than real prophecies that may raise my hopes. Happiness, whether in a high or low degree, is the same thing. And I desire no more. And this perhaps is more within anybody's reach than is vulgarly imagined.

In my last I gave you some intimation of Mr. Bligh's ball. The Marlborough's family being there disgraced him with the Tories, his friends at the Cocoa-tree, whither he constantly goes. And soon after it there was an advertisement published in one of the printed papers, giving an account that the Duchess of Marlborough had left a hundred guineas to be laid out in a ball at Duke Hamilton's House, as a triumph over his Grace's memory.

This affront, which robbed him of the glory of his ball, could not but be uneasy to Mr. Bligh. Dr. Swift (whom I met by chance at my Lord Pembroke's two nights agone) told me Mr. Bligh had applied to the author of the *Post-Boy*, to publish contradiction to his former advertisement ; but that he refused to do it without the Duchess of Hamilton's consent. Mr. Bligh prevailed with Dr. Swift to introduce him to the Duchess in order to obtain it. But her Grace being a smart woman, and the Dr. (as he says himself) very ill naturedly taking part with her against Dr. Bligh, they proved to him the unreasonableness of his request, and sent him away in no small confusion.

It is reported we shall have the peace proclaimed this week. Both Whigs and Tories give out, either that six new peers are to be created, or more than that number of young noblemen called up into the House of Lords.

You will soon hear of Mr. Steele under the character of the ' Guardian ' ; he designs his paper shall come out every day as the *Spectator*. He is likewise proposing a noble entertainment for persons of a refined taste. It is chiefly to consist of the finest pieces of eloquence translated from the Greek and Latin authors. They will be accompanied with the best music suited to raise those passions that are proper to the occasion. Pieces of poetry will be there recited. These informations I have from Mr. Steele himself. I have seen the place designed for these performances : it is in York Buildings, and he has been at no small expence to embellish with all imaginable decorations. It is by much the finest chamber I have seen, and will contain seats for a select company of 200 persons of the best quality and taste, who are to be subscribers. I had last night a very ingenious new poem upon Windsor Forest given me by the author, Mr. Pope. This gentleman is a Papist, but a man of excellent wit and learning, and one of those Mr. Steele mentions in his last paper as having writ some of the *Spectators*.

I am extremely honoured by my Lady and Mrs. Parker that they have not quite forgot me. Pray give my best humble service to them, and let them know that notwithstanding the great distance between us they are every day present to my thoughts. Sir Philip and Mr. Clerke are very well. We were a day or two agone at Mr. Clerke's remembering our friends in Ireland.

I am, Dr Sr John,

Yr most humb. & affect. Servt,

G. Berkeley.

London, March 27th, 1712/13

Dr Sr,

I received your letter about three days since. Your opinion of Mr. Steele I take to be very just, and am persuaded a man of his discernment and insight into men will know how to value an acquaintance so much to be courted as that you design to honour him with. His wit, natural good sense, generous sentiments, and enterprising genius, with a peculiar delicacy and easiness of writing, seem those qualities which distinguish Mr. Steele. Mr. Addison has the same talents in a high degree, and is likewise a great philosopher, having applied himself to speculative studies more than any of the wits that I know.

After what I have formerly told you of the apprehensions those gentlemen had, I think myself obliged to let you know that they are now all over. Mr. Steele having told me this week that he now imagines my Lord Treasurer had no design of bringing in the Pretender, and in case he had, that he is persuaded he could never perform it ; and this morning I breakfasted with Mr. Addison at Dr. Swift's lodging. His coming in whilst I was there, and the good temper he shewed, was construed by me as a sign of an approaching coalition of parties, Mr. Addison being more earnest in the Whig cause than Mr. Steele (the former having quitted an employment, rather than hold it under the Tories, which by a little compliance he might have done), and there having passed a coldness, if not a direct breach, between those two gentlemen and Dr. Swift on the score of politics. Dr. Swift's wit is admired by both of them, and indeed by his greatest enemies ; and if I were not afraid of disobliging my Lady and Mrs. Parker I should tell you that I think him one of the best natured and agreeable men in the world.

Mr. Steele's entertainment at York Buildings only waits the finishing of two pictures, the one of truth, the other of eloquence, which are designed as part of the ornaments of the place where it is to be. He tells me he has had some discourse with the Lord Treasurer relating to it, and talks as if he would engage my Lord Treasurer in his project, designing that it shall comprehend both Whigs and Tories. A play of Mr. Steele's, which was expected, he has now put off to next winter. But *Cato*, a most noble play of Mr. Addison's, and the only one he writ, is to be acted in Easter

week. The town is full of expectation of it, the boxes being already
bespoke, and he designing to give all the benefit away among
the actors in proportion to their performing. I would send you
the *Guardians* and two very fine poems, one of them being
writ by an Irish Clergyman, Dr. Parnell, if you would direct
me how.

My humble service to my Lady and Mrs. Parker.

Yr most hum. Servt,
G. BERKELEY.

31   TO PERCIVAL

London, Apr. 16th, 1713

Dr Sr,

If I had sooner known of my Lady's being delivered of
a daughter, I should sooner have congratulated you upon that
good fortune. I say this that you might not think me insensible
of your happiness, though you were not pleased to impart it
to me.

For public news I suppose the public papers sufficiently inform
you as to that. However I shall tell you two or three particulars
which I believe you have not heard. About three weeks ago my
Lord Treasurer was at a meeting of Whigs at my Lord Halifax's
house. The Duke of Argyle and some other Tory Lords who
were jealous of this taxed my Lord Treasurer with it in a private
company, and were curious to know what was the business of
that conference ; to which he answered no more than this :
What ! am I not fit to be trusted ? I would not be understood
to apprehend a change by this, but only tell it as an instance of
that man's secrecy, and to shew that he is not on such violent
terms with those of the other party as may be imagined. I was
informed of this by a gentleman that was present at what passed
between my Lord and the Duke of Argyle &c. The same person
is very acquainted with all the ministers and with my Lady
Masham and declared to me that he never heard the least expression drop from any of them (and he makes one in almost all
their partys of private meetings) that looked like an inclination
to the Pretender.

On Tuesday last Mr. Addison's play entitled Cato was acted
the first time. I am informed the front boxes were all bespoke

for nine days, a fortnight before the play was acted. I was present with Mr. Addison, and two or three more friends in a side box, where we had a table and two or three flasks of burgundy and champagne, with which the author (who is a very sober man) thought it necessary to support his spirits in the concern he was then under ; and indeed it was a pleasant refreshment to us all between the acts. He has performed a very difficult task with great success, having introduced the noblest ideas of virtue and religion upon the stage with the greatest applause, and in the fullest audience that ever was known. The actors were at the expence of new habits, which were very magnificent, and Mr. Addison takes no part of the profit, which will be very great, to himself. Some parts of the prologue, which were written by Mr. Pope, a Tory and even a Papist, were hissed, being thought to savour of whiggism, but the clap got much [the better of] the hiss. My Lord Harley, who sat in the next box to us, was observed to clap as loud as any in the house all the time of the play. Though some Tories imagine his play to have an ill design, yet I am persuaded you are not so violent as to be displeased at the good success of an author (whose aim is to reform the stage) because his hero was thought to be a Roman whig.

This day I dined at Dr. Arbuthnot's lodging in the Queen's palace. The Dr. read part of a letter from a friend in France, which gave an account that the French king is now forming a company of merchants to whom he will grant great privileges and encouragements to import into his kingdom sixty thousand head of black cattle alive. The gentleman who wrote the letter (whose name I am obliged not to mention) says that he was offered to be made director of this affair but that he refused it, being of the opinion it would prove very prejudicial to Her Majesty's dominions, and particularly to Ireland, whence they propose to import the greatest part of the cattle. This looks as if the stock of France was exhausted, and perhaps it may not be amiss if the Council of Ireland would enter on some measures to prevent the exhausting the stock of their own country by supplying France.

This Dr. Arbuthnot is the first proselyte I have made by the Treatise I came over to print, which will soon be published. His wit you have an instance of in his *Art of Political Lying*, and the tracts of *John Bull* of which he is the author. He is the Queen's domestic physician, and in great esteem with the whole Court. Nor is he less valuable for his learning, being a great philosopher, and reckoned among the first mathematicians of the age. Besides which he has likewise the character of very uncommon virtue and probity.

D. Dering is so full of business that I can hardly ever see him. My humble service to my Lady and Mrs. Parker. Pray inform me of the children in your next.

> Your most hum. Servt,
> G. BERKELEY.

32 TO PERCIVAL

London, 7th May 1713

Dr Sr,

I am very glad to hear that Miss has pleased the world so well upon her first appearance in it, and foresee there is not a pair in the Queen's dominions to whom the public will have greater obligations for propagating a healthy and beautiful race, than to my Lady and yourself.

By the account I gave you in my last, I did not apprehend that the French would be able to rival us in our beef trade, but the danger that I and others apprehended from their project was, that the exporting so many head of black cattle out of Ireland might lessen the stock there, and by that means occasion an effect in its consequences much more prejudicial to the kingdom, than the present pistoles they would import might be of advantage to it.

Mr. Molyneux has been this considerable time gone for Utrecht, whence he designs to continue his travels into Italy &c., and Mr. Bligh is gone to France.

Mr. Addison's play has taken wonderfully, they have acted it now almost a month, and would I believe act it a month longer were it not that Mrs. Oldfield cannot hold out any longer, having had for several nights past, as I am informed, a midwife behind the scenes, which is surely very unbecoming the character of Cato's daughter. I hear likewise that the principal players are resolved for the future to reform the stage, and suffer nothing to be repeated there, which the most virtuous persons might not hear, being now convinced by experience that no play ever drew a greater concourse of people, than the most virtuous.

Pray let my Lady and Mrs. Parker know that I converse

much with Whigs. The very day on which the peace was proclaimed, instead of associating with Tories, I dined with several
of the other party at Dr. Garth's, where we drank the Duke of
Marlborough's health, though they had not the heart to speak
one word against the peace, and indeed the spirit of the Whigs
seems quite broken, and is not likely to recover.

I believe as you do that I shall stay longer here than I at
first designed, and am much obliged to you for your kind offer,
but, I thank God, that way of life which best suits with my circumstances is not disagreeable to my inclinations. There is here a
Lord of my name, a man of letters and a very worthy man, from
whom I have received great civilities ; I dine two or three times
a week at his table, and there are several other places where I
am invited, which lightens my expence, and makes it easier living
here than I expected. I saw Sir Philip Parker yesterday. He
is resolved upon going to Ireland the latter end of this, or the
beginning of next, month. My humble service to my Lady and
Mrs. Parker.

I am, Dr Sir,
Your most obliged & most humb. Servt,
G. Berkeley.

33   TO PERCIVAL

London, 2nd June 1713

Dr Sr,

Your letter wherein you desire me to assist Mr. Daniel
Dering in the choice of a telescope for you came to my hands
after his departure for Ireland. If in that or any other affair
you will lay your commands upon me, I hope I need not tell you
that I should be glad to serve you. As to what you mention of
a dispute on foot here, concerning the invention of some notions
that I have published, I do not know of anything which might
give ground for that report, unless it be that a clergyman of
Wiltshire has lately put forth a treatise, wherein he advances
something which had been published three years before in my
Treatise concerning the Principles of Human Knowledge. D. Dering
brings you one of the books I printed the other day. I shall
be very glad to hear your opinion of it, and that you thought
it worth your perusal. I have discoursed with Mr. Addison,

Dr. Smalridge, and several others since my coming hither, upon the points I have endeavoured to introduce into the world. I find them to be men of clear understandings and great candour.

Having mentioned Dr. Smalridge I cannot but take notice to you that I think myself very happy in the acquaintance I have made with him. He is a man no less amiable for his cheerfulness of temper and good nature, than he is to be respected for his piety and learning. He and Bishop Atterbury are mentioned for the Bishopric of Rochester and Deanery of Westminster, which go together. If Atterbury is preferred before him, people will look on it as owing to a division between that Dean and the Canons of Christchurch, Oxon, which the government is willing to put an end to.

The Scotch are in a great ferment, occasioned by the malt tax, insomuch that they have proposed the breaking of the Union. And it is now in the mouth of everyone that the Duke of Argyle and the rest of them are fallen off from the Court interests. It is reported that they had lately a meeting with the Whigs at the Duke of Devonshire's, wherein they promised to vote with them for bringing over the heir of Hanover, and running down the Treaty of Commerce, in case the Whigs would join them in taking off the malt tax. This trafficking for votes looks very dishonourable. Love of their country is pretended to be the motive that stirs up the Scots, but others think it is love of places and pensions which they propose to get by bullying the Court.

My most humble service to my Lady and Mrs. Parker.

I am, in haste,

Your most humble & affect. Servant,

GEORGE BERKELEY.

34 TO PERCIVAL

Oxford, 19th July 1713

Dr Sr,

I have been now almost a month in this town and think it to be the most delightful place I have ever seen, as well as for the pleasantness of its situation, as that great number of ancient and modern buildings which have a very agreeable effect on my eye, though I came from London and visited Hampton Court and Windsor by the way.

It may perhaps be some entertainment to give you an account of the solemnity with which the Act has been celebrated in this place. For several days together we have had the best music of all kinds in the theatre performed by the most eminent persons of London, from the Opera, Queen's Chapel &c., joined with some belonging to the chorus of Oxford ; and with the music there were intermixed public exercises as disputations in the several facultys, speeches, declamations, and verses. These performances drew together a great concourse both from London and the country, amongst whom were several foreigners, particularly about thirty Frenchmen of the Ambassador's company, who (it is reported) were all robbed by one single highwayman as they were coming from London, who is since taken. The town was so crowded that lodgings at other times not worth half a crown were set for a guinea the week. It was computed that at once there were two thousand ladies in the theatre. During the time of the Act and since, there was nothing but feasting and music in the several colleges. Plays are acted every night, and the town is filled with puppet-shows, and other the like diversions. But there is no part of the entertainment so agreeable to me as the conversation of Dr. Smalridge, who is in all respects a most excellent person. Two days since he was installed Dean of Christ Church. The same day a young gentleman of Christ Church College was found drowned in the public house of office. He fell in about four days before, through the holes which were too wide, and by some groans that were heard it is computed that he lived about five hours in that miserable condition.

The weather is extremely bad, I think no better than we had last summer at Burton. And indeed in this particular I have been very much disappointed ever since my coming into England.

My most humble respects to my Lady, Mrs. Parker, your little son and daughters. I should be glad to hear how Mr Johnny speaks, and what he says. If you favour me with a line, direct to Mr. Ives's over against All Souls College,

         I am, Sr,

            Your most humble & affect. Servant,

               G. BERKELEY.

Oxford, Aug. 7th, 1713

Dr Sr,

It makes me have a better opinion of my book that you have thought it worth your while to read it through, and not dislike the notions it contains the more for having attended to them. As it was my intention to conceal or smother nothing that made against me I endeavoured to place all objections in the fairest light, and if either you or any other ingenious friend will communicate any which are not answered, I shall not fail to consider them with all the impartiality I can.

As to what you write of Dr. Arbuthnot's not being of my opinion, it is true there has been some difference between us concerning some notions relating to the necessity of the laws of nature, but this does not touch the main point of the non-existence of what philosophers call material substance, against which he has acknowledged he can object nothing.

I cannot imagine what should give occasion to the report of my not designing to go back to Ireland, since I have never written one word to that purpose to any friend there. I thank you for your kind concern for my advancement in the world, though I assure you it is not any prospect of that kind that detains me here. The steps I have taken since my coming hither, having been rather in order to make some acquaintance with men of merit, than to engage myself in the interests of those in power. Besides the greatest satisfaction which I proposed by living in England, I am utterly disappointed in, I mean fair weather, which we have had as little of here as ever I knew in the worst season in Ireland. And this circumstance makes me more in love with my own country than I was before. There is another motive which would give the preference in my thoughts to Ireland, viz. the conversation of yourself and the good company you have with you ; but when I consider it is likely you will spend as much of your time here as there, I look on that point as making for neither side. The more I think on it, the more I am persuaded that my happiness will not consist in riches and advancement. If I could prosecute my studies in health and tranquillity, that would make me as happy as I expect to be in this life, but in the College I enjoyed neither in that degree I do at present.

Pray give my most humble service to my Lady and Mrs. Parker, and her nephew and nieces.

I am, Dr Sr,

Yr most affect. & most obliged humble Servt,

GEO. BERKELEY.

36   TO PERCIVAL

London, Aug. 27th, 1713

Dr Sr,

Last night I came hither from Oxford. I could not without some regret leave a place which I had found so entertaining, on account of the pleasant situation, healthy air, magnificent buildings, and good company, all which I enjoyed the last fortnight of my being there with much better relish than I had done before, the weather having been during that time very fair, without which I find nothing can be agreeable to me. But the far greater affliction that I sustained about this time twelvemonth in leaving Burton made this seem a small misfortune. The first news I heard upon my coming to town was that two or three nights since Mr. Bligh was married to the Lady Theodosia Hide, daughter of the Earl of Clarendon. I am told she is a great beauty, and has to her fortune about two thousand pound per annum : but I believe this is magnified. She is Baroness of Clifton, which title will descend to her son. I went to see him this morning when it was past ten o'clock, but he was not then stirring. Mr. Bligh has not been above ten days come from France, so that the match must have been very sudden. The Provost who knows Lady Thodosia says she is of a brisk and lively temper. I hardly find anyone that I used to converse with in town. But I was obliged to come here in order to solicit a licence for absence from the College, at the Secretary's Office, the house thinking themselves obliged to put me to the expence and trouble of it. Mr. Clerke I am informed went yesterday to the Bath. Pray give my humble respects to my Lady, Mrs Parker, Sir Philip, and the little pledges of your and my Lady's love.

I am, Dear Sir,

Your most humble & most affect. Servt,

G. BERKELEY.

Dr Sr,   London, 2nd Oct. 1713

The description you favoured me with of your little off-spring was very entertaining, and though slightly amiable has, I am persuaded, nothing of a father's fondness in it : what shall we think of your family which had before the greatest charms of any that I ever knew, when it is enriched by the accession of these growing wits and beauties.   As I cannot but think your condition to be envied for the present, since you have so much good company within your own walls, so I am troubled when I consider, that you must lose it in a little time ; your son will distinguish himself in the University, and at Court, and your daughters will be forced from you by men of the greatest merit and fortune in England.

Lady Theodosia Bligh is I think the most airy young creature I ever saw : she detests the thought of going to Ireland, and Mr. Bligh is about taking a house, and purchasing the furniture of it from myDr. Stairs.

I am informed that the Queen and Council at Windsor have decided the affair in dispute between the Government and city of Dublin in favour of the latter, to me it is surprising that you should begin a contest with the aldermen which you were not able to go through with.

I have good hopes that the public welfare will be better provided for by our treaty of peace and commerce than you seem to apprehend.   My reason for this is, that on all hands it is agreed the Tories have incomparably the majority in the elections for parliament men, which could hardly be, in case they were thought to pursue methods destructive of the nation.   Since I have been obliged to get a licence from the Queen for absence from the college, I shall probably stay longer than I intended, and do not now think of returning before Christmas.

Mr. Steele having laid down his employments, because (as he says) he would not be obliged to those to whom he could not be grateful, has of late turned his head towards politics and published a pamphlet in relation to Dunkirk, which you may perhaps have seen by this time.

My humble service to my Lady and Mrs. Parker.
                    Dr Sr,
                              Your most humble & affect. Servant,
                                        G. BERKELEY.

38 TO PERCIVAL

London, 15th Oct. 1713

Dr Sr,

I have just time to take my leave of you and let you know that I am now on the point of going to Sicily, where I propose seeing the new king's coronation. I go Chaplain to my Lord Peterborough who is the ambassador extraordinary sent thither on this occasion. We take France, &c. in our way. There is not any place that I have a greater curiosity to see than Sicily. I cannot now make a certain judgment of things, how they are likely to go with me, but when I am there in case I find myself pressed I shall have recourse to the kind offer you have often made me. This notion is very sudden. Pray give my respects to my Lady, Mrs. Parker, &c.

I am, Dr Sr,

Your most affect. & obed. Servt,

G. BERKELEY.

39 TO PERCIVAL

Paris, 24th Nov. N.S. 1713

Dr Sr,

On the 25th Oct. O.S. I set out from London in company of a Frenchman, a Spaniard, and a Flandrian, with three English servants of my Lord's. I was glad of this opportunity of going before with Col. Du Hamel, my Lord's aide-de-camp, that I may have time to see Paris etc. before my Lord's arrival ; besides I found a great benefit in travelling with foreigners, which obliged me to speak the French language. The 29th about four in the morning after a very narrow escape we landed at Calais. Here my Lord's chariot, which brought the Colonel and me from London to Dover, was to wait his coming ; and it was left to my choice either to ride fast with the Col. (who was obliged to go before to provide lodgings &c. in Paris), or stay till the stage coach went. I chose the latter, and on the 12th Novr N.S. em-

6

barked in the stage-coach with a company who were all perfect
strangers to me. There happened to be one English gentleman
and two Scotch, among whom was Mr. Martin, the author of
The Voyage to St Kilda. He also published an account of the
other western islands of Scotland. We were very cheerful on the
road, and the inhabitants of St Kilda did not a little contribute
to our diversion. For certain reasons I omit saying anything
of the country, the towns, or the people that we saw in our seven
days' journey from Calais to Paris, where we arrived on the 17th
N.S. in the evening. The next day I dined with the Ambassador
of Sicily, where there were several Sicilian and Piedmontese
persons of quality. Since that I have visited Mr. Prior, and am
to dine with him today. He is a man of good sense and learning,
and lives magnificently as becomes the Queen's Plenipotentiary.
My time is thus divided between foreigners and statesmen, and
the intervals of time are filled up with thinking on my absent
friends, and viewing the noble buildings and pieces of painting
and statuary, which are here very numerous, and so far as I can
judge excellent.

I have here met with a pleasant ingenious gentleman, Monsr
l'abbé d'Aubigne, Chevalier of the order of St Lazarus, who has
undertaken to shew me everything that is curious. I have spent
the two last days with him : today he is to introduce me to Father
Mallebranche, a famous philosopher in this city ; and tomorrow
we go together to Versailles. It were endless to recount particulars,
all I shall say is, that the magnificence of their churches and
convents surpasses my expectation. The day before yesterday I
visited the place de Vendome, le place de Victoire, and le place
Regale, and the Louvre, le convent des Capucins, le Feuillant,
l'Eglise des Minims, l'Eglise des Celestins, where are the tombs
of the ancient kings. Yesterday we saw the monastery of Ste
Genevieve, with its library and cabinet of rarities ; the English
college where the body of King James and that of his daughter
are still to be seen exposed in their coffins. The people who take
the king for a saint have broke off several pieces of the coffin, &c.
for relics. We saw likewise the Irish college, and the Sorbonne,
where we were present at their Divinity disputations. All is
wonderfully fine and curious, but the finest of all is the Chapel
in the Church of the Invalides, which the Abbé d'Aubigne assured
me was not to be surpassed in Italy. We now expect my Lord
every minute in Paris ; so that I am in a great hurry, being
willing to profit of the little time I stay here ; however, I snatched

the present moment to write you this scrawl, which I hope you will excuse.

Dr Sr,

Your most humle & most affect. Servt,

G. BERKELEY.

My most humble service to my Lady and Mrs. Parker.

40   TO PRIOR

Paris, November 25, 1713, N.S.

Dear Tom,

From London to Calais I came in the company of a Flamand, a Spaniard, a Frenchman, and three English servants of my Lord. The three gentlemen being of those different nations obliged me to speak the French language (which is now familiar), and gave me the opportunity of seeing much of the world in a little compass. After a very remarkable escape from rocks and banks of sand, and darkness and storm, and the hazards that attend rash and ignorant seamen, we arrived at Calais in a vessel which, returning the next day, was cast away in the harbour in open daylight, (as I think I already told you). From Calais, Colonel du Hamel left it to my choice either to go with him by post to Paris, or come after in the stage-coach. I chose the latter ; and, on November 1, O.S., embarked in the stage-coach with a company that were all perfect strangers to me. There were two Scotch, and one English gentleman. One of the former happened to be the author of the *Voyage to St. Kilda*, and the *Account of the Western Isles*. We were good company on the road ; and that day se'ennight came to Paris.

I have been since taken up in viewing churches, convents, palaces, colleges, &c., which are very numerous and magnificent in this town. The splendour and riches of these things surpasses belief ; but it were endless to descend to particulars. I was present at a disputation in the Sorbonne, which indeed had much of the French fire in it. I saw the Irish and the English colleges. In the latter I saw, inclosed in a coffin, the body of the late king James. Bits of the coffin, and of the cloth that hangs the room, have been cut away for relics, he being esteemed a great saint by the people. The day after I came to town, I dined at the ambassador of Sicily's ; and this day with Mr. Prior. I snatched an opportunity to mention you to him, and do your character justice. To-morrow I intend to visit Father Malebranche, and discourse him on certain points. I have some reasons to decline speaking of the country or villages that I saw as I came along.

My Lord is just now arrived, and tells me he has an opportunity of sending my letters to my friends to-morrow morning, which occasions my writing this. My humble service to Sir John Rawdon, Mrs. Rawdon, Mrs. Kempsy, and all other friends. My Lord thinks he shall stay a fortnight here.

I am, dear Tom,
Your affectionate humble servant,
G. BERKELEY.

I must give you the trouble of putting the inclosed in the penny-post.

41   TO PERCIVAL

Lyons, Dec. 28th, 1713

Dr Sr,

Lyons has been filled all this day with rejoicings of all sorts, on account of the king's statue, which was placed this morning on its pedestal in the middle of the great place. Some part of the solemnity was pretty singular, the mayor, aldermen, and sheriffs were drawn out in their formalities, and bare-headed to salute the statue. The mayor made a speech to it, I am told it will be printed. The fireworks are now beginning to play, but I have more pleasure in snatching the present opportunity of writing to you than I should in seeing that spectacle. This is a very noble city, and more populous and rich in proportion than Paris. It has several fine buildings and antiquities, which made the week I have spent here pass very agreeably. The opera here is magnificent enough, but the music bad. I was introduced to the Assembly of Madame d'Intendante ; when I was there I could not but observe, in my thoughts, how much her apartments and furniture as well as her person were inferiour to those of my Lady Percival. The month I spent at Paris was not so entertaining as I hoped on account of the extreme sharpness of the weather, which however did not prevent my visiting the king's palaces and country seats &c., though it must be owned it spoilt my relish and made them appear worse than they would have done in a better season.

I had forgot to tell what seems odd to strangers, that the clergy game in these public assemblys. Play is the general humour of the French, and it runs high. Mr. Oglethorpe, an ingenious English gentleman that goes with us to Sicily, lost fifty guineas last night at the Intendants. He and Col. Du Hamel and I set forward tomorrow morning for Turin, and thence to Genoa, where we meet my Lord, who goes by sea from Toulon. For my own part I am glad of this opportunity of seeing Italy, though it be at the expence of passing the Alps in this rude season. I go armed with furred gloves, a furred bag to put my legs in, and the like necessaries to withstand the prodigious cold we must expect in this journey, which has already pretty well hardened my constitution.

I will not congratulate with you, but with your country, that has you for its representative in Parliament. I am sure it were to be wished there were many such representatives at this time when the parties there run so high, and are so much incensed against each other, though (God knows) at bottom for little reason, and to no other purpose than to hurt their country. I have only time to add my humble respects to my Lady and Mrs. Parker (perhaps now Mrs. Domville, my Lady Poorscourt, or some other name) and remain,

Dr Sr,

Yr most humbe & affect. Servt,

G. BERKELEY.

42   TO PRIOR

Turin, Jan. 6, N.S. 1713/14

Dear Tom,

At Lyons, where I was about eight days, it was left to my choice whether I would go from thence to Toulon, and there embark for Genoa, or else pass through Savoy, cross the Alps, and so through Italy. I chose the latter route, though I was obliged to ride post, in company of Colonel du Hamel and Mr. Oglethorpe, Adjutant-General of the Queen's forces, who were sent with a letter from my Lord to the King's mother at Turin.

The first day we rode from Lyons to Chambery, the capital

of Savoy, which is reckoned sixty miles. The Lionnois and Dauphiné were very well ; but Savoy was a perpetual chain or rocks and mountains, almost impassible for ice and snow. And yet I rode post through it, and came off with only four falls ; from which I received no other damage than the breaking my sword, my watch, and my snuff-box.

On New Year's Day we passed Mount Cenis, one of the most difficult and formidable parts of the Alps which is ever passed over by mortal men. We were carried in open chairs by men used to scale these rocks and precipices, which in this season are more slippery and dangerous than at other times, and at the best are high, craggy, and steep enough to cause the heart of the most valiant man to melt within him. My life often depended on a single step. No one will think that I exaggerate, who considers what it is to pass the Alps on New Year's Day. But I shall leave particulars to be described by the fireside.

We have been now five days here, and in two or three more design to set forward towards Genoa, where we are to join my Lord, who embarked at Toulon. I am now hardened against wind and weather, earth and sea, frost and snow ; can gallop all day long, and sleep but three or four hours at night. The court here is polite and splendid, the city beautiful, the churches and colleges magnificent, but not much learning stirring among them. However, all orders of people, clergy and laity, are wonderfully civil, and everywhere a man finds his account in being an Englishman, that character alone being sufficient to gain respect. My service to all friends, particularly to Sir John and Mrs. Rawdon, and Mrs. Kempsy. It is my advice that they do not pass the Alps in their way to Sicily.

I am, dear Tom,

yours, &c.,

G. B.

43   TO PERCIVAL

Genoa, 4th Feb., N.S., 1714

Dear Sir,

I staid about a month at Paris, eight days at Lyons, and eleven at Turin, and I have been now almost three weeks at Genoa. I writ to you from each of the fore mentioned places, but know not whether my letters came to your hands, being in some doubt that the posts are not yet regulated, between France and England. This makes my letter shorter than otherwise it would be ; for I have a thousand things to tell you of my travels by sea and land, by coach, horse, boat chaise, and in all kind of companies. I have not seen any town that pleased me more than this. The churches, palaces, and indeed the ordinary houses are very magnificent. It has nevertheless one fault, that the streets are generally very narrow, but I should not pretend to describe it to you, believing you have been here yourself.

I made it my business to visit the colleges, libraries, booksellers' shops, both at Turin and here, but do not find that learning flourishes among them. Nothing curious in the sciences has of late been published in Italy. Their clergy for the most part are extremely ignorant ; as an instance of it, they shewed me in the library of the Franciscans in this town a Hebrew book, taking it to be an English one.

My Lord Peterborough joined us here, about a week since. He came by water from Toulon. He is a man of excellent parts, and frank cheerful conversation. We are to set out to-day in a felucca for Leghorn, where we are to embark for Sicily in two Maltese vessels, the man of war and yacht with my Lord's equipage not being yet arrived.

I reckon it is now time that I congratulate you and my Lady on the birth of a new son, and Mrs. Parker on her marriage. I long to hear some news from your fireside and am with the truest respect to those that sit about it,

Dr Sr,

Your most obedt & affect. Servt,

G. BERKELEY.

44   TO PERCIVAL

Leghorn, 19th Feb., N.S., 1713/14

Dear Sir,

Ireland is certainly one of the finest countries and Dublin one of the finest cities in the world ; the further I go, the more I am convinced of this truth. But if you have the advantage of these countries in point of plenty, government, and religion, it must be owned you fall infinitely short of them, in respect of concord, and unanimity. By nature and constitution you should be happy, but faction and jealousy make you miserable in spite of both. These reflections are occasioned by my seeing the newspapers filled with an account of the dissensions at present reigning between the citizens, lords, commons, and clergy of Ireland. I now fancy that your estate is converted into a ship filled with all necessaries for the voyage to Mascarenes, and that you and our friends of that party are on the point of embarking. I beg you will turn aside to the left and take me up at Leghorn, though if I were not afraid of diverting you from such an agreeable project, I could assure you that the French nation is so impoverished and dispeopled by the war, that we need not entertain any apprehensions of having a Pretender imposed upon us by their power. I speak this of my own knowledge having passed through the heart of France, and been an eyewitness of its misery.

I shall not pretend to give you my description of Italy, who knows it so much better than myself. There is nothing in it that pleases me more than the clear sky and warm weather so universal with us in this season. This town is the neatest and most regular that I have seen in Italy. It is very populous and a place of great trade. There are several English families of merchants, who are very rich and live at a much greater rate than the Italian nobility.

My Lord Ambassador, who is a man of excellent parts and good humour, not thinking fit to wait the arrival of his equipage, which is coming by sea from London, parted from hence about ten days since on board a Maltese vessel bound to Palermo, where he designs to stay but a short time, and put off his public entry till his return. He has taken with him but two or three servants, and left orders for my diet and lodging here with his secretary, and some others of his retinue. The secretary is an Italian and a very good-natured gentleman, as well as a man of sense. There are already no less than nine different nations among my Lord's domestics. This gives me a good opportunity of improving myself in French and Italian. They are very civil to me, and in that respect make me as easy as I hope to be in any company besides those who used to rejoice my heart in Dublin.

A thought comes into my head that the restless state of affairs at home may put you (like Atticus) upon seeking repose in Italy, till the storm is overblown. This climate I am sure would contribute very much to your health as well as to that of my Lady and the children. Though in this suggestion I know I consult my own satisfaction more than the public interests. I shall probably stay a considerable time in this town or hereabouts, and should be overjoyed to hear you were on this side the Alps. I writ to you when I was at Paris, at Lyons, at Turin, and at Genoa, at each of which places I made a considerable stay. I long to see a line from you. When you do me that favour pray be particular, and rather with respect to domestic than public affairs. I can read in the Gazette that the Bishop of Raphoe is made Primate, and the Lord Chancellor under the displeasure of the Commons ; but it says nothing of my Lady's health, your son's learning, your daughter's beauty, Mrs. Parker's being married, Mrs. Dering's being recovered of the gout, or Mrs. Percival's breeding, or Mr. Dering's getting a good employment. If you send your letter to the Secretary's office in London to be enclosed in my Lord Peterborough's pacquet, or (in case there be a ship coming from Dublin to Leghorn) direct it for me, to be left at the English consul's here, it will come to my hands.

I am, Sr,

Yr most humle & affect. Servt,

G. BERKELEY.

45   TO PRIOR

Dear Tom,

Mrs. Rawdon is too thin, and Sir John too fat, to agree with the English climate. I advise them to make haste and transport themselves into this warm clear air. Your best way is to come through France ; but make no long stay there ; for the air is too cold, and there are instances enough of poverty and distress to spoil the mirth of any one who feels the sufferings of his fellow-creatures. I would prescribe you two or three operas at Paris, and as many days amusement at Versailles. My next recipe shall be, to ride post from Paris to Toulon, and there to embark for Genoa ; for I would by no means have you shaken to pieces, as I was, riding post over the rocks of Savoy, or put out of humour by the most horrible precipices of Mount Cenis, that part of the Alps which divides Piedmont from Savoy. I shall not anticipate your pleasure by any description of Italy or France ; only with regard to the latter, I cannot help observing, that the Jacobites have little to hope, and others little to fear, from that reduced nation. The king indeed looks as he neither wanted meat nor drink, and his palaces are in good repair ; but throughout the land there is a different face of things. I staid about a month at Paris, eight days at Lyons, eleven at Turin, three weeks at Genoa ; and am now to be above a fortnight with my Lord's secretary (an Italian) and some others of his retinue, my Lord having gone aboard a Maltese vessel from hence to Sicily, with a couple of servants. He designs to stay there incognito a few days, and then return hither, having put off his public entry till the yacht with his equipage arrives.

I have wrote to you several times before by post. In answer to all my letters, I desire you to send me one great one, close writ, and filled on all sides, containing a particular account of all transactions in London and Dublin. Inclose it in a cover to my Lord Ambassador, and that again in another cover to Mr. Hare at my Lord Bolingbroke's office. If you have a mind to travel only in the map, here is a list of all the places where I lodged since my leaving England, in their natural order : Calais, Boulogne, Montreuil, Abbeville, Poix, Beauvais, Paris, Melun, Ville Neufe le Roi Vermonton, Saulieu, Chalons, Maçon, Lyons, Chambery, St Jean de Maurienne, Lanebourg, Susa, Turin, Alexandria, Campo Maro, Genoa, Sestri di Levante, Lerici, Leghorne. My humble service to Sir John, Mrs. Rawdon, and Mrs. Kempsy, Mr. Digby, Mr. French, &c.

I am, dear Tom,
>   your affectionate humble servant,
>   G. BERKELEY.

Leghorn, Feb. 26, N.S. 1713/14

46   TO POPE

Leghorn, May 1, 1714

As I take ingratitude to be a greater crime than impertinence, I chose rather to run the risk of being thought guilty of the latter, than not to return you my thanks for the very agreeable entertainment you just now gave me. I have accidentally met with your *Rape of the Lock* here, having never seen it before. Style, painting, judgment, spirit, I had already admired in your other writings ; but in this I am charmed with the magic of your invention, with all those images, allusions, and inexplicable beauties which you raise so surprisingly, and at the same time so naturally out of a trifle. And yet I cannot say that I was more pleased with the reading of it, than I am with the pretext it gives me to renew in your thoughts the remembrance of one who values no happiness beyond the friendship of men of wit, learning, and good nature.

I remember to have heard you mention some half formed design of coming to Italy. What might we not expect from a muse that sings so well in the bleak climate of England, if she felt the same warm sun, and breathed the same air with Virgil and Horace.

There is here an incredible number of poets that have all the inclination, but want the genius, or perhaps the art of the ancients. Some among them, who understand English, begin to relish our authors ; and I am informed that at Florence they have translated Milton into Italian verse. If one who knows so well how to write like the old Latin poets came among them, it would probably be a means to retrieve them from their cold trivial conceits, to an imitation of their predecessors.

As merchants, antiquaries, men of pleasure, &c., have all different views in travelling, I know not whether it might not be worth a poet's while to travel, in order to store his mind with strong images of nature.

Green fields and groves, flowery meadows and purling streams, are nowhere in such perfection as in England ; but if you would know lightsome days, warm suns, and blue skies, you must come to Italy ; and to enable a man to describe rocks and precipices, it is absolutely necessary that he pass the Alps.

You will easily perceive that it is self interest makes me so fond of giving advice to one who has no need of it. If you came into these parts, I should fly to see you. I am here (by the favour of my good friend the Dean of St. Patrick's) in quality of chaplain to the Earl of Peterborough, who about three months since left the greatest part of his family in this town. God knows how long we shall stay here.

I am yours, &c.

47   TO PERCIVAL

Leghorn, 1st May 1714

Dr Sr,

Since my last to you dated from this town, I have had an opportunity of seeing Pisa, Lucca, Pistoia, Florence &c. But

I have not seen anything that should make me desirous to live out of England or Ireland. The descriptions that we find in the Latin poets make me expect Elysian fields and the golden age in Italy. But in my opinion England is a more poetical country, the spring there is forwarder and lasts longer, purling streams are more numerous, and the fields and groves have a cheerfuller green, the only advantage here, is, in point of air, which as you know is warmer and dryer than with us, though I doubt whether it be generally more wholesome.

There is here together in a family about a dozen of my Lord's domestics, among whom is the secretary (an Italian) and myself. Last week I received a letter from my Lord, dated at Palermo. He talks of coming soon to Leghorn. We have so long waited the vessel that brings the coaches and equipage, that (though it be now arrived here) yet I doubt whether we shall have a public entry in Sicily. As my Lord is Plenipotentiary to all the Courts in Italy, I know not whither we shall go next. I wish it may be homewards. I have already seen enough to be satisfied, that England has the most learning, the most riches, the best government, the best people, and the best religion in the world. Amongst two thousand clergymen that are reckoned in this town, I do not hear of any one man of letters worth making an acquaintance with. The people here are much dissatisfied with the hard government of the Grand Duke. The family of the Medici is now on the point of being extinct, and they know not to whom they shall be next a prey. But in that matter they are easy, being sure they cannot fall into worse hands.

This letter I suppose will find you at London, where I hope to see you together with my Lady, and Mrs. Parker, to whom pray give my humblest respects.

I am, Sr,

Yr most humble & most obed. Servt,

G. Berkeley.

48   to percival

Paris, 13th July 1714

Dr Sr,

I am just come from Mr. Southwell, who told me the joyful news of your being in London and my Lady being delivered

of a son. As I have a sensible pleasure in all your good fortune
I could not defer congratulating with you on that happy event
till my seeing you, which I hope will be very soon. Nothing could
have pleased me more than the hearing of your family's being
in London, with a purpose of continuing there twelve months.
I am sure it will be a strong motive for doing so too. I parted
with my Lord Peterborough at Genoa where I embarked with
Mr. Molesworth the late envoy at Florence, and the Col. his
brother, and have had a very pleasant journey in their company
to Paris, where I came about three days agone. My Lord took
post for Turin, and thence designed passing over the Alps, and
so through Savoy and France in his way to England.

I have here met with an Irish gentleman of my acquaintance
who designs returning to England through Flanders and Holland :
being glad of an opportunity to see those countries, I have taken
a place in the Brussels' coach with him. We are to set out next
week.

I know not whether you received my letters from Paris, Lyons,
Turin, Genoa, Leghorn, Florence. Last month I received one
of yours dated in Novr last, being then in Italy, whence I answered
it. I shall trouble you with no more at present, but with my
humble respects to my Lady and Mrs. Parker,

I am, Dr Sr,

Yr most humble & affect. Servt,

G. BERKELEY.

49   TO PERCIVAL

London, 6th July 1715

My Lord,

I am in hopes that this letter will find your Lordship and
my Lady safe arrived in Dublin. Things have been pretty much
at a stand here since your departure. This by many is imputed
to the difficulty which the Duke of Shrewsbury's case gave the
impeaching party. If this be all, the difficulty is now over, that
peer being displaced from his office of Lord Chamberlain, which
speaks him deserted by the Court. It had indeed been hard that
a person who was deep in the late measures, and concluded the
peace with France, should be employed and favoured at Court,

whilst others against whom nothing appears lie under a disgrace, e.g. Lord Peterborough.

I promised your Lordship some Tory news, not doubting but that you are sufficiently furnished with Whig reports by other hands. But the truth is I hear little news at present to be depended on. People speak uncertainly, and seem to be in a suspense. As to my own opinion, men seem tired of baiting one another, the spirit of party begins to cool among us, and in a little time there is hopes we may be a quiet and united people. I am persuaded a little address at this juncture might make the Tories all what they ought to be, true friends to the King, which would put an end to our fears, but this advice must come from cooler heads than those who advise infringing Charters of Universities for the extravagances and crimes of a few young lads. I need not tell you what I hint at. You know what hath passed with regard to our University better than myself. All I can say is that the thing is represented here much to the disadvantage of the Court, and I am credibly informed that Oxford and Cambridge are both alarmed at it.

Of late I have had some symptoms of a return of my ague, but am now upon the point of going to Gloucestershire, for about a fortnight or three weeks, which will I hope entirely cure me. Mrs. Parker and Mr. Phill are both, as I suppose you know, much better than when you left them. For the rest, all friends are as well as could be expected in your and my Lady's absence. For my own part I comfort myself with the thought that I shall see you soon there or here. In the meantime
I am, My Lord,
     Yr Lordship's Most obedient and most Obliged Servant,
        G. BERKELEY.

50   TO POPE

July 7, 1715

. . . . Some days ago three or four gentlemen and myself, exerting that right which all the readers pretend to over authors, sat in judgment upon the two new translations of the first Iliad. Without partiality to my countrymen, I assure you they all gave the preference where it was due ; being unanimously of opinion that yours was equally just to the sense with Mr. ——'s, and without comparison, more easy, more poetical, and more sublime. But I will say no more on such a threadbare subject as your late performance at this time. . . .

51   TO PERCIVAL

Flaxley, July 23rd, 1715

My Lord,

I have now spent about a fortnight in Gloucestershire in a very agreeable place, and with the most entertaining company that I know out of your family, and propose going to London next week. The news of that place I doubt not you are well informed of. But I may perhaps give you some account of riots in the neighbouring counties, Worcester, Stafford &c. the particulars whereof are not published in the papers. A servant of the Lady with whom I am, having gone to receive some money at Bromingham, gives a dismal relation of tumults there. He says there have been twenty eight of the rioters slain. He saw seven of their bodies lying unburied in the fields. There are likewise eight of the principal Dissenters missed. He met in one squadron above five hundred rioters in a field. And says that being in the town of Bromingham he saw a man on horseback ride through the streets with a horn, which he publicly sounded to raise the mob, whereof four thousand immediately got together and joined him. They obliged the constable who at first came to seize the horseman to go with them and join in pulling down a meeting-house. Of a great number of meeting-houses there are now but three left standing in Worcestershire and Staffordshire. In a neighbouring town he says the Dissenters, who guarded the meeting-house with firearms, got one of the Tory mob, and upon his refusing to curse Dr. Sacheverel they slit his mouth from ear to ear, and gave him other wounds of which he died, and that this hath terribly incensed the riotry and increased their numbers. That an eminent Presbyterian's son is now in gaol at Bromingham for having proffered sixty pounds to some fellows to pull down the meeting-house, and that a Dissenter assured him that he himself doubted these insurrections were at bottom set on foot and favoured by Whigs for a pretence to ruin the Tory party. Whether this be so or no, God knows. But I can tell you of my own know-

ledge that the mob of Gloucester would have pulled down the
meeting-house there, if they had not been dissuaded by the
principal Tories of that town, who use all possible methods to
keep them quiet, as knowing these riots can in no wise advantage
their cause. It is said there are above twenty thousand men of
Bromingham and the parts adjacent ready to take arms against
the Government if there was any one to head them. This falls
out the more unluckily because of the vast number of firearms
and all sorts of weapons which make the great trade of that town.
It is the opinion of most people that the nation is ready to break
out into a flame, and to do the Tories justice (with whom I principally converse here) they express an honest detestation of these
proceedings, as I hope I need not tell you I do myself. This
with my humble respects to my Lady is all I shall trouble you
with at this time.
     My Lord,
          Yr Lordship's most obedt & most obliged Servt,
            GEO. BERKELEY.

52   TO PERCIVAL

                      London, Aug. 9th, 1715
My Lord,
     I am now to thank your Lordship for the favour of two
letters which I received since my coming to town. I will endeavour to return it by sending you an account of such news as
is current here. Mr Kenedy, secretary to the Duke of Ormond,
and Col. Butler, uncle to the Lord Ikerrin, were both seized at
Dover as they were going to the Duke. They have been before
the Council and are released from custody.
     The High-gate cobbler was whipped on Thursday last, and
notwithstanding the Act against riots, there was a mob of several
thousands got together on the occasion, who threatened to pull the
executioner to pieces in case he did not perform his office gently.
     I hear my Lord Peterborough left the Kingdom on Friday
last with the King's pass. I do not know the occasion, having
had no discourse with his Lordship since my coming to town.
On the same day articles of high treason and high crimes and
high misdemeanors against the Duke of Ormond were exhibited
and agreed to in the House of Commons. They are six in number,

in substance as follows : Acting against orders. Corresponding with the enemy. Not concurring in the siege of Quesnoy. Informing M. Villars what foreign troops withdrew with him. Advising the Queen to disappoint the Dutch in their design on Newport and Furnes. Imposing on her Majesty by a double letter to Lord Bolingbroke. I was in the house during part of the debate. General Lumley made a long speech in defence of the Duke, shewed that what he did was pursuant to orders, and that had it been his own case, he would have followed the same measures. Mr. Spencer Cooper in answer alleged that the orders were not valid, as not having been signed by the Queen, and added that if Lumley had done the same things he should have met with the same fate. Mr. Bromley spoke much in honour of his Grace, and in the close of his speech said that the Duke's noble qualities had endeared him to all the nation, except those who envied him the having those qualities which they themselves wanted. He was answered with great warmth by Lord Coningsby. Those who spoke against the Duke insisted on his flight into France, upon which the Speaker interposed saying that was a point that did not appear to the house and which they were not to take notice of. Mr. Bromley added that flight was no certain argument of guilt, and instanced Lord Clarendon and the Earl of Danby, who formerly withdrew themselves (as he said), not out of guilt but from the violence of the times. Several others spoke, but some Lord appearing in the gallery we were all ordered to withdraw. Upon the division on the first article, the Tories left the house.

The reason assigned for the Duke of Montrose's laying down is that the Duke of Argyle got himself made Lord Lieutenant of that shire where his interest and estate lay. It is said Lord Ilay will succeed him. Lord Oxford continues very ill in the tower. I have it from a good hand that the court have discovered an association amongst several great men here to bring over the Pretender. It is talked too that the French king is to dismiss all the Scotch and Irish forces in his service, and to give them six months pay as a reward for past service. And that one Fitzgerald an Irish merchant at St Malo's will furnish four men of war at his own charges. A little time will shew what there is in these reports.

What your Lordship observes that the clergy should open their mouths as well as eyes is certainly very just. For my part I think it my duty to disclaim perjury and rebellion on all occasions.

7

Nothing surely can give a deeper wound to the church than that her pretended sons should be guilty of such foul practices. What advantage some great men here out of employ may purpose from the Pretender's coming among us, they best know ; but it is inconceivable what shadow of an advantage an Irish Protestant can fancy to himself from such a revolution.

I cannot well leave this country for Ireland before next month, when I hope to find you there. I cannot imagine why they should murmur at my absence in the College, considering all the persons absent. I am the only one who has the royal authority to be so. Not to mention that I am no Senior Fellow, nor consequently concerned in the material part of governing the College.

The other day when I saw the children they were very well, except Philly who is much worn away. Mr. Bligh lost his son last Saturday.

My humble respects to my Lady.

I am, My Lord,

Your Lordship's most obedient humb. Servant,

G. BERKELEY.

53   TO PERCIVAL

London, August 18th, 1715

My Lord,

This is to inform you of two remarkable pieces of news that I heard this day. The French King is either dead or at least past hopes of recovery, of which an express from Lord Stairs has brought advice this morning, gangrene having begun in the leg and thigh of that Prince. What I am further to tell you is that the rumour of the Pretender's invasion is revived and credited more than ever. And indeed it does not seem improbable that the Anjou-faction in France should incline to give England a diversion at this juncture to prevent their assisting the Duke of Orleans in his claim to the Regency. My Lord Mar's, Sr William Wyndham's, Sr Thomas Hanmer's and several others withdrawing into the country seems to strengthen the suspicion. At least I know it strengthens the hopes of the only Jacobite I am acquainted with here.

If this news prove true, and the Tories openly engage in the attempt, I shall think them guilty of as barefaced perjury and dishonesty as ever could be imputed to any set of men.

I am very sorry to hear of my Lady's illness. I hope it is only what owes it original to you. The most comfortable prospect I have in Ireland is that I shall find her Ladyship and you there.

I am, My Lord,

Yr Lordship's most affect. humble Servt,

G. BERKELEY.

54   TO PERCIVAL

London, September 8th, 1715

My Lord,

I agree with your Lordship that there never was a more important juncture, or that justified a curiosity after news more than the present. It was my province to inform you what the Tories say. For Whig news, I doubt not, you have enough from other hands. They say then that Col. Paul, who you must have heard is committed to Newgate, was always known to be a Whig, and consequently is innocent of what is laid to his charge. They add that the Serjeant, his accuser, is a noted villain, who suffered thirteen years imprisonment in Dublin on account of former crimes, and so not to be depended on. But notwithstanding all this, the discovery of many others engaged in the same black design makes me think him guilty, which seems more probable because I am assured he is a silly man, and one likely to be prevailed on by the hopes of commanding the second battalion of guards, which is said was promised him by the Pretender. There could not certainly have been a more subtle and mischievous project set on foot by the Jacobites, and I doubt it has spread further than is commonly imagined : I mean tampering with the soldiers and new levies. This occasions my calling to mind what I observed about a fortnight agone. As I walked through St. James's park, there was an odd looking fellow in close conference with one of the sentinels. I heard him mention the words, *hereditary right* ; and think the entire sentence was : *But sure you are for hereditary right.* I observe likewise that the few I suspect for Jacobites are not so dispirited or desperate, as the late accident of the French King's death and the succession of the Duke of Orleans in the Regency would incline one to think they should be. Add to this the general ferment in men's mind, the artifice with which it is kept up by those that wish ill to the present establishment, and the indiscretion of some of its well wishers, which perhaps may no less contribute to the same effect, and our prospect must seem very dismal. I once little imagined that any considerable number of Church of England-men could be moved either by passion or interest to so wicked an undertaking as that must be which includes both rebellion and perjury. For my part I condemn both them and their practices.

The best of it is, that the vigilant measures taken at Court and the perfect seeming good disposition of France gives hopes that any impious design to embroil the nation may be soon defeated and turned on the heads of the contrivers. There is now a strict inquiry making into the characters of all persons in the army, private men as well as officers. And tomorrow the Duke of Argyle, Duke of Roxburgh, and Lord Sutherland are to set out for Scotland. There must have been some pressing reason for this, it having been much against the inclination and endeavours of the Duke of Argyle. The Bishop of Bristol assured me the other day that the Court expect the Duke of Orleans would, in case of need, supply them with forces against the Pretender. And I myself have seen two letters, one from the Duke Regent, the other from the new King of France to the Prince of Wales, containing assurance of friendship and affection.

I reckon it is no news to tell you the two pretty children are well and grow every day more like their mother and father, that is more pretty and wise. Mrs. Parker is well. Mr. Dering goes this day to meet his mother at Chester.

Argyle and Sutherland are set out today.

I am, My Lord,
Yr Lordship's most humble and most affect. Servt,
G. BERKELEY.

55   TO PERCIVAL

London, September 22nd, 1715

My Lord,
We are in a very ill condition, the rage and resentment of the Tories having at length broke out into an open flame. You are I doubt not already well informed of this. Be pleased

however to take things as I hear them. The Rebellion in Scotland is differently represented as to the force and number of the rebels. Some reckon twenty eight thousand, others seventeen thousand, and others ten thousand. The last account came three days ago by an express from the Duke of Argyle, who complains much of the disparity of numbers, having only fifteen hundred to oppose ten thousand that were then come within thirty miles of Edinburgh, and designed proclaiming the Pretender at Dundee, yesterday was sennight. The Duke was then in suspense whether he should retire towards Berwick, or intrench near Stirling. The unhappy misunderstanding between our Courtiers, particularly the Duke of Marlborough and Argyle, prevents the Court from forming any resolute judgment on these informations, many being of an opinion that Argyle magnifies the force of the rebels with a design to oppose and distress the Duke of Marlborough, who is they say of a humour inclined to starve any service wherein he is not employed himself. On the other hand other well wishers of the King are afraid the Duke of Marlborough's jealousy might make him propose such measures as may destroy the Duke of Argyle. Thus as in most other cases the public is neglected while ministers pursue and indulge their private piques and passions.

This account you may depend on for I had it from a very good hand who knows the Court, and whose interest and inclinations engage him to be heartily zealous for the King's safety. We are informed that the rebels increase daily, that they have seized and plundered the custom house of Leith, and that they have taken three companies of the King's forces, the major part whereof have listed under them. They have with them the Generals Dillon and Hamilton, and some say the Duke of Berwick. Expresses come to Court thick one upon another, and their being kept secret makes one suspect they bring no good news. But the worst sign of all is the cheerful insolent behaviour of the Jacobites, and the downcast melancholy looks of the Loyal party, which last was very observable yesterday in the House of Commons. It is not doubted that the rebels will march directly into England, and then it is very much feared that there will be a general insurrection in all parts of the land. It is this general bent of the people towards Jacobitism, that occasions the raising of so few forces at home, which might prove to be raising the King's enemies. However, this is certain, that Brigadier Preston is sent into Holland to demand the ten thousand soldiers which they were to furnish by the Barrier treaty, and they talk here of listing several thousand

French refugees under Lord Galloway. Yesterday the Lords Landsdowne and Duplin were seized here ; Lord Jersey was likewise sought for, but made his escape. There are warrants said to be issued for the seizing twenty Lords more, and six Commoners.

I wish your Lordship, my Lady and a dozen more friends safe at Mascarenes out of this corrupt part of the world, where the resentment, the perjury, and breach of faith of one side, and the private piques and interested views of the other, are in a fair way of ruining our King and country, if Providence does not interpose in a manner we nowise deserve. It is believed the Pretender is in England.

I am, My Lord,
　　　　Yr Lordship's most Obedt and affect. humble Servant,
　　　　　　G. Berkeley.

56　to percival

London, 26th Sept. 1715

My Lord,

My last, according to the intelligence I then had, gave you a dismal prospect of our affairs. This is to make amends by assuring you there is ground to hope that all the bloodshed and desolation which then threatened us will be prevented by the discovery the Court has made of the persons and designs of the conspirators.

Mr. Harvey of Combe, a man of 7000 pounds a year, has been taken up and examined before a Committee of Council. At first he spoke resolutely and denied all that he was charged with, but upon Lord Townshend's producing his own handwriting he was struck dumb, and being sent away in custody of a messenger he soon after stabbed himself with a penknife in three places. I hear that Lord Nottingham, his uncle, was with him today, and that he seemed desirous to live, but it is thought, if he be not dead already, that he will soon die of his wounds.

You have heard that Sir William Wyndham made his escape out of the hands of a messenger ; there is a report about town that he is again taken, but I do not find it gains credit. It was rumoured likewise yesterday that a warrant was issued out to apprehend the Bishop of Rochester, but I hear nothing of it since. Lord Duplin is in the hands of a messenger. Lord Landsdowne is committed to the tower. Our great security is that the Duke of Orleans seems steady to the interest of the King, and that our last advices from Lord Stairs bring assurances of the Pretender's continuing still at Bar-le-duc.

For my part I see no hopes for him or his pretensions. His shyness in point of danger will sacrifice them, and their being sacrificed will discourage others from rising in his favour. What better could be hoped from so wicked management; but the most lamentable evil is the great dishonour they have done to the Church and religion by public perjury and rebellion.

This is so clear and plain a case now, that no honest man can pretend to justify them.

It is very late and I have only time to say

> I am, My Lord,
>> Yr Lordsp's most obedt and affect. humble Servant,
>>> GEO. BERKELEY.

My humble respects to my Lady. I suppose I need [not] tell you Mrs. Dering is recovered, and that Mrs. Parker and the children are well.

57   TO PERCIVAL

London, 20th October 1715

My Lord,

I have but little inclination to write to your Lordship at present upon politics : the scene every day opening and discovering new cause to apprehend a popish power, and all the dismal consequences of it. You will therefore excuse me if I am backward to be the messenger of ill news. In a late letter to you I was of opinion we had no more to fear from the intended conspiracy. But things have since taken a different turn from what I then expected.

The rebellion in Northumberland is said to be two thousand men strong and daily increasing. It is not doubted that as many more have passed the Firth under General Hamilton. The Court indeed gives them out to be a thousand only, but the other account is most credited. The Dutch forces, which I thought would set all things right, are not likely to be here until the game is over. It is at least certain that the Jacobites make a jest of them, saying, that if they do come, they will prejudice King George's affairs more than anything that has been done yet. Some say the Dutch have been threatened by the Duke of Ormond and a certain foreign count in case they furnish us with any forces. But whatever the cause is you may depend on it, they are not expected here by any body in a fortnight. I must own I cannot account for these dilatory proceedings. The seizing Lord Landsdowne and Sir William Wyndham has not given all the light I first imagined. Sir William, when he was asked by the Council whether he knew anything of an association, answered that he knew of no association but that of the whole nation against the present ministry, upon which he was sent to the tower, and this, I know not why, is resented by the old Duke of Somerset, his father-in-law. It is thought the Duke of Ormond is landed in Scotland. In a word the chief cause of my apprehensions is the pert confidence of the Jacobites, who are now more spirited than ever.

If my Lady and your Lordship continue thoughts of Mascarenes I will gladly become one of your subjects, for I assure you I ever did and ever shall abhor a Popish Government.

I thought to have seen you before now, but have been prevailed with some friends to stay here a little upon a prospect of something in England, so that I believe I shall see you here again.

        I am, Yrs and my Lady's

                Most obedt and most humble Servt,

                    GEO. BERKELEY.

58 TO PERCIVAL

                 London, 3rd November 1715

My Lord,

There is a high Torie (which is now reckoned the same thing with a Jacobite) of my acquaintance, who used to serve me instead of a political weather glass. When his spirits were high I concluded our affairs went wrong, and the contrary when they were low. I never knew him so high in spirit as he was when I writ last to your Lordship ; but since that time things are altered, and we have now reason to thank God that the enemies of our Constitution hang down their heads. Whatever I might have apprehended of late, at present I think their game desperate.

Your Lordship will be of my mind when I tell you that the Duke of Ormond is gone back to France, after having lain one night ashore at one Cary's in Devonshire. My Lord Stairs has sent to Court a letter intercepted from him to the Pretender, wherein the Duke tells his pretended Majesty that he would embark and make his signalls on the coast of England, which if answered he did not doubt being at the head of a body of his subjects able to do him justice, otherwise he would be himself the messenger of the ill news to his Majesty. In the same letter he exhorts the Pretender to be in a readiness to embark in case occasion should serve.

For the future I shall never be scared at the vauntings of a few fellows who have all the villany, without the sense or courage necessary to carry on a conspiracy. The forces under Lord Mar nobody doubts will languish and disperse in a little time. To do my Lord Peterborough justice, this was the opinion he always declared himself to have of the rebels and their project.

Dr. Friend, who got the £20000 prize in the lottery, is disposed to give up a living in the presentation of his Lordship. By what I hear he will resign it in a few months in which case it may be worth my acceptance. I wish your Lordship a good voyage and hope to see you here in less than a month. Two days ago I saw the children very well in the Pall Mall, as are Mrs. Parker and Mr. Dering.

I am, My Lord,
    Yr Lordship's most obliged & most humble and affect. Servt,
                    G. BERKELEY.

59   TO PERCIVAL

London, 17th Nov. 1715

My Lord,
        I wish your Lordship and my Lady Percival joy of the victory which his Majesty's forces have gained over the rebels in Preston, the particulars whereof the newspapers tell you. I hope this blow hath put an end to or prevented the calamities we had too much cause to apprehend from an obstinate and bloody civil war. The want of spirit and conduct in the rebels deserves our scorn, as much as the unjustice of their cause and the mischiefs they were going to involve us in did our abhorrence. They seem to have been intimidated and struck from heaven, which, it is to

be hoped, will speedily open the eyes of their accomplices, and teach them their own and the nation's true interest.

I reckon it none of the least misfortunes of these troublesome times, that books and literature seem to be forgotten, conversation being entirely turned from them to more disagreeable and less innocent topics. Even the most retired men and who are at the bottom of fortune's wheel are too much interested in our public broils to be attentive to other things. This makes me doubt your application to the classics hath been intermitted since your going to Ireland. If it hath not and you are at leisure, I would much rather correspond with you on the beauties of the Latin authors, than on the subject of news of which the public papers tell you all that is certain, and for other surmises they are hardly worth troubling. But of what do I talk, you have perhaps left Dublin already.

I wish you and my Lady a good voyage and long to see you safe in London.

My Lord,

Your Lordship's most obedt and most obliged Servt,

GEO. BERKELEY.

60   TO PERCIVAL

London, May 1716

My Lord,

I am sorry to hear you pass the time so pleasantly at Bath. I am afraid it may keep you too long from us. However, I hope to see you before I go to Ireland, which is likely to be soon, the Prince having recommended me to succeed Charles Carr in the Living of St Paul's, in Dublin. I suppose you have heard that Mr. Carr is named to the Bishopric of Killaloe, that the Bishop of Killaloe is removed to Raphoe, and the Bishop of Raphoe to the Archbishopric of Tuam. The letter from the Prince is enclosed and seconded by Mr. Secretary Stanhope, so that I think it cannot fail of success. The living is reckoned to be worth about a hundred a year, but I put the greater value on it because it is consistent with my Fellowship.

We had yesterday a very remarkable piece of news. An express arrived at Court from Constantinople with proposals to the King to mediate a peace between the Turk and the Venetians.

This falls out very unexpectedly, and gives some credit to the opinions of the Bishop of Worcester, and the rest of our expositors who judged it inconsistent with their scheme that the Grand Seignior should carry his arms any farther westward.

I hope the waters agree well with my Lady, Mrs. Parker, and the children. Pray give my humble service to them all.

My Lord,

Yr Lordship's most obedt and most affect. humble Servt,

G. BERKELEY.

61 TO PERCIVAL

My Lord, London, May 26th, 1716

If it be what your Lordship can properly do I beg the favour of you to write a letter next post to the Duke of Grafton, imparting your acquaintance with me, and your confidence of my being well affected to his Majesty's Government. Were it necessary I might produce several instances of this, as well as from my endeavours to serve the present establishment by writing, which are more than I care to mention, as from the offer I refused in the times of the late ministry. I make you this request because I have some reasons to think my competitors have wronged my character on the other side of the water. The government of Ireland have yet made no answer to the recommendation of the Prince and Secretary Stanhope, which if they refuse to comply with I am assured it will be taken very ill, I am likewise told that their not complying may prove an advantage to me. But be that as it will, I cannot but be solicitous to have my character cleared to the Lords Justices and others there, who are probably misled by the calumny of interested persons who are strangers to me.

This is all that I desire of your Lordship. As for recommending me, or desiring any favour for me from his hands, I ask no such thing, because I do not think I want it, having been so well recommended already.

Please to give my humble service to Lady Percival and Mrs. Parker. I am glad to hear from your Lordship that they and the children are well, and hope to see you all in town next week.

I am, My Lord,

Your Lordship's most obedient and most affect. Servt,

G. BERKELEY.

Turin, 24th Novr 1716.   N.S.

My Lord,

I did not think it prudent to make reflections of the state of France while I was in the country, but now I am got out of it I may safely impart my mind to your Lordship and assure you that it is in a very bad condition : the Regent is generally disliked by the people, and his alliance with England has perhaps contributed to make him so as much as any other article of his conduct.

The French seemed to have recovered their tongues, and speak with a freedom unusual in the late King's reign. They scruple not to say the Duke hath done more mischief in two, than his predecessor in seventy years. They exclaim against the demolition of Mardyke as a thing dishonourable to their nation ; and against his recoining their money as a project that has ruined them, and has cut off all correspondence with foreigners who are sure to lose four livres in the pound on the present foot of exchange. This project, however, hath filled the Regent's coffers by robbing the subjects of a fourth part of the money.

I was assured there appeared a disposition in several, as well clergy as laity, to embrace the protestant communion.

We travel with all the ease and convenience possible. Mr. Ashe is a modest, ingenious, well natured, young gentleman, whom the more I know the more I esteem, and we have unlimited letters of credit so that we want for nothing. I never thought I should pass Mount Cenis a second time in winter. But we have now passed in a worse condition than it was when I saw it before. It blew and snowed bitterly all the time. The snow almost blinded us and reached above the waists of the men who carried us. They let me fall six or seven times, and thrice on the brinks of horrid precipices, the snow having covered the path so that it was impossible to avoid making false steps. The porters assured us they never in their lives had passed the mountain in such an ill road and weather. However, blessed be God, we arrived safe at Turin two nights ago, and design to set out from hence towards Milan tomorrow.

I forgot to tell you that we saw two avalanches of snow (as the men called them) on the mountain : I mean huge quantities of snow fallen from the side and tops of rocks, sufficient to have overwhelmed a regiment of men. They told us of fourteen, and about fifty mules that were some time since destroyed by an accident of that kind. I must not omit another adventure in Dauphine. A huge dark coloured Alpine wolf ran across an open plain when our chaise was passing, when he came near as he turned about and made a stand with a very fierce and daring look, I instantly drew my sword and Mr. Ashe fired his pistol. I did the same too, upon which the beast very calmly retired looking back ever and anon. We were much mortified that he did not attack us and give us an opportunity of killing him.

The route we design to take is through Milan, Parma, Modena, Bologna, Florence, Siena, Rome &c., which will be a means of seeing the best part of the cities of Italy. We hear of banditti, rivers overflown, mountains covered with snow, and the like difficulties in this winter expedition, but our resolution is fixed.

Whatever become of me and wherever I am you may assure yourself I shall always be most sincerely,

My Lord,

Yr Lordship's most obliged and most affect. humble Servt,

G. BERKELEY.

My humble service to the ladies.

63   TO PERCIVAL

Rome, 1st March 1716/17

My Lord,

It is with a great deal of pleasure that I hear my Lady hath been safely delivered of a daughter. I wish you and her Ladyship joy of this happy event, and hope it may facilitate your projected journey into these parts this summer. I can give you no temptations to effect this design so long talked of, but what you know by your own experience better than I can possibly describe them to you. The climate, the music, the pictures, the palaces &c. are things so enchanting that I am afraid if my Lady sees them she will be more backward to return than ever she was to come abroad.

Though I would not pretend to inform you of anything to be seen in Italy, yet a picture in the gallery of the Duke of Parma, at Parma, may possibly have escaped your observation. I mean the original of your Danae, which is esteemed one of the finest

pieces that ever Titian did.   We have staid at Rome much longer
than we intended, being constrained partly by the extreme rigour
of the season for about three weeks together, and since that by
the illness of our valet de chambre.   As soon as ever he can travel
we design for Naples where I long to be.   I have got eyes but
no ears.   I would say that I am a judge of painting though not
of music.   Cardinal Ottoboni has let off his entertainments, and
Prince Rospoli is the man who now gives music every week to
strangers, where I am sure to fall asleep as constantly as I go.
Perhaps when I reach Naples I may be able to tell you of something you have not seen.

In the meantime give me leave to inform you of a piece of
secret history that I learned the other night from one who I
doubt not knew the truth, and I have reason to think told it me.
In England there are now seven hundred clergymen in all of the
Church of Rome, of which one hundred Jesuits, three hundred
priests, and the rest friars of several orders.   In Wales there are
50 clergy, in the west 10, in the north 200.   In London and the
environs 150, of which in London 20 Jesuits, 12 Benedictines,
5 Capuchins, 3 Carmelites.   The Jesuits have at least £8000 a
year terra firma in England (some say £30000).   The secular
priests have £3000 per annum.   The number of Papists in England is 70000.

Pray give my humble service to my Lady, Mrs. Parker, Mrs.
Dering (whose health I should gladly be informed of), Mrs.
Minshull and Mr. Dering, with the rest of those friends who are
so good as to remember me.

I am, My Lord,
Your Lordship's most obliged and most humble Servant,
G. BERKELEY.

64   TO PERCIVAL

Naples, 6th April 1717

My Lord,
I know not whether I ought to reckon it to your good or
ill fortune that when you were abroad you missed seeing the
Kingdom of Naples.   This in itself one of the worst accidents
and disappointments of your life may become by prudent management a great piece of good fortune to you and your whole family.

I mean, in case it should be the occasion of your wisely resolving to visit again the regions on this side the Alps, and bring them with you. Your Lordship hath many motives of pleasure to invite you to home ; but I have now solid reasons for bringing your further southward. The health of all that is most dear to you, my Lady and the pretty children, and yourself depend on it. The air of this happy part of the world is soft and delightful beyond conception, being perfumed with myrtle shrubs and orange groves, that are everywhere scattered throughout the country ; the sky almost constantly serene and blue ; the heat tempered to a just warmth by refreshing breezes from the sea. Nor will this serene and warmth of the climate have a better effect on the spirits, than the balsamine particles of sulphur which you breathe with the common air will have on your blood, correcting those sharp scorbutic humours that molest the inhabitants of these bleak islands. If enchanting prospects be a temptation, surely there are not more and finer anywhere than here, rude mountains, fruitful hills, shady vales, and green plains, with all the variety of sea as well as land. Prospects are the natural ornaments of this Kingdom. *Nullus in orbe sinus Baiis praelucet amoenis* was the opinion of one who had a very good taste. It would fill a volume to describe the wonders of nature and antiquity that adorn that whole coast. Every hill, rock, promontory, creek, and island, is sung by Homer and Virgil, and renowned as well for having been the scene of the travels of Ulysses and Aeneas as for having been the delicious retreat of all the great men among the Romans, whenever they with-drew from the fatigue of public affairs. The Campania felecie is a different scene ; but surely nothing can be more beautiful than the wild Apennine on one hand and the boundless plain without enclosures on the other covered with a most delightful verdure and crowned with fruit trees scattered so thinly as not to hinder the prospect of the wide-extended green fields. Here grew the famous Falernian wine, and in the same plain stands the once famous city of Capua whose pleasures were destructive to Hannibal. To describe the antiquities and natural curiosities of these places would perhaps seem tedious to you, and I would not forestall the pleasure you will take in seeing them yourself.

It may be perhaps a more prevailing tune with my Lady, the informing you that there is here a very numerous nobility, who think of nothing but how to amuse themselves agreeably, and are very civil in admitting strangers to share with them in their entertainments of music and refreshments, though to say the truth they are not the politest people in the world. Today I had the honour to dine with three Princes, besides half a dozen Counts and Dukes, the first nobility in the land, and I assure you it was not without some surprise that I found myself to be one of the politest persons at table. You will believe me disinterested and sincere in what I have said, when I tell you that I cannot propose to myself the happiness of seeing you here during my own stay in this country.

My humblest respects to my Lady, Mrs. Parker and the rest of our friends.

> My Lord,
> Yr Lordship's Most obedt humble Servt,
> G. BERKELEY.

65 TO PERCIVAL

Naples, June 18th, 1717

My Lord,

I am lately returned from a tour through the most remote and unknown parts of Italy.

The celebrated cities your Lordship is perfectly acquainted with. But perhaps it may be new to you to hear that the most beautiful city in Italy lies in a remote corner of the heel. Lecce (the ancient Aletium) is the most luxuriant in all ornaments of architecture of any town that I have seen. The meanest houses are built of hewn stone, have ornamented doors, rustics. Doric, Corinthian, are ornaments about the windows, and balustrades of stone. I have not in all Italy seen so fine convents. The general fault is they run into a superfluity of ornaments. The most predominant are the Corinthian, which order is much affected by the inhabitants, being used in the gates of their city, which are extremely beautiful.

The town being inland and consequently without trade hath not above 16000 inhabitants. They are a civil polite people, and seem to have among them some remains of the delicacy of the Greeks who of old inhabited these parts of Italy.

You know that in most cities of Italy the palaces indeed are fine, but the ordinary houses of an indifferent gusto. 'Tis so even in Rome, whereas in Lecce there is a general good *gout*, which descends down to the poorest houses. I saw many other remarkable towns, amongst the rest five fair cities in one day, the most part built of white marble, whereof the names are not known to Englishmen. The season of the year (which was much more moderate than I expected) together with the various beautiful landscapes throughout Apulia, Peucetia, and the old Calabria, made this journey very agreeable. Nor should I pass over the antiquities that we saw in Brundisium, Tarentum, Venusia (where Horace was born), Cannae famous for the great victory obtained by Hannibal, and many other places in all which we were stared at like men dropt from the sky, and sometimes followed by a numerous crowd of citizens, who out of curiosity attended us through the streets. The fear of bandits which hinders strangers from visiting these curiosities is a mere bugbear.

Upon my return to Naples I found Vesuvius in a terrible fit which is not yet over.

I beg your Lordship to let me know what way you, my Lady, and Mrs. Parker design to take, that I may continue to meet you in our return. My humble service to them.

I am,

Yr Lordship's most obedt Servt,

G. BERKELEY.

66   TO PERCIVAL

Testaccio in the Island Inarime,
1 September N.S. 1717

My Lord,

Your Lordship's letter found me very ill in the Island Inarime, a remote corner of the world where we have now spent three months. When we go to Naples or Rome I shall make it my business to provide the prints &c., there being nothing more agreeable to me than your Lordship's commands. My illness, a flux, after about six weeks continuance, hath now quite left me, and in a better state of health than it found me. I am thank God very well.

Though your Lordship is well acquainted with other parts of Italy perhaps you may be a stranger to the Island Inarime (now vulgarly called Ischia). It is situate about six leagues from the city of Naples to the southwest : about eighteen miles in circuit,

containing sixteen thousand souls, the air temperate and wholesome, the soil extremely fertile. Apples, pears, plums, and cherries,
are not worth the naming, besides apricots, peaches, almonds,
figs, pomegranates, and many other fruits that have no English
names, together with vines, wheat, and Indian corn, cover almost
every spot in the Island. The fruit lying everywhere exposed
without enclosures makes the country look like one great fruit
garden, except some parks which are covered with chestnut groves
and others that produce nothing but thickets of myrtle. Nothing
can be conceived more romantic than the forces of nature, mountains, hills, vales, and little plains, being thrown together in a wild
and beautiful variety. The hills are most of them covered to the
top with vines, of which you will believe there is a prodigious
abundance in the Island, when I assure you there are no less than
sixty thousand hogsheads of wine made every year in so small
a spot. Here are also mountains very high, having towns and
villages on their sides placed in steep situations one above another,
and making a very odd prospect. And though the roads among
the hills are often steep and unequal, yet the asses of the Island
(the only *voiture* used here) carry us everywhere without danger.
We have two considerable towns or cities, one of which contains
six thousand souls : the rest are villages. The houses are real
and lasting, being everywhere built of lime and stone, flat roofed.

As riches and honours have no footing here, the people are
unacquainted with the vices that attend them, but in lieu thereof
they have got an ugly habit of murdering one another for trifles.
The second night after our coming to the Island a youth of 18
years was shot dead by our door ; but we have had several
instances of the like since that in several parts of the Island.
Last year thirty six murders were compounded for by the
Governour ; the life of man being rated at ten ducats.

In old times Inarime was inhabited by a Grecian colony from
the Euboea. And Hiero, King of Syracuse, resided here some
years, but the volcanoes and eruptions of fire in several parts
of the Island obliged the ancient inhabitants to quit it. We see
the remains of these eruptions in many places, which gave occasion
to the poets feigning that Typhoeus lay under it :

Inarime Jovis imperiis inposta Typhoeo.
Virg. *Aen.* ix. 716.

My humble service to my Lady, Mrs. Parker, Miss Kitty,
Master Johnny, the little stranger, Mrs. Dering, Miss Minshull,

Dan. Dering, Ch. Dering, the two Mr. Shutes, Sir David, &c.
I writ a long letter to Dan. Dering but never had an answer.
Mr. Ashe gives his humble service to your Lordship.

My Lord,

Your Lordship's most obliged &c.,

G. BERKELEY.

67 TO POPE

Naples, Oct. 22, N.S. 1717

I have long had it in my thoughts to trouble you with a letter,
but was discouraged for want of something that I could think
worth sending fifteen hundred miles. Italy is such an exhausted
subject that, I dare say, you'd easily forgive my saying nothing
of it ; and the imagination of a poet is a thing so nice and delicate
that it is no easy matter to find out images capable of giving
pleasure to one of the few, who (in any age) have come up to
that character. I am nevertheless lately returned from an island
where I passed three or four months ; which, were it set out in
its true colours, might, methinks, amuse you agreeably enough
for a minute or two.

The island Inarime is an epitome of the whole earth, containing within the compass of eighteen miles, a wonderful variety
of hills, vales, ragged rocks, fruitful plains, and barren mountains,
all thrown together in a most romantic confusion. The air is,
in the hottest season, constantly refreshed by cool breezes from the
sea. The vales produce excellent wheat and Indian corn, but are
mostly covered with vineyards intermixed with fruit-trees. Besides
the common kinds, as cherries, apricots, peaches, &c., they produce oranges, limes, almonds, pomegranates, figs, water-melons,
and many other fruits unknown to our climates, which lie every
where open to the passenger. The hills are the greater part
covered to the top with vines, some with chesnut groves, and
others with thickets of myrtle and lentiscus. The fields in the
northern side are divided by hedgerows of myrtle. Several
fountains and rivulets add to the beauty of this landscape, which
is likewise set off by the variety of some barren spots and naked
rocks. But that which crowns the scene, is a large mountain
rising out of the middle of the island, (once a terrible volcano,
by the ancients called Mons Epomeus). Its lower parts are

adorned with vines and other fruits ; the middle affords pasture
to flocks of goats and sheep ; and the top is a sandy pointed rock,
from which you have the finest prospect in the world, surveying
at one view, besides several pleasant islands lying at your feet,
a tract of Italy about three hundred miles in length, from the
promontory of Antium to the Cape of Palinurus : the greater part
of which hath been sung by Homer and Virgil, as making a considerable part of the travels and adventures of their two heroes.
The islands Caprea, Prochyta, and Parthenope, together with
Cajeta, Cumae, Monte Miseno, the habitations of Circe, the
Syrens, and the Laestrigones, the bay of Naples, the promontary
of Minerva, and the whole Campagnia felice, make but a part
of this noble landscape ; which would demand an imagination
as warm and numbers as flowing as your own, to describe it.
The inhabitants of this delicious isle, as they are without riches
and honours, so are they without the vices and follies that attend
them ; and were they but as much strangers to revenge as they
are to avarice and ambition, they might in fact answer the poetical
notions of the golden age. But they have got, as an alloy to their
happiness, an ill habit of murdering one another on slight offences.
We had an instance of this the second night after our arrival,
a youth of eighteen being shot dead by our door : and yet by the
sole secret of minding our own business, we found a means of
living securely among those dangerous people.

   Would you know how we pass the time at Naples ? Our chief
entertainment is the devotion of our neighbours. Besides the
gaiety of their churches (where folks go to see what they call *una
bella Devotione*, i.e. a sort of religious opera), they make fireworks
almost every week out of devotion ; the streets are often hung
with arras out of devotion ; and (what is still more strange)
the ladies invite gentlemen to their houses, and treat them with
music and sweetmeats, out of devotion : in a word, were it not
for this devotion of its inhabitants, Naples would have little else
to recommend it beside the air and situation.

   Learning is in no very thriving state here, as indeed nowhere
else in Italy ; however, among many pretenders, some men of
taste are to be met with. A friend of mine told me not long since
that, being to visit Salvini at Florence, he found him reading
your Homer : he liked the notes extremely, and could find no
other fault with the version, but that he thought it approached
too near a paraphrase ; which shews him not to be sufficiently
acquainted with our language. I wish you health to go on with

that noble work ; and when you have that, I need not wish you success. You will do me the justice to believe, that whatever relates to your welfare is sincerely wished by your, &c.

68   TO TOMMASO CAMPAILLA

Messanae, Februarii 25, 1718

Clarissime Vir,

     Ex itinere per universam insulam instituto jam tandem, favente numine, reversus, animum jucundissima memoria Siculorum hospitum, atque amicorum, praesertim quos ingenio atque eruditione praestantes inviserim, subinde reficio. Porro inter illos quanti te faciam, vir doctissime, facilius mente concipi, quam verbis exprimi potest. Id unum me male habet, quod, exaudito tuo colloquio diutius frui per itineris festinationem non licuerit. Clarissimos ingenii tui fructus, quos mihi impartiri dignatus sis, quam primum Londinium pervenero, aequius illiusmodi Rerum Aestimatoribus distribuendos, curabo. Si quid interim aliud occurrat, quod ad Societatem Regiam Londiniensem transmitti cupias, id, modo mittatur ad D. D. Portem. Hoare & Allen Anglos, negotii causa Messanae commorantes, ad me, ubicunque tandem sim, perveniet ; Porro Neutoni nostri Naturalis Philosophia Principia Mathematica, si quando in patriam sospes rediero ad te transmittenda dabo, vel si qua alia ratione commodis tuis inservire possim, reperies me, si minus potentem, promptum tamen, omnique ossequio

Humillimum servum,
G. BERKELEY.

69   TO PERCIVAL

Rome, 26th April 1718

My Lord,

     Upon my arrival here I had the good fortune to meet with Mr. Hamilton who brought me a letter from your Lordship, which was very agreeable as everything is that assures me of the welfare of your family. Among the many obligations I have to your Lordship I must reckon your making me acquainted with a gentleman of Mr. Hamilton's merit. I gave him a recommendation to some friends of mine in Naples where he intends to make a short stay, and upon his return I hope to enjoy more of his company.

It would I believe be no news to your Lordship to give you an account of the functions of the Holy Week, which has drawn a great confluence of strangers from all parts of Europe, particularly several of the nobility and gentry of Great Britain, enough to fill two coffee houses. The well affected part meet at that in Piazza d'Espagna ; and the rebels have another part to themselves. Among the latter are the Lords Mar, Southesk &c. Methinks it is no ill sign to see them loiter about town as if they had nothing to do. Though it must be owned, men of good sense, understanding, and friends to King George, are in these parts alarmed with apprehensions more from divisions at home than from any power or foreign foes. Your Lordship hath seen too much of Italy not to know that every indifferent man who travels must be heartily concerned at any accident that should seem to make way for introducing among us, that sort of government and religion that hath made the inhabitants of these parts the greatest fools and slaves from the wisest and bravest men in the world. But I hope the breach is not so wide, nor the consequences likely to prove so fatal, as is commonly feared or imagined at this distance.

During the functions of the Holy Week and the Easter holidays it was impossible to look out for prints or books ; but my next shall bring your Lordship an account of what I have procured for you, in which I hope my gusto will shew itself somewhat improved since coming abroad.

I must beg your Lordship to give my humblest respects to my Lady, Mrs. Parker, the children, and all friends who are so kind as to remember me, and to believe, that
            I am, My Lord,
                    Your Lordship's most obedt and most humble Servt,
                            GEO. BERKELEY.

The general talk here is of a peace between the Emperour and King Philip.

Rome, 28th July 1718

My Lord,

My last to your Lordship I have some suspicion might not have come to your hands, but having now got a correspondent at Leghorn to forward our letters I am in hopes this will. Upon the ill news of my Lord Bishop's death we were resolved to go directly homewards, but a few days after Mr. Ashe received letters from his friends with directions to continue longer this side the Alps, which together with the extreme heats that render travelling insupportable hath determined us to stay some months longer at Rome, where we have at present about thirty English gentlemen and noblemen, most of them men of good sense and very sober. This makes the *séjour* as agreeable as it is possible to be out of England, whither I long for liberty to return on many accounts, particularly that I may have a part in the contrivance of the house you design to build this winter, for you must know I pretend to an uncommon skill in architecture, as you will easily imagine when I assure your Lordship there is not any one modern building in Rome that pleases me, except the wings of the capitol built by Michael Angelo and the colonnade of Berninies before St Peter's. The Church itself I find a thousand faults with, as indeed with every other modern Church here. I forget the little round one in the place where St Peter was beheaded built by Bramante, which is very pretty and built like an ancient temple. This gusto of mine is formed on the remains of antiquity that I have met with in my travels, particularly in Sicily, which convince me that the old Romans were inferior to the Greeks, and that the moderns fall infinitely short of both in the grandeur and simplicity of taste.

I have bought for your Lordship prints of the Churches, palaces, and statues of Rome, a great number. I had likewise bought those of the Colonne Trajane and Antonina, which in many large sheets display the Roman antiquity, but shewing them to a judicious friend here who informed me that the plates are much worn out, and very coarsely retouched, which had spoiled the prints, I returned them. The rest are sent on board an English ship, safe packed up with some things of Mr. Ashe's, with directions to lie at the custom house in London till our return.

As for books there is no sort of learning flourishes here but

civil and canon law.   Not but there is enough too of divinity and
poetry, but so very bad that I can meet with nothing in either
kind worth buying.   The truth is the Italians of the last and present
age are not worth importing into England.   Those of the golden
age of Pope Leo the tenth are scarce, and very hard to be met
with.   But those I presume you are already provided with.   However, if there be any particular authors or editions that you want,
please to let me know, and when I come to Padua or Venice,
I shall make it my business to enquire for them.

I have had several letters from Lord Pembroke with directions
to enquire for about thirty books of which I have not in a years
time with my utmost diligence been able to procure above three.
If at Venice which is the great mart for books I meet with anything new worth buying, I intend to purchase it for your Lordship.   As to old authors I would gladly know which you want,
that I might not buy those you have already.

Your Lordship's letter under cover to George Ashe Esq., and
directed to Messrs. Bates Campion and Mitchel at Leghorn, will
at any time come safe to me, and can never bring any news more
agreeable than that of the welfare of yourself and family.

My best respects to my Lady and Mrs. Parker and the rest
of those who remember me, particularly Mrs. Dering.   I beg
your Lordship to believe me,
              My Lord,
                    Your Lordship's most obedt and most obliged Servant,
                                G. BERKELEY.

                         71   TO PERCIVAL

                                          Rome, 13th November 1718
My Lord,
              I know not by what accident the letter your Lordship
favoured me with from Paris came to my hands, being enclosed
in a cover to Mr. St George instead of Mr. Ashe.   My surprise to
hear your Lordship and the Ladies were at Paris was attended
with no small mortification to think I should miss the happiness
of seeing you there.

The Pretender is hourly expected in this city where he designs
to make his residence.   The greatest part of his followers are
already come and swarm in all public places, which must make

Rome an uneasy place to men of different principles. So we are now in a hurry proposing to set out from hence in a day or two, which makes me fear I shall not have time to enquire about the medals and other things your Lordship mentioned in your last. But I design to leave directions with a friend here to inform himself as to the price of them and where they may be had. He is one who having an excellent genius for painting designs to continue a year longer at Rome, and will gladly serve me in anything that lies in his power. So that by his means I hope to procure anything your Lordship shall have occasion for. I remember to have heard your Lordship speak of certain models in plaster of Paris cast from busts at Florence which miscarried in their way home, and having met with a man in the Villa Medici who has some moulds taken from celebrated antique busts, I have got him to form eight of them in terra cotta (as they call it), which is much more durable than plaster of Paris or giesso, being as hard as brick. Two painted after bronze antique are Julius Caesar and the Antinous in the Vatican, the other six busts have their names on billets affixed to them and are painted of a leaden colour, which seems to me more natural, though perhaps I had done better not to have had them painted at all. These I have seen carefully boxed up and sent to Leghorn, with directions from Mr. Ashe to his correspondents there to send them to London to Mr. Cairns (Sir Alexander's brother) with orders to deliver them to your Lordship, wishing they may in any measure repair the loss of those who had ordered yourself. You will have nothing to pay Mr. Cairns but the carriage from Leghorn to London.

I find the outside of your Lordship's house is finished and doubt not it will answer your fine taste. Within I hope to find a stone staircase, tiled floors, and vaulted roofs, with oval or square oblong pictures in the middle.

We are going to Venice in our way homewards and hope to kiss your Lordship's hands this Spring in London. My humble respects to the Ladies.

I am, My Lord,

Yr Lordship's most obedt hum. Servt,
GEO. BERKELEY.

Florence, 9/20 July, N.S. 1720

My Lord,

I have at length the pleasure to let you know of having procured for you what they called *serie mezana* of brass medals from Julius Caesar down to Galienus, which they tell me is the period of the good work. They are fifty odd heads fair, about a dozen copies. I have never studied medals so was obliged to follow the judgment of others. I hoped to have been able to have sent you this advice long since, having employed an English gentleman who passed this way to Rome (for my friend who I left there was returned to England). That gentleman after a long delay wrote me word he could get a series at a reasonable rate, but the heads would be very blind, and the sizes unequal. This put me upon trying what may be done here, and employing persons to pick up what originals may be had in Florence and making copies of the rest : but you know how tedious it is to deal with Italians. I never knew people so ready to promise and so slow to perform.

It is not Magnolfi but one Bianchi who hath care of the painters' heads. But upon enquiry I find it impracticable to have them copied, the great Duke being very jealous in that point lest they should be made public.

I have been with Soldani to know what the busts were which he did for you, but having at different times done things for English gentlemen, he remembers nothing in particular which he did for you.

Since the making those busts I sent you, I had got some others much finer being made of scaglione (a hard composition that looks and shines like marble). These packed up with the greatest care to prevent breaking I ordered to be sent to Mr. Cairns at London, but find they are gone without my knowledge to Lisbon with some things of Mr. Ashe's in order to embark there for Ireland ; but I have desired Mr. Ashe to write to his merchant in Dublin to send them back to London.

You wrote to me for a series of marbles. I have been told this was the proper place to get them in ; accordingly I have made it my business to enquire for them, but could find only one set in the whole town. It contains about one hundred sorts, being small oval pieces. I shall either send them or bring it myself.

As to the figured stones which you wrote for, when I was here before, I bought several of them which I designed for you. They are now in London ; but these as well as the prints are put up promiscuously with Mr. Ashe's things, so that I can give no directions for coming at them till we come to London, which I hope will be before the cold weather comes on. I have indeed been detained so long against my expectations and wishes on this side the Alps that I have lost patience. Every month these six months we have designed to begin our journey and have been as often disappointed. We are now resolved to set out in two days, but shall travel slowly because of the heats which are intolerable except a few hours in the morning and evening.

The advice you were so kind as to forward to me, and for which I return my hearty thanks, having by mistake lain many months at Brussels, came too late to be of any use. This and the like disappointments have had the good effect to harden me against any future mishaps. I hope to find that yourself and other friends there, particularly Mrs. Parker and Mrs. D. Dering, have had better fortune in the general scramble for the wealth of the nation ; nothing else can reconcile the French projects now on foot in England to

My Lord,
        Your Lordship's most obedt and most humble Servt,
        GEORGE BERKELEY.

Mr. Ashe presents his humble service to your Lordship, and I must desire you to present mine to the Ladies and all friends. I was particularly obliged for the account you were pleased to give me of your hopeful offspring, which must be very entertaining to one who by inclination as well as gratitude thinks himself interested in all that concerns your family. Your Lordship cannot do a better service to the public than to get and breed up sons like your self and daughters like my Lady.

73   TO PERCIVAL

Trin. Coll., Dublin, 12th Oct. 1721

My Lord,
    I have been now a month in Ireland without writing to your Lordship, not that I am in the least insensible of many

favours received from you and good Lady Percival, and the acknowledgments I ought to make for them. But the truth is I deferred it every post, in hopes I should have been able before the following to let you know, I was in possession of the preferment which of all those in the Lord Lieutenant's gift would have been the most agreeable to me, which the goodness I have constantly experienced in your Lordship made me flatter myself would have proved welcome news ; but his Grace still imagining himself obliged in point of policy to keep that affair in suspence, I can no longer delay what I should otherwise have done upon my first arrival.

I had no sooner set foot on shore, but I heard that the Deanery of Dromore was become vacant, which is worth about £500 a year, and a sinecure : which circumstance recommends it to me beyond any preferment in the kingdom, though there are some Deaneries of twice that value. I instantly applied to his Grace, and put him in mind of his promises. He answered me very civilly, but in general terms, saying that he meant to do more than he cared to say, and more to the same purpose, from which I could gather that he designed to dispose of nothing during the session, in order to create a dependence, though at the same time he create much trouble to himself and others by encouraging more hopes and solicitations than he can satisfy. I have represented this matter in a letter to my Lord Burlington, but can hardly hope his Lordship will write to the Duke, since he told me in England that he was willing to serve me in any other instance, but that he thought it below him to solicit his Grace any further.

The Duchess is very civil, and, were this affair in her disposal, would I believe bestow it to my liking which I owe to my Lady Percival. Mr. Fairfax also befriends me much. But notwithstanding all these things, and the Duke's repeated promises, it must be owned the importunities he exposeth himself to on all hands by this unnecessary delay make me uncertain of the event. One thing I believe is pretty sure, that it will not be determined before the recess, which can hardly be these three weeks yet, it being probable the debates about the bank will hardly be over before that time. I do not find that this new project meets with many partisans here besides those who are immediately interested in it, and I am inclined to think it may come to nothing.

I cannot conclude without recommending to you and your family a preservative against the plague, which I am told alarms you much at present, it is no more than the Jesuits bark taken as against the ague. This I had from Dr. Arbuthnot just before I left London, who is resolved his whole family shall make use of it, and I cannot but think for the reasons he gave me, too long to be repeated, it would be of great benefit.

Mr. Dering, who has gathered flesh and mended his complection very sensibly in the little time that I have been here, has given me the agreeable news of my Lady Percival's being well. God grant that she may continue so, and bring forth to your Lordship another fine boy, which I hope shortly to hear.

If there be any nonsense in this letter I beg your Lordship will have the goodness to excuse : the truth is, I am more than half asleep as I write, having been up very early this morning. Pray present my humble service to my Lady, to her sister, and to Mrs. Dering, and believe me to be, my Lord,

Yr Lordship's most obedt and most humble Servt,

G. BERKELEY.

If I get this Deanery I hope to see your Lordship soon.

74 TO PERCIVAL

Trinity Coll., Dublin, 23rd Oct. 1721

My Lord,

I remember to have read with a great deal of pleasure a very clear and instructive piece of your Lordship's concerning the Bank, or rather concerning Banks in general. I must now make it my request to your Lordship to favour me with a copy of it. It may be sent conveniently in two covers. I cannot but think your discourse would be very serviceable to the public at this time, when men's thoughts and conversation are almost entirely turned towards a subject they are generally speaking very ignorant of. It would even have its use if it were shewn only to two or three leading men in manuscript. I must therefore beg leave to press you on this head, the rather because the bank scheme is not quite laid aside, and may still one way or other be very important.

The love of your country will I doubt not be a sufficient

motive to your Lordship to comply in this particular with, my
Lord,

> Yr Lordship's
>> Most obedt and most humble Servt,
>> G. BERKELEY.

I long to hear how my Lady does and the rest of your family,
to all whom pray give my humble service. The affair which I
mentioned last is not yet come to an issue.

---

75   TO PERCIVAL

Trinity Coll., Dub. [Dec.] 1721

My Lord,

I just now received the favour of your Lordship's letter,
together with your dissertation on the Bank, for which I most
heartily thank your Lordship. After a long dearth of news we
have had ten packets this evening at once, which alone could
occasion my being so late in my acknowledgment. I shall make
the use you prescribe of what you have been pleased to send me,
and must ask your pardon if I persist in thinking very differently
of it from what you seem to do. And to say no more, this I will
venture to affirm, that I never saw anything so proper as to give
me an easy insight into the several sorts of banks as your Lordship's papers. We have had two or three things printed here
about the late project, particularly one by Mr. Maxwell, and an
answer to it by Mr. Rowley, both Parliament men, the first for,
the latter against the Bank, which I would have sent to you, had
I judged such large pamphlets worth the postage. But that affair
is in such a declining way, that it is to be questioned whether it
will be resumed this session, which commences next week.

The Deanery still continues in suspense, and is likely to remain
so till the parliament is up, which probably will not be before
middle of Jan'y.

Your Lordship's amusement in planting trees for the use of
a stranger is so far from culpable, that it shews a refined taste
and a disinterested benevolence to mankind, a thing not the less
excellent because it is rare and perhaps ridiculous in this corrupt
age.

Three days hence we are to have the honour of entertaining
the Duke of Grafton at the College, and I am appointed to make

the Latin speech to him, which employs my thoughts for the present, so I shall give you no further trouble, but concluding with my best good wishes for yourself, my good Lady Percival, and all the rest of your family.

I remain, My Lord,
Yr Lordship's most obedt & most humble Servt,
G. Berkeley.

76   TO PERCIVAL

Tr. Coll. Dublin, 9th Jany. 1721/22

My Lord,

It is very obliging in your Lordship to think of me and my interests in the kind manner you do. This makes me think it will not be altogether impertinent to lay before you a short account of our Irish vacancies in the Church. There are vacant besides the Bishopric of Leighlin and Fernes, the Deaneries of Downe, Dromore, Limerick and Cork, and also some smaller benefices. I applied at first for that of Dromore, and have not since altered my application, the Bishopric and rich Deanery of Downe being above my desires, and the others below them. The Deanery of Dromore exactly suits my wishes, and I have had encouragement to hope for it. At first I forced myself to be a pretty constant courtier, but of late have remitted somewhat of my diligence, being tired out with delays. I do nevertheless still see the Duke and Duchess once in ten days. The truth is, the assurances I have had from both ought in good manners to make me easy till the time comes when things can be declared, which cannot be far off if the Parliament rises in a fortnight.

For news I hear none, but that the Commons have been uneasy at their bills being altered in the Council here. This it was thought would have produced some resolutions, but their heat I am now told is now over. For some time past I have been afflicted for the death of Mr. Ashe who died at Brussels.

I am glad to hear your family are all well, and am in hopes when you next favour me to have an account of my Lady's safe deliverance. So wishing you and all yours all happiness,

I remain, My Lord,
Yr Lordship's most obedient and most humble Servt,
G. Berkeley.

77   TO PERCIVAL

Trin. Coll., 10th Feb. 1721/22

My Lord,

Your Lordship hath been always so partial to my interests, that I persuade myself it will be welcome news to you that my patent is now passing the seals for the Deanery of Dromore. As upon all other accounts so especially on my Lady Duchess' favour and friendly interposition on my behalf, I am very sensible of the obligations I have to my good Lady Percival. I shall be in pain till I hear she is well delivered of a child, that from my heart I wish may rival Mr. Johnny in learning, or Miss Helena in beauty, and I can hardly wish more. I shall then request another favour from her Ladyship, and that is to acknowledge those I have received from my Lady Duchess. I believe I have formerly told your Lordship the Deanery of Dromore is worth £500 p. ann. It is what were I in possession would please me beyond anything, but the worst of it is, the Bishop, pretending a title, hath put in a presentee of his own, which unavoidably engages me in a lawsuit ; but if I succeed, my pains will be abundantly recompensed.

I am, my Lord,
Yr Lordship's most obedient Servt,
G. BERKELEY.

78   TO PERCIVAL

Trin. Coll. 13th Feb. 1721/22

My Lord,

As among all your friends there is nobody hath better reason to be pleased with any good fortune that befalls your Lordship or good Lady Percival than I have, so I beg leave to assure you there is no one employs more sincere and constant wishes for your prosperity. You will therefore do me the justice to believe it was most agreeable news to me which I heard this day of my Lady's being safely delivered of a fine boy. I could not omit congratulating your Lordship on this happy event, and at the same time wishing you may live to procure many of the same

kind to your own comfort, and the joy of all your friends, particularly,
    My Lord,
               Yr Lordship's most obedient & most humble Servt,
                     G. BERKELEY.

79   TO PERCIVAL

                         Dublin, 15th March 1721/22
My Lord,
    It was very kind in your Lordship to wait on the Lord
Lieutenant and acknowledge the favour his Grace has been pleased
to confer on me, which I am very sensible was in great goodness
designed for my advantage, though in the event it may possibly
prove otherwise. I had indeed £50 Concordation money given
towards carrying on the suit at the last Council the Duke held.
Twenty-five of that is gone already in seeing lawyers, and making
searches and extracts in several offices, though the suit be not yet
commenced ; which upon enquiry I find will be more tedious,
and the event much more doubtful, than I was at first aware of,
but with a sure expense on my side, if I am informed right, of
several hundred pounds besides what I am likely to get from the
Government, which will go but a little way to fee eight lawyers
(for so many I have engaged), and defray all other expenses of
a suit against a man who is worth £1200 p. ann. beside the Deanery
which he is in actual possession of, and who hath been practised
in lawsuits five and twenty years together. This being the case,
my friends think it would be no unreasonable request for me to
desire the Chantership of Christ Church now vacant by the death
of the Dean of Armagh, and said to be worth somewhat more than
one hundred pounds p. ann. This Chantership is consistent with
my fellowship, and might enable me to carry on the suit with ease,
and perhaps recover the right of the Crown. And as it is in his
Grace's gift, who hath on all occasions shewn great humanity and
goodness, I have hopes he may comply with my request, if it be
speedily laid before him in a proper manner. As there is no one
can do this better than your Lordship, so there is no one on
whose friendship and protection I can better depend. I must
likewise recommend myself to good Lady Percival whose speaking
to the Duchess will be of service, her Grace having been always

favourable to me on her account. If your Lordship could speak yourself, or (if unacquainted with him) could get another to speak to Mr. Hopkins, it would be very proper and useful on this occasion.

Your Lordship will do me the justice to believe, that as I have the sincerest gratitude for the favour his Grace hath already conferred upon me, so I should not presume to solicit for a new one, if I were in possession of that, and not under just apprehensions of a long, uncertain, and expensive suit, in no sort proportioned to my circumstances, which nevertheless I may be enabled to prosecute to the utmost by the addition of this small preferment.

I should be glad to hear your family are all well, and that Mrs. Dering was out of danger.

You see, my Lord, the trouble your good natured inclination to serve your friends has drawn upon you. I have a particular reason why I would not trouble my Lord Burlington in this affair, and I thought it would be more respectful to get a friend to state the case to the Duke than to write myself to him upon it. If in desiring this from your Lordship I ask anything improper, you are the best judge in what manner to act or whether to act at all ; so begging ten thousand pardons, I conclude,

Yr Lordship's most obedt and most obliged Servt,
GEO. BERKELEY.

80   TO PERCIVAL

Trinity College, 14th April 1722

My Lord,

I humbly thank your Lordship for the trouble you have taken on my account, not doubting but you have laid my affair before his Grace in the properest and kindest manner that good nature and good sense should suggest.

I make no question that the Duke will think it reasonable my cause should be supported out of the treasury during his Lieutenancy, but I much fear it will survive his government.

Your Lordship is surprised at the number of my lawyers, and truly so am I myself, having at first little thought that I should have occasion for so many. They are six counsellors, two attorneys, and a civilian. The former are Rogerson, Marlow,

Malone, Nuttley, Stannard, and Howard. The attorneys are Mr. Smith of the King's Bench, and Mr. Stanton who is my solicitor. My civilian is Dr. Hawkshaw. The cause is a great cause, and I was told that fewer would not do. My adversary, if I am informed right, hath as many, and had the advantage to pre-engage the best, before I had got my Patent.

Tuesday last I had a meeting of my lawyers, who direct that I should proceed by *quare impedit*, and I am to serve my adversaries the Bishop and Dr. Lesley with a writ this week.

God preserve your Lordship from law and lawyers. Had the Deanery been disposed of when first vacant, I had been in possession and avoided all this trouble, but now the Bishop's clerk is in, I fear it will be a very difficult matter to dispossess him : so difficult and so doubtful that I heartily wish instead of my present Patent I had a promise of the next Deanery that falls.

One of the most disagreeable effects of my lawsuit is that it detains me from England, and consequently from Charlton, where I proposed being happy this summer, and where I hope your Lordship, my good Lady Percival and your delightful offspring now enjoy all those domestic pleasures which constitute the true and solid comforts of life.

I am, my Lord,

&c.

G. BERKELEY.

81 TO PERCIVAL

Dublin, Trinity College, 29th July 1722

My Lord,

Not having the honour of a line from your Lordship since my last, I am well pleased to find by Mr. Percival that you and my Lady and the rest of the family are well.

Your Lordship knows this barren bleak island too well to expect any news from it worth your notice. The most remarkable thing now going on is a house of Mr. Conolly's at Castletown. It is 142 feet in front, and above 60 deep in the clear, the height will be about 70. It is to be of fine wrought stone, harder and better coloured than the Portland, with outhouse joining to it by colonnades &c. The plan is chiefly of Mr. Conolly's invention, however, in some points they are pleased to consult me. I hope it will be an ornament to the country.

On Thursday next the King's equestrian statue is to be un-covered and exposed to view ; the several companys will ride the fringes on that day, and our magistrates appear in their utmost magnificence. I hear six guineas are given for a floor to see the show. I was desired to make the Latin inscription for the statue, which I did, being willing to distinguish my zeal for his Majesty, and in consequence thereof had the honour to dine at my Lord Mayor's on last great day.

I heartily wish my lawsuit was at an end, that I may pay a visit to my friends in England, especially yourself and my good Lady, whom I long to see ; but as it is, it unluckily detains me here from seeing my friends, or prosecuting my interest in England. I do nevertheless conceive hopes it may be cut short by a project contained in the enclosed, which when you have read, I must entreat you to seal and deliver or send to Mr. Molyneux. I take the liberty to give you this trouble, having cause to suspect that some former letters of mine to him might have miscarried, and as this is of importance, I would fain have it go sure and speedy. My Lord, I am out of countenance for the trouble I have given you, and remain with a hearty sense of all your favours,

Yr Lordship's

Most obedt & most humble Servt,
GEO. BERKELEY.

82   TO PERCIVAL

Trinity Coll. Dubl., 7th Sept. 1722

My Lord,

I am to return my thanks to your Lordship for your obliging letter, and your care in conveying mine to Mr. Molyneux, though as it happens I might have spared my friends and myself that trouble. I flatter myself with hopes of seeing your Lordship in London this winter, if I can steal so much time from my lawsuit ; which besides that it gives me but a very discouraging prospect (the only way of getting possession of the Deanery being I am fully persuaded to make Dean Lesley a Bishop) hath this incon-venience, that it keeps me from friends in England, though I have a letter of absence.

I shall then give you the best account I can of Mr. Conolly's House ; in the meantime you will be surprised to hear that the building is begun and the cellar floor arched before they have agreed on any plan for the elevation or façade. Several have been made by several hands, but as I do not approve of a work conceived by many heads so I have made no draught of mine own. All I do being to give my opinion on any point, when consulted.

We are much alarmed here by the seizing of the Bishop of Rochester, which makes men think the plot more considerable than was at first imagined. Providence hath hitherto baffled all schemes for introducing popery and arbitrary power, and I trust in God will continue to do so. I am sorry and ashamed to see a Protestant Bishop accused of so foul a conspiracy.

I remain with my humblest services to Lady Percival and best wishes to all your family,

My Lord,

Yr Lordship's most obedt and most obliged Servt,

GEO. BERKELEY.

83   TO PERCIVAL

Trin. Coll. Dub. Oct. 1722

My Lord,

I have still hopes of seeing your Lordship this winter, when I flatter myself with the prospect of rejoicing by your fireside, where I have spent so many agreeable hours.

The information you were so good to send me about the Bishop of Rochester was very acceptable : it is an affair that holds us all in suspense, everyone longing to see the event and know his accomplices.

As to my own affair, I could wish it were one brought to any conclusion, being prepared for the issue, be it what it will, and I think as indifferent about it as one can well be supposed to be on a like occasion.

My Lord Duke hath taken one step of late that pleases every one, I mean the presenting Dr. Bolton to the Bishopric of Clonfert. He could not possibly have pitched upon a person more universally esteemed and unenvied. There is another of that name Dean of Derry, who lieth dangerously ill of a palsy, and is indeed past hopes of recovery. My friends think that in case of a vacancy I may have some pretensions to my Lord Lieutenant's favour ;

especially if his Grace shall not think fit to recommend my adversary to a Bishopric, without which I have little or no prospect of succeeding to the Deanery of Dromore.

As to Mr. Payzant's copying pieces out of our Library, it is at present so old and ruinous, and the books so out of order, that there is little attendance given ; beside it is unusual for strangers to be admitted to copy in it. The only way is for me to borrow in my own name, and under caution any book that you would have copied, and so for Mr. Payzant to transcribe it at home, which I will gladly do. Let me therefore know what your Lordship would have, and I will enquire if it be in our MS. library, which to speak the truth is but indifferently furnished. This with my respects to my good Lady Percival, your Lordship and all your family, not forgetting Mr. Dering and Mrs. Dering, is what occurs from,

Yr Lordship's, &c.,
G. Berkeley.

84   TO PERCIVAL

London, 16th Dec. 1722

My Lord,

After so dangerous a voyage, and so long a journey, it is a great mortification to find myself disappointed of the principal pleasure I proposed in London, by your Lordship's and my Lady's absence at Bath. But the occasion is still more mortifying. I hope my good Lady finds the benefit she expected from those waters. If the Bath doth not perfect her cure, I know a place within a thousand leagues that I am persuaded will, if I can persuade her Ladyship to go thither. But more of this when I have the happiness to see you.

For the present I have made an excursion into England, partly to see my friends, and partly to inform myself in some points of law which are not so well known in Ireland. I am heartily sorry that my suit is likely to call me back before your return to London, but if it should, I shall not be long without making another attempt to see you.

I know not whether you have heard of our abandoned condition at sea. For thirty-six hours together we expected every minute to be swallowed by a wave, or dashed in pieces against a rock. We sprung and split our mast, lost our anchor, and heaved our guns overboard. The storm and the sea were outrageous beyond description, but it pleased God to deliver us.

I have services to you and my Lady from Mr. Percival and Mrs. Percival, as also an Irish prayer-book which your brother sends as a specimen of our good printing.

The first house I went to was yours in Pall Mall, where I found the children very well, and was particularly well pleased with my new acquaintance, your youngest son, who is as fine a boy as the sun shines on. My humble service to my Lady and Mrs. Dering.

I am,

My Ld,

Yr Lordship's most obedt & affect. Servt,

G. BERKELEY.

85 TO PERCIVAL

London, March 4th, 1722/23

My Lord,

It is now about ten months since I have determined with myself to spend the residue of my days in the Island of Bermuda, where I trust in Providence I may be the mean instrument of doing good to mankind. Your Lordship is not to be told that the reformation of manners among the English in our western plantations, and the propagation of the Gospel among the American savages, are two points of high moment. The natural way of doing this is by founding a college or seminary in some convenient part of the West Indies, where the English youth of our plantations may be educated in such sort as to supply the churches with pastors of good morals and good learning, a thing (God knows !) much wanted. In the same seminary a number of young American savages may be also educated till they have taken their degree of Master of Arts. And being by that time well instructed in Christian religion, practical mathematics, and other liberal arts and sciences, and early endued with public spirited principles and inclinations, they may become the fittest missionaries for spreading religion, morality, and civil life, among their countrymen, who can entertain no suspicion or jealousy of men of their own blood and language, as they might do of English missionaries, who can never be so well qualified for that work. Some attempts have been made towards a college in the West, but to little purpose, chiefly I conceive for want of a proper situation wherein to place such college or seminary, as also for want of a sufficient number of able men well qualified with divine and human learning, as well as with zeal to prosecute such an undertaking. As to the first, I do think the small group of Bermuda Islands the fittest spot for a college on the following accounts. 1. It is the most equidistant part of our plantations from all the rest, whether in the continent, or the isles. 2. It is the only Plantation that holds a general commerce and correspondence with all the rest, there being sixty cedar ships belonging to the Bermudians, which they employ as carriers to all parts of the English West Indies, in like manner as the Dutch are carriers in Europe. 3. The climate is by far the healthiest and most serene, and consequently the most fit for study. 4. There is the greatest abundance of all the necessary provisions for life, which is much to be considered in a place of education. 5. It is the securest spot in the universe, being environed round with rocks all but one narrow entrance, guarded by seven forts, which render it inaccessible not only to pirates but to the united force of France and Spain. 6. The inhabitants have the greatest simplicity of manners, more innocence, honesty, and good nature, than any of our other planters, who are many of them descended from whores, vagabonds, and transported criminals, none of which ever settled in Bermudas. 7. The Islands of Bermuda produce no one enriching commodity, neither sugar, tobacco, indigo, or the like, which may tempt men from their studies to turn traders, as the parsons do too often elsewhere.

It would take up too much of your Lordship's time minutely to describe the beauties of Bermuda, the summers refreshed with constant cool breezes, the winters as mild as our May, the sky as light and blue as a sapphire, the ever green pastures, the earth eternally crowned with fruits and flowers. The woods of cedars, palmettos, myrtles, oranges &c., always fresh and blooming. The beautiful situations and prospects of hills, vales, promontories, rocks, lakes and sinuses of the sea. The great variety, plenty, and perfection of fish, fowl, vegetables of all kinds, and (which is in no other of our Western Islands) the most excellent butter, beef, veal, pork, and mutton. But above all, that uninterrupted health and alacrity of spirit, which is the result of the finest weather and gentlest climate in the world, and which of all others is the most effectual cure for the cholic, as I am most certainly assured by the information of many very credible persons of all ranks who have been there.

In case I carry Deanery (as I have good hopes I shall) I design to erect a charity school in Dromore, and to maintain ten savages and ten whites in the Bermudan University. But whatever happens, go I am resolved if I live. Half a dozen of the most agreeable and ingenious men of our college are with me in this project. And since I came hither I have got together about a dozen English men of quality, and gentlemen, who intend to retire to these islands, to build villas and plant gardens, and to enjoy health of body and peace of mind, where they have a soft freestone like that at Bath, and a soil which produces everything that grows in America, Europe, or the East, and where a man may live with more pleasure and dignity for £500 p. annum than for £10,000 here : in short where men may find, in fact, whatsoever the most poetical imagination can figure to itself in the golden age, or the Elysian fields.

I have been proposing every day this month past to trouble you with this narrative, and have at last ventured to do it, tho' I run the risk of being thought mad and chimerical. But I beg your Lordship not to determine anything of me or my project till I have the honour of seeing you at Charlton, which I hope for this summer, and thereto lay before you a thousand things relating to the scheme, the method of carrying it on, and answering objections against it. In the meantime I am going to Ireland, for three months, or four at most, by which time my lawsuit will probably be ended. If I can make a convert of your Lordship to Bermuda, I doubt not my Lady will be pleased to pass a few years there for the perfect recovery of her health, to which that climate will contribute beyond anything in the world. My heartiest good wishes and best respects to her Ladyship.

I am, &c.,

G. BERKELEY.

86 TO PERCIVAL

Trinity College, Dublin, 4th June 1723

My Lord,

The kind concern you have always shewn for my interests hath made it become my duty to inform you of any great advantage that should befall me. Some thing of that sort is just now come to pass, that probably will surprise your Lordship as much as it doth me. Mrs. Hester van Omry, a Lady to whom I was a perfect stranger, having never in the whole course of my life, to my knowledge, exchanged one single word with her, died on Sunday night. Yesterday her will was opened, by which it appears that I am constituted executor, the advantage whereof is computed by those who understand her affairs to be worth three thousand pounds, and if a suit she had depending be carried, it will be considerably more. But this is only a confused gross reckoning; in a little time I hope to see more distinctly into the state of her affairs. If this had not happened, I was determined to write to your Lordship by this post on my Lady's account. I am heartily sorry to hear she is not so well recovered of her cholic by the Bath as I could wish, and do therefore repeat and insist on the advice I formerly gave her Ladyship to go and drink the waters of Geronster near Spa. If this does not perfect her cure, there is nothing left but your and her going to Bermuda, where to enjoy the company of you all in good health, would be as great a blessing as I can figure to myself upon earth.

I know not what your thoughts are on the long account I sent you from London to Bath of my Bermuda scheme, (which is now stronger on my mind than ever, this providential event having made many things easy in my private affairs which were otherwise before). But I hear that Mr. Moore reports that you are terrified with the apprehension of earthquakes. Upon the word of a priest, I am thoroughly convinced that an earthquake was never known to have happened in Bermuda. The Summer Islands are all to my certain knowledge freer from earthquakes than that on which you now live. There is not (I may say without vanity) a man in the world, who never was in the Summer Islands, that knows so much of them as I do; and this of the earthquakes is a most villanous calumny, set about by somebody who wants objections against the scheme, as I could easily prove by arguments and testimonies to your Lordship; but that I am in a prodigious hurry, the Lady being to be buried in a little more than an hour's time. Her funeral is under the direction of the King at arms, where I am to act I know not what part, which puts an end to this hasty scrawl.

I am, my Lord,

Yr Lordship's most obedt and most humble Servt,

GEO. BERKELEY.

87   TO TOMMASO CAMPAILLA

Londinii Kalendis Julii 1723

Clarissime Vir

Post longam quinque ferme annorum peregrinationem, variosque casus, et discrimina, nunc demum in Angliam redux, nihil antiquius habeo, quam fidem meam tibi quondam obligatam. Deus bone ! Ab illo tempore quot clades, quot rerum mutationes, tam apud vos, quam apud nos ! Sed mittamus haec tristia. Libros tuos, prout in mandatis habui, viro erudito e Societate Regia tradidi, qui, cum solertiam, et ingenium tuum pro meritis extimet [*sic*], tum id plurimum miratur, tantum scientiae lumen in extremo Siciliae angulo tam diu delituisse. Telescopium quod attinet catoptricum, e metallo confectum, id quidem olim aggressus est Neutonus ; verum res ex voto non successit ; nam impossibile erat, nitidum chalybis splendorem usque eo conservare, ut stellarum imagines distincte exhiberet ; proinde hujusmodi telescopia nec in usu sunt, nec unquam fuere ; nec praeter unicum illud, quod Author experimenti causa fabricavit, ullum factum esse unquam, vel fando accepi. Hodie certe apud nostrates non reperiuntur. Caeterum librum clarissimi istius philosophi juxta ac mathematici, quem spondebam missurum, ad te mitto, quem tanquam sincerae amicitiae pignus accipias, quaeso. Tu, interim, vir clarissime, promovere rem litterariam pergas ; artesque bonas et scientias in ea insula serere et propagare, ubi felicissimae terrae indoles frugibus, et ingeniis apta ab omni aevo aeque fuit. Scito me tibi semper futurum

Addictissimum et humillimum servum

G. BERKELEY.

88 TO PERCIVAL

Trinity College, Dublin, 19th Sept. 1723

My Lord,

I heartily congratulate your and good Lady Percival's safe arrival at Charlton, though I must own the pleasure this incident would otherwise have given me is not a little alloyed by the account I hear of her Ladyship's not receiving all the benefit she expected from the Spa waters. I hope however that she is considerably eased, but for a perfect cure of so rooted a disorder, it must I believe under God be the effect of time and change of air. Besides my best wishes and prayers for her Ladyship's health, I will venture to contribute my mite of advice, how extravagant however it may seem, and that is to try the air of the Summer Islands which I am thoroughly satisfied is the best in the world, and particularly good for the cholic. And in good earnest what is a year's or two years' confinement there in competition with her health, which I am sure your Lordship can never be easy without.

In my last I gave an account of a legacy left me by a Lady. Since that, looking into her affairs we find her debts to have been considerably greater than we imagined. I am, nevertheless, still likely to make two thousand pound clear, not reckoning in the law suit depending between the executors and Mr. Partinton.

As to the suit about the Deanery of Dromore, I despair of seeing it end to my advantage. The Deanery of Down is now vacant, but there is such a crowd of competitors for everything, that I cannot promise myself success without such assiduity and attendance as I hardly think it deserves. The truth is, my first purpose of going to Bermuda sets me above soliciting anything with earnestness in this part of the world, which can now be of no use to me, but as it may enable me the better to prosecute that design : and it must be owned that the present possession of something in the Church would make my application for an establishment in these Islands more considered. I mean a Charter for a College there, which of all things I desire, as being what would reconcile duty and inclination, making my life at once more useful to the public and more agreeable to myself than I can possibly expect elsewhere. And as I am to run into visions on this subject, I have sometimes thought it not quite impossible that you and my Lady may sometime or other take a fancy to retire to that part of the world. But I dare only think this possible, and if it be otherwise should be sorry to be undeceived. I am with all respect,

> My Lord,
>> Yr Lordship's most obedt most humble & affect. Servt,
>>> GEORG. BERKELEY.

89   TO PERCIVAL

Trin. Coll. Dublin, 5th May 1724

My Lord,

After a long silence which was purely occasioned by my not knowing what to say, and expecting every day to be able to say something with certainty of my affairs (which I flattered myself might not be disagreeable to one from whom I have received so many instances of favour and goodness), I can now tell your Lordship, that yesterday I received my patent for the best Deanery in this kingdom, that of Derry. The affair of Dromore is still undecided, and likely to be so for some years, but it is now in other hands, God be praised.

I have had powerful competitors, who used many arts to undermine me : but two livings worth £700 per ann. happening to fall in the gift of the College, which the House, to further my promotion, was so kind as to put into the disposal of my Lord Duke, this gave a strong turn in my favour. I am very sensible how much the Duchess hath been my friend, and as sensible how much I am indebted for that to good Lady Percival.

This Deanery is said to be worth £1500 p. ann., but then there are four curates to be paid, and great charges upon entering, for a large house and offices, first fruits, patent, &c. which will consume the first year's profit, and part of the second. But as I do not consider it with an eye to enriching myself, so I shall be perfectly contented if it facilitates and recommends my scheme of Bermuda, which I am in hopes will meet with a better reception when it comes from one possessed of so great a Deanery. I am the fonder of Bermuda because I take it to be the likeliest means under heaven to re-establish my Lady's health, which I know your just tenderness for her will put you on restoring by all possible methods. I intend to-morrow for the North in order to my instalment and taking possession. When that is over

I may trouble your Lordship with another letter, till when, I conclude,

My Lord,
Yr most, &c.,
GEORGE BERKELEY.

90   TO PERCIVAL

Elphin, 8th June 1724

My Lord,

I am now on my return from Derry, where I have taken possession of my Deanery, and farmed out my tithe lands, &c. for £1250 a year. I am assured they are worth two hundred pounds per ann. more, but thought it better to have men of substantial fortunes engaged for the punctual payment of the foregoing sum, than by keeping them in my own hands to subject myself to all that trouble, and all those cheats which Dissenters (whereof we have many about Derry) are inclined to practice towards the clergy of our Church.

The city of Londonderry is the most compact, regular, well built town, that I have seen in the King's Dominions, the town house (no mean structure) stands in the midst of a square piazza from which there are four principal streets leading to as many gates. It is a walled town, and has walks all round on the walls planted with trees, as in Padua. The Cathedral is the prettiest in Ireland. My house is a fashionable thing, not five years old, and cost eleven hundred pounds. The Corporation are all good churchmen, a civil people, and throughout English, being a colony from London. I have hardly seen a more agreeable situation, the town standing on a peninsula in the midst of a fine spreading lake, environed with green hills, and at a distance the noble ridge of Ennishawen mountains and the mighty rocks of Maghilligan form a most august scene. There is indeed much of the *gusto grande* in the laying out of this whole country, which recalls to mind many prospects of Naples and Sicily.

After all I may chance not to be twopence the richer for this preferment, for by the time I have paid for the house and first fruits, I hope I shall have brought the Bermuda project to an issue, which, God willing, is to be my employment this winter in London, where I long for the pleasure of waiting on your

Lordship and good Lady Percival, to whom with the rest of the family I beg you to give my most humble and affectionate respects.

I remain,

&c.,

GEO. BERKELEY.

91   TO PERCIVAL

Trin. Coll. Dub. 9th Sept. 1724

My Lord,

I am now, bless God, quite at ease from a cruel periodical cholic which seized me after my return from Derry. For several days it was very violent, but the loss of thirty-six ounces of blood with about a dozen purgings and vomitings, reduced both it and me to a very weak state. I have now and then inclinations of a relapse which hath made me entertain thoughts of going to Bath, Bristol, or Tunbridge. I am not yet determined which, but propose going the first opportunity for England, where I hope to find your Lordship, my Lady, and all your good family, if not so well as I could wish, at least in a way of being thoroughly recovered and established in good health by a year's or two years' residence in Bermuda, which I earnestly recommend to you. This I must own looks like a selfish proposal. But though I cannot deny that it would delight me beyond measure, yet I doubt not when I see you to prove by good arguments that your own and my Lady's interest is as much consulted in this project as my satisfaction. I have so many things to say on this head that if I once begun I should soon exceed the bounds of a letter, and shall therefore only add (with my best respects to your Lordship, my Lady, and all your family), that in the hopes of seeing you soon, I remain with the greatest sincerity,

My Lord,

Yr Lordship's most obedt and most obliged humble Servt,

G. BERKELEY.

Yesterday Wood's effigy was carried in procession by the mob through most of the streets of this town in order to be hanged or burnt, but it is given out by them that the Lord Mayor hath reprieved him till Wednesday. It is hardly possible to express the indignation which all ranks of men shew on this occasion.

92   TO PRIOR

London, December 8, 1724

Dear Tom,

You wrote to me something or other, which I received a fortnight ago, about temporal affairs, which I have no leisure to think of at present.   The L. Chancellor is not a busier man than myself; and I thank God my pains are not without success, which hitherto hath answered beyond expectation.   Doubtless the English are a nation *très éclairée*.   I have only time to tell you, that Robin will call on you for thirteen pounds.   Let me know whether you have wrote to Mr. Newman whatever you judged might give him a good opinion of our project.   Let me also know where Bermuda Jones lives, or where he is to be met with.

I am,

Your, &c.,

G. Berkeley.

I lodge at Mr. Fox's, an apothecary in Albemarle Street, near St. James's.

Provided you bring my affair with Partinton to a complete issue before Christmas day come twelvemonth, by reference or otherwise, that I may have my dividend, whatever it is, clear, I do hereby promise you to increase the premium I promised you before by its fifth part, whatever it amounts to.

93   TO PRIOR

April 20, 1725

Dear Tom,

Nothing hath occurred since my last worth writing; only Clarke affirms the jewels were part of the father's goods, to be divided as the rest.   He saith they were claimed as such from Partinton by the daughters, and that this may appear by the writings.   I long to hear that Mr. Marshal and you have agreed on what is due, and taken methods to pay it, &c.

Pray give my service to Caldwell; and let him know that in case he goes abroad with Mr. Stewart, Jaques, who lived with Mr. Ashe, is desirous to attend upon him.   I think him a very proper servant to travel with a gentleman ; but believing him sufficiently known to Caldwell, I shall forbear recommending him in more words.

I have obtained reports from the Bishop of London, the Board of Trade and Plantations, and the Attorney and Solicitor General, in favour of the Bermuda scheme, and hope to have the warrant signed by his Majesty this week.   Yours,

G. BERKELEY.

94   TO PRIOR

Dear Tom,

I have been this morning with Mr. Wogan, who hath undertaken to inform himself about the value of our South Sea stock, and what must be done in order to impower him to receive it.   I have nothing more to add to my last letter ; only to desire you to transact with Marshal and Partinton so as may dispose them to terminate all matters by a speedy arbitration, I care not before whom, lawyer or not lawyer.   I very much wish that we could get the reversionary lands off our hands.   If Partinton's own inclination for them should be a stop to the sale, I wish he had them.   But the conduct of all these matters I must leave to your own care and prudence :   Only I long to see them finished for our common interest.   I must desire you to give yourself the trouble of sending me by the very next post a bill of forty pounds, payable here at the shortest sight.   Pray fail not in this ; and you will oblige,

Dear Tom,

Yours sincerely,

G. BERKELEY.

Yesterday the Charter passed the Privy Seal.   This day the new Chancellor began his office by putting the *Recepi* to it.

London, June 3, 1725

95   TO PRIOR

London, June 12, 1725

Dear Tom,

I wrote to you some time since for forty pounds to be transmitted hither.   I must now beg you to send me another forty

10

pounds. I have had no answer to my last ; so if you have not yet negotiated that bill, make the whole together fourscore pounds ; which sum I shall hope for by the first opportunity. Mr. Wogan hath not yet found out the South Sea stock, but hath employed one in that office to inquire about it. As soon as I am informed myself, I shall let you know. He is also to make inquiry at Doctors' Commons to know what must be done in order to prove the present property in us, and to empower him to receive it. In order thereunto, I have given him a memorial of what I knew. I hope, as soon as he sends these directions, they will be complied with on that side the water. It was always my opinion we should have such an agent here. I am sure, had he been appointed a year agone, our affairs would have been the better for it.

The Charter hath passed all the seals, and is now in my custody. It hath cost me 130 pounds dry fees, besides expedition-money to men in office.

Mr. Percival writes that he hath given you the bonds. I must intreat you, dear Tom, to get the residue of last year's rent, with an account stated from Alderman M'Manus.

I am,
Yours sincerely,
G. BERKELEY.

96 TO PRIOR

London, July 20, 1725

Dear Tom,

I have been of late in much embarrass of business, which, with Mr. Wogan's being often out of town, hath occasioned your not hearing from me for some time. I must now tell you that our South Sea stock, &c, is confirmed to be what I already in-formed you, *viz.* 880 pounds, somewhat more or less. You are forthwith to get probates of Alderman Pearson's will, Partinton's will, and Mrs. Esther Van Homrigh's will, in which names the Exchequer annuities were subscribed, transmitted hither, together with two letters of attorney, one for receiving the stock, the other for the annuities. You will hear from Mr. Wogan by this post, who will send you more particular directions, together with a copy of such letters of attorney as will be necessary. In case Pearson refuses to sign the letter, let him send over a renunciation to any right therein, which will do as well. It may suffice, without going through all the steps, to tell you that I have clearly seen it made out how the Exchequer annuities, subscribed in the name of the three forementioned persons, came (through various mutations incident to stock) to be worth this money, and likewise to have begot other annuities ; which annuities, stock and dividends un-received make up the sum. But before you get Partinton and Marshal to sign the letters of attorney, or make the probates, nay, before you tell them of the value of the subscribed annuities, you should by all means, in my opinion, insist, carry and secure, two points ; *first*, that Partinton should consent to a partition of this stock, &c. (which I believe he cannot deny) : *secondly*, that Marshal should engage not to touch one penny of it till all debts on this side the water are satisfied. I even desire you would take advice, and legally secure it in such sort that he may not touch it if he would till the said debts are paid. It would be the wrongest thing in the world, and give me the greatest pain possible, to think we did not administer in the justest sense. Whatever therefore appears to be due, let it be instantly paid ; here is money sufficient to do it. And here I must tell that Mrs. Hill hath been with me, who says the debt was the mother's originally, but that Mrs. Esther made it her own, by giving a note for the same under her hand, which note is now in Dublin. Mr. Clarke hath likewise shewn me a letter of Mrs. Esther's (writ by him, but signed by her), acknow-ledging the debt for her mother's funeral. And indeed it seems she must have necessarily given order for that, and so contract the debt, since the party deceased could not be supposed to have ordered her own burial. These things being so, I would see Marshal brought to consent to the payment of them, or good reason assigned why they should not be paid. Mrs. Philips *alias* Barret (a very poor woman) is in great want of her dues. She saith Clarke and Baron can attest them, besides that they appear in Mrs. Esther's accompt-book. I must therefore intreat you, once for all, to clear up and agree with Marshal what is due, and then make an end, by paying that which it is a shame was not paid sooner. Query, Why the annuities should not have been subscribed in Prat's name, if B. V. Homrigh had a share in them ? For God's sake, adjust, finish, conclude any way with Partinton ; for at the rate we have gone on these two years, we may go on twenty. In your next, let me know what you have proposed to him and Marshal, and how they relish it. I hoped to have been in Dublin by this time ; but business grows out of business. I have wrote lately to Alderman M'Manus to clear accounts with you.

I am, dear Tom,

Yours sincerely,

G. Berkeley.

Bermuda prospers.

97   TO PRIOR

London, September 3, 1725

Dear Tom,

 I suppose you have long since received the draughts of the letters of attorney, &c., from Mr. Wogan, with his letter and mine. I must now add to what I there said, that it will be necessary for me to administer here in order to obtain the money out of the South Sea. This is what Mr. Wogan tells me, and this is a step that I cannot think of taking till such time as the debts on this side the water are agreed on by Mr. Marshal and you ; for, having once taken out an administration on this side the water, I may be liable to be put to trouble here by the creditors more than I am at present. To be short, I expect the business of the debts will be ascertained before I take any steps on my part about the stock or annuities. I must further tell you, that in case Mr. Marshal does not send orders to pay all the debts really due, with particular mention of the same, I must e'en put them all (pretenders as well as just creditors) upon attaching or securing the whole effects here, in South Sea, &c., to their own use, wherein I shall think myself obliged to be aiding to the best of my power. Clarke hath brought me from time to time the pretensions of divers creditors, all which I directed him to send to you ; and he saith he hath sent them to you. I think Mr. Wogan should be constituted attorney for paying the debts here, as well as for getting the stock. If my brother Robin calls upon you for ten pounds, you will let him have it.

I am, dear Tom,

Yours,

G. Berkeley.

 I wrote long since to Caldwell about his going to Bermudas, but had no answer, which makes me think my letter miscarried.

I must now desire you to give my service to him, and know whether he still retains the thoughts he once seemed to have of entering into that design. I know he hath since got an employment, &c. ; but I have good reason to think he would not suffer in his temporalities by taking one of our fellowships, although he resigned all that. In plain English, I have good assurance that our College will be endowed beyond any thing expected or desired hitherto. This makes me confident he would lose nothing by the change ; and on this condition only I propose it to him. I wish he may judge right in this matter, as well for his own sake as for the sake of the College.

98   TO PRIOR

Dear Tom,

It is an age since I have heard from you. You have long since received instructions from Mr. Wogan and from me what is to be done. If these are not already complied with, I beg you will lose no more time, but take proper methods, out of hand, for selling the South Sea stock and annuities. I have very good reason to apprehend that they will sink in their value, and desire you to let Van Homrigh Partinton,[1] and Mr. Marshal, know as much. The less there is to be expected from them, the more I must hope from you. I know not how to move them at this distance but by you ; and if what I have already said will not do, I profess myself to be at a loss for words to move you. I shall therefore only mention three points (often mentioned heretofore) which I earnestly wish to see something done in. 1st, The debts on this side the water stated, if not with concurrence of Mr. Marshal without him ; for sure this may be done without him, by the papers you have already seen, where Clarke saith they all appear. 2d, A commission of attorney sent to Wogan (who I am assured is an honest and capable man) to transact all affairs here. 3d, Matters somehow or other concluded with Partinton. You have told me he was willing to refer them to an arbitration, but not of lawyers, and that Marshal would refer them only to lawyers. For my part, rather than fail, I am for referring them to any honest knowing person or persons, whether lawyer or not lawyer ; and if Marshal will not come into this, I desire you will do all you can to oblige him, either by persuasion or otherwise : particularly

[1] Lit. Rel. reads V. Homrigh, Partinton.

represent to him my resolution of going (with God's blessing) in April next to Bermuda, which will probably make it his interest to compromise matters out of hand ; but if he will not, agree if possible with Partinton to force him to compliance in putting an end to our disputes. Partinton Van Homrigh, I remember, expressed a desire to purchase the reversionary lands. I beg he may be allowed to do it, or any other means be used to bring him to consent to the sale of them.

I have been these five weeks in a ramble through England. I came hither two or three days since, and propose leaving this place in a day or two, and being in London by the time answer may come from you ; but not being sure where I shall lodge, must desire you to direct to be left with Mr. Bindon, at the Golden-glove in Jermyn's Street, near Piccadilly.

And now I must desire you to pay to my brother Robin seventeen pounds, for which his receipt will be sufficient.

I am, dear Tom,

Yours sincerely,

GEOR. BERKELEY.

Flaxley, Oct. 15, 1725

99   TO PRIOR

December 2, 1725

Dear Tom,

I am just returned from a long ramble through the country to London, where I am settled in my old lodging at Mr. Fox's, and where I have met with two letters from you, after a very long and profound silence, which made me apprehensive of your welfare.

I presume you have by this time a commission for the administration of Mr. Marshal, which was to have gone last post to you from Messrs. Wogan and Aspinwall. I do think it necessary that Mr. Marshal should act, both as he hath acted hitherto and hath right to act, and as my attention to other affairs makes it more inconvenient for me. You will therefore take care that Mr. Marshal perform his part without delay. There is another point to be managed, without which no step can be taken towards transferring the stock, and that is, a full renunciation (since he will not act) from Mr. Pearson, provided he be sole heir to his father : if not, the other heirs must concur therein. Was there any authentic paper or declaration by which it legally appeared that old Mr. Pearson was only a trustee concerned in the stock ? This alone would do ; but I knew of none such. I beg you to dispatch this affair of the stock, and the other points relating thereto, which I formerly recommended to you, and which I hope you have not forgot. I long to hear what you and Mr. Marshal have resolved about the creditors : it is a shame something is not done. The woman of St James's coffee-house claims a debt upon the family, for coffee, tea, &c. I promised to acquaint you with it : the particular sum I do not know, but suppose you are not unacquainted with any of the debts. If this be a debt that we ought to pay, I desire it be immediately taken care of. I must repeat to you, that I earnestly wish to see things brought to some conclusion with Partinton, both with respect to the suit and the sale of the reversion. Dear Tom, it requires some address, diligence, and management, to bring business of this kind to an issue, which should not seem impossible, considering it can be none of our interests to spend our lives and substance in law. I am willing to refer things to an arbitration, even vote, of lawyers. Pray push this point, and let me hear from you upon it.

I am,

Your affectionate humble servant,

G. BERKELEY.

100   TO PRIOR

Dear Tom,

I have not time to repeat what I have said in my former letters. I shall now only say one thing, which I beg you to see dispatched by all means, otherwise we may be great losers. There must have been heirs to Alderman Pearson (whether his son alone, or his son with others) ; but there must of necessity be heirs ; and those heirs must have administered, otherwise they could not be entitled to his effects. Now, what you are to do, is to get a full renunciation (or declaration that they and the Alderman had no concern otherwise than as trustees in the South Sea stock and annuities) from the said heir or heirs, with a proper proof that they are such heir or heirs to Alderman Pearson. It is now near three months since I told you there were strong reasons for haste ;

and these reasons grow every moment stronger. I need say no more—I can say no more to you.

I am, dear Tom,

Yours,

G. B.

London, Dec. 11, 1725

101   TO PERCIVAL

London, 28th December 1725

My Lord,

Nothing could be more elegant or suitable to my fancy than the present I have the honour to receive from your Lordship. I cannot pretend to thank you with the same politeness and good taste with which you confer your favours, and shall only say as often as I cast my eye on the great men of antiquity, I shall have the pleasure to think of your Lordship who was one of the few (*antiquis moribus*) that can appear without disadvantage in such company.

I wish your Lordship, my Lady, and all your good family, a happy new year, and as nothing can contribute to make it so more than her Ladyship's health, I shall for a new year's gift send you a receipt for curing or giving sudden ease to a fit of the cholic, which I learned the other day from the Bishop of Asaph. He assured me a clergyman in Wales had tried it on forty or fifty persons in very violent fits and never knew it once to fail. It is only drinking a pint of good fresh coffee. A lesser quantity may give ease, but this is said entirely to take away the pain and put an end to the fit. I knew that coffee is commonly thought to cause a trembling in the nerves, and yet I have known some very good drinkers of it, who never were affected with any such symptom. But allowing it to be prejudicial, it can only be so upon habitual drinking of it ; and there is no medicine whatsover that would not be prejudicial, if one was constantly to breakfast on it. Whereas if coffee be only taken medicinally now and then in a painful fit of the cholic, I am persuaded such a use of it cannot induce an ill habit on the nerves, nor be a hundredth part so dangerous as laudanum. This medicine was recommended in such strong terms, from so good a hand, and such manifold experience, that from the first moment I heard of it, I was resolved to send you this account. I heartily wish it may be found useful to my Lady.

My long stay in town and great hurry of business had made fresh air and exercise necessary for my health. In this view I set out in September on a journey through eight or nine counties of England. I never travelled in worse roads or worse weather, so that all the advantage I got must be imputed to the motion. I doubt the same may be said of my Lady who at Paris is (as to the air) but one remove from the dirt and fog and smoke of London. Fine air and proper diversions together cannot be hoped for on this side Bermuda. Now I have mentioned Bermuda, I must acquaint your Lordship (who is so good a friend to it) that the subscriptions amount to £3400, though the town hath been very thin ever since I obtained the Charter. On the meeting of Parliament I have good hopes of seeing our affairs thrive. The desiring of that and His Majesty's absence have been such drawbacks, that I begin to fear it will not be possible for me to visit the Island this spring. I conclude with my humblest service and best wishes to you all.

My Lord,

Yr Lordship's most obedt and most obliged Servt,

GEO. BERKELEY.

102 TO PRIOR

Dear Tom,

I received your letters, and have desired Messrs Wogan and Aspinwall (for they act in concert in all things) to look into the act of parliament you mention, though I doubt it cannot be to any great purpose ; for though, by the act, it should appear that Pearson was a trustee, yet as that was passed long before the South Sea subscriptions, it will not, I fear, thereby appear that the said subscriptions were part of his trust. You have informed us there will be no difficulty in obtaining Mr. Pearson's renunciation. If the time be expired since the old gentleman's (his father's) death that by law is limited for taking out letters of administration, then I am told such single renunciation may be sufficient, without troubling the sisters. This you will inform yourself in there. Since Mr. Marshal is averse to it, he need not act at all ; only send back the will and probate hither for me to administer by. I know not what trouble this may expose me to, but I see it is a thing must be done in justice one time or other. One thing, nevertheless, I must repeat and insist on ; that is, that you must order matters so with Mr. Partinton Van Homrigh so that Mr· Marshal's share and mine of the South Sea, &c., may be applied to the payment of English debts (as you formerly have assured me it should). If it were not in this view, I might incur great difficulties by administering here, and this money's lying by undivided, as the Duchess of Tyrconnel's reversion would quite disappoint this view. I have not yet been able to find Mr. Levinge at his lodgings in the Temple. I must desire you to pay the sum of fifty pounds to my brother Robin, who will call on you for it. I must also desire you to send me an account of what money is in Mr. Synge's hands and yours belonging to me, as likewise of the draughts that I have made for money upon either of you. You'll be so good as to call on Mr. Stanton, and pay his bill when in Dublin. I called several times, but could not find him, to know what it came to. You will also inform yourself whether Coll. Maccasland demands any thing for the running of my horse, and pay it ; as likewise whatever is due for the other horse belonging to me ; and I make you a present of them both.

I am exceedingly plagued by these creditors, and am quite tired and ashamed of repeating the same answer to them, that I expect every post to hear what Mr. Marshal and you think of their pretensions, and that then they shall be paid. It is now a full twelve-month that I have been expecting to hear from you on this head, and expecting in vain. I shall therefore expect no longer, nor hope nor desire to know what Mr. Marshal thinks, but only what you think or what appears to you by Mrs. V. Homrigh's papers and accounts, as stated by Clarke, and compared with the claims of creditors long since transmitted from hence. This is what solely depends on you, what I sued for several months ago, and what you promised to send me an account of long before this time. I have likewise sent you several hints and proposals, tending, as I thought, to shorten our affair with Partinton, which, at the rate it hath hitherto gone on, is never likely to have an end ; but to these points I have never received any answer at all from you. I hope you have not overlooked or forgot them. Had I more time I would repeat them to you ; but I have only time to add at present that

   I am, dear Tom,

      Your affectionate humble servant,

       GEOR. BERKELEY.

  London, Dec. 30, 1725

London, Jan. 20, 1725/26

Dear Tom,

I am wearied [1] to death by creditors : I see nothing done, neither towards clearing their accounts, nor settling the effects here, nor finishing affairs with Partinton. I am at an end of my patience, and almost of my wits. My conclusion is, not to wait a moment longer for Marshal, nor to have (if possible) any further regard to him, but to settle all things without him, and whether he will or no. How far this is practicable, you will know by consulting an able lawyer. I have some confused notion that one executor may act by himself ; but how far, and in what case, you will thoroughly be informed. It is an infinite shame that the debts here are not cleared up and paid. I have borne the shock and importunity of creditors above a twelvemonth, and am never the nearer ; have nothing now [2] to say to them : judge you what I feel. But I have already said all that can be said on this head. It is also no small disappointment to find, that we have been near three years doing nothing with respect to bringing things to a conclusion with Partinton. Is there no way of making a separate agreement with him ? Is there no way of prevailing with him to consent to the sale of the reversion ? Let me entreat you to proceed with a little management and dispatch in these matters ; and inform yourself particularly, whether I may not come to a reference or arbitration with Partinton, even though Marshal should be against it?—Whether I may not take steps that may compel Marshal to an agreement ?—What is the practised method when one of two executors is negligent or unreasonable ? In a word, Whether an end may not be put to these matters one way or other ? I do not doubt your skill ; I only wish you were as active to serve an old friend as I should be in any affair of yours that lay in my power. All the papers relating to Mrs. V. Homrigh's affairs were in the closet ; and this I understand you have broke open, as likewise my bed-chamber (which last, having none of these papers in it, but only things of another nature, I had given no directions for breaking it open) ; but I do not find the effect I proposed from it, viz. a clear account of the debts transmitted hither, though, by what Clarke tells me, it would not take up an hour to do it. Mrs. Hill is very noisy : I mention her as the last

[1] worried—Stock   [2] new—Stock

that was with me. Pray let me know your thoughts of her, and all the rest of them together. Clarke demands to be considered for service done, and for postage of letters. You know wherein, and how much, you have employed him (for I have not employed him), and will concert with Marshal and Partinton what he should have. Qu. Had not Mrs. Hill commenced a suit, and how that matter stands ? But again, I desire to hear from you a distinct answer to the claim of every creditor sent over by Clarke. As to the money in the South Sea, I have already told you, that the thing to be done, is the obtaining the renunciation from Pearson, which may do in case the old gentleman be dead a year and a day (which you may inform yourself, whether it be the time after which no other body can set up for heir). I hope to have this by the next post. I must also repeat to you, that I very much desire to have my last letter answered, particularly as to the money matters ; which, depending only on Synge and you, I flatter myself you will not defer.

I am, dear Tom, your affectionate humble servant,
GEOR. BERKELEY.

By the next post I shall hope for an account of my own money, though it should require a day or two more before you can write satisfactory on the other points. My last letters I directed to the Free Mason Coffee-house, and inclosed as you ordered ; but not hearing, am in doubt whether you received them.

104   TO PRIOR

Dear Tom,

I received yours of the 13th, a little after I had wrote my last, directed to the Custom-house coffee-house. You say the letter of attorney for subscribing the annuities into the South-Sea stock, show these annuities to have been old Van Homrigh's. This would make all easy. I beg therefore that you would transmit that letter hither, or let us know how we may come at it. As to my administering to Pearson, I do not understand the consequences of it ; therefore hope it will not be necessary. You say that if you cannot prevail on Marshal to come in to an allowance of the just debts, you will send me your opinion of them, that I may govern myself accordingly. As to me, I know not how to act or govern myself : I depend upon your compelling Marshal by legal methods and that you will take advice thereupon, and act accordingly. That was the advantage that I proposed by your undertaking to act for me, and as my attorney in the management of those affairs, viz. that you would see that justice was done to the creditors and to me by Mr. Marshal, to whom I was as much a stranger as to the business. I have said this and many other things to you in my last, which I suppose you have received ere now ; and as I am very earnest and instant, I doubt not you will soon let me see that you exert yourself, and answer all my desires specified in that and the foregoing letters. Dear Tom, I am at present exceedingly embarrassed with much business of a very different kind. I shall nevertheless administer as soon as I see that nothing else is wanting in order to sell the stock, and pay the debts herewith : for every other step I shall depend on you. I need not tell you what I formerly hinted to you. You see I was too true a prophet, and that we have already lost considerably by this delay.

I must desire you to pay forty pounds to my brother, Cornet William Berkeley, quartered in Sligo, or to his order in Dublin, for which you will take a receipt, and place it to my account. You will, I presume, soon hear from him.

In your next, pray let me know your opinion about the way of transmitting about five hundred pounds hither, whether by bill or by draught, from hence, or if there be any other way more advantageous. I must once more entreat you, for the sake of old friendship, to pluck up a vigorous active spirit, and disincumber me of the affairs relating to the inheritance, by putting, one way or other, a final issue to them.

I thank God I find, in matters of a more difficult nature, good effects of activity and resolution ; I mean Bermuda, with which my hands are full, and which is in a fair way to thrive and flourish in spite of all opposition. I shall hope to hear from you speedily ; and am,

Dear Tom, yours affectionately,

GEOR. BERKELEY.

London, Jan. 27, 1725/26

Dear Tom,

Messrs. Wogan and Aspinwall have not yet been able to
see the act of parliament, which I am pretty sure could be of little
or no use if they had seen it ; for as it passed several years before
the South-Sea business, it would never prove that Pearson acted
as trustee in the subscriptions.   But if there be any paper (as you
seem to intimate in your last), that sets forth his trust in that
particular, you need only procure the sight thereof, and the
business is done ;   otherwise, for ought I can see, it is necessary
that Mr. Alderman Pearson's heir or heirs renounce, and that I
admininister as to his effects in this province ;   otherwise nothing
can be done, as I suppose you see by the paper of instructions sent
you from Doctors' Commons.   Now that I may see my way in
this matter, I must desire you to inform me particularly what
the nature of administering is, what it obliges one to, and to what
it may expose a man.   I have not yet taken out letters of administration to Mrs. V. Homrigh here, nor shall I, until I see that it can
be of use ;   that is, until I see that every other step is accomplished
towards the immediate selling the stock, and applying it as it should
be applied.   What I wrote in my former concerning the year and
a day for administering, &c., has, I find, nothing in it, as I am
now told by Mr. Aspinwall, from whom I had it, and who, it
seems, was mistaken.   I think I ought to tell you these things,
that you may see where the stop is, and that you may act accordingly.   The affair of the creditors I must recommend to you of
course ;   though I have nothing new to say, but only that I
earnestly refer you to what I have already written upon that and
other matters ;   which, after all that hath been said, I need not
repeat.   I hope, dear Tom, that you will exert yourself once for
all, and give a masterly finishing stroke to the whole business of
the executorship.   If it be not such a stroke as one could wish at
law, yet a finishing one of any sort, by arbitration of lawyers, or
not lawyers, before I leave this part of the world, would be very
agreeable.

My brother hath informed me that Dr. Ward tells him Colonel
M'Casland is not inclined to add to the trouble of his other business
that of taking any further care of my tithes, &c.   I must desire,
if you can find out the truth of this, to let me know it ;   for it will
be time for me to look out for other farmers.   I had once thought

of employing a brother of my own, but have now no thought of that kind. I must desire you to send me fifty pounds by the next post.

I am in a fair way of having a very noble endowment for the College of Bermuda, though the late meeting of parliament, and the preparations of a fleet, &c., will delay the finishing things, which depend in some measure on the parliament, and to which I have gained the consent of the government, and indeed of which I make no doubt ; but only the delay, it is to be feared, will make it impossible for me to set out this Spring. One good effect of this evil delay, I hope, may be, that you will have disembarrassed yourself of all sort of business that may detain you here, and so be ready to go with us. In which case, I may have somewhat to propose to you that I believe is of a kind agreeable to your inclinations, and may be of considerable advantage to you. But you must say nothing of this to any one, nor of any one thing that I have now hinted concerning endowment, delay, going, &c. I have heard lately from Caldwell, who wrote to me in an affair in which it will not be in my power to do him any service. I answered his letter, and mentioned somewhat about Bermuda, with an overture for his being Fellow there. I desire you would discourse him as from yourself on that subject, and let me know what your thoughts are of his disposition towards engaging in that design.

I am, dear Tom, Your affectionate friend and humble servant,
GEOR. BERKELEY.

London, Feb. 6, 1725/26

106   TO PERCIVAL

London, 10th Feb. 1725/26

My Lord,
I am now in a great hurry of business preparing an interest in the House of Commons against the introducing my affair to St. Christopher's among them. The spirits of the ministry have been hitherto and are still so entirely possessed with fleets, subsidies, &c., that it hath not yet been thought proper to insist on that point, which however I hope will be soon carried, there being very good interest made among malcontents, and the Court being quite for it.

It is this hurry (which hardly allows me a moment to myself) that hath so long delayed my acknowledgment of your Lordship's letter, &c. In it you desire to be informed by me what there is in the report you have heard of Mr. Lesley's going to Bermuda and bestowing a good part of his fortune on that design. All I can say is, that this gentleman upon reading the Proposal was struck with it and expressed himself in words to that effect. His affairs are I understand, at present in some disorder. As soon as those are settled I believe he may entertain thoughts of going to Bermuda and be a benefactor. In the interim nothing is done of what you heard was performed.

The subscriptions amount to about four thousand pounds. Lord Palmerston is desirous that nine hundred and odd pounds in his hands should be disposed of to this our college for breeding up young negroes agreeable to Mr. Delon's will. The trustees for directing the disposal thereof are your Lordships, Dr. Bray, Mr. Hales, his brother, and Mr. Beleitha. The majority of these are of Lord Palmerston's mind, and your Lordship's concurrence hath been applied for.

You have annexed a poem * wrote by a friend of mine with a view to the scheme. Your Lordship is desired to shew it to none but of your own family, and suffer no copy to be taken of it.

I am glad to hear your family, and particularly my Lady, are so well.

I am, My Lord,
       Yr Lordship's most obedt and most humble Servant,
              G. BERKELEY.

* AMERICA OR THE MUSE'S REFUGE

A Prophecy

The muse, offended at this age, these climes
    Where nought she found fit to rehearse,
Waits now in distant lands for better times,
    Producing subjects worthy verse.

In happy climes where from the genial sun
    And virgin earth fair scenes ensue,
Such scenes as shew that fancy is outdone,
    And make poetic fiction true.

In happy climes, the seat of innocence,
    Where nature guides and virtue rules,
Where men shall not impose for truth and sense
    The pedantry of Courts and schools.

There shall be sung another golden age,
    The rise of Empire and of arts,
The good and great inspiring epic rage
    The wisest heads and noblest hearts.

Not such as Europe breeds in her decay,
    Such as she bred when fresh and young,
When heavenly flame did animate her clay,
    By future poets shall be sung.

Westward the course of Empire takes its way,
    The four first acts already past,
A fifth shall close the drama with the day,
    The world's great effort is the last.

107   TO PRIOR

Dear Tom,

    I have wrote to you on several points to which I have had no answer. The bill indeed of fifty pounds I have received ; but the answer to other points you postponed for a few posts. It is not yet come to hand, and I long to see it. I shall nevertheless not repeat now what I have so often insisted on, but refer you to my former letters, which I hope are not forgotten, and that I shall be convinced they are not in a post or two.

    In your last you mention your design of coming to London this summer. I must entreat you to let me know by the first opportunity whether you persist in that design, and in what month you propose to execute it, and as nearly as possible the very time. Pray fail not in this ; I have particular reasons for desiring it.

    There is one point that will not admit of any delay ; I mean the setting my Deanery to farm. I told you that Dr. Ward had informed my brother that Col. M'Casland (who hath his hands full of other business) cared not to be any farther concerned in it. I must desire you, without loss of time, to inform yourself whether this be so, and to let me know what instrument I must send to you to empower you to set it. This by all means I would be informed of the next post, that it may be set either to the same

11

persons who held it last, or else to Mr. Bolton, or some other person of sufficient credit and substance and good reputation. I do not doubt your setting it to the best advantage ; only there is one thing which I desire you to insist on, viz. that instead of the first of April and the first of June, the days of payment for the current year, be the first of December and the first of February, that so I may have the money against my voyage to Bermuda, which possibly may not be till this time twelvemonth. Whatever trouble you are at in this affair, I shall acknowledge in the proper manner, and shew myself thankful for it. I thought I should be able to have gone to Ireland, and transacted this affair myself.

I had even once thought I should be able to have set out for Bermuda this season ; but his Majesty's long stay abroad, the late meeting of parliament, and the present posture of foreign affairs, taking up the thoughts both of ministers and parliament, have postponed the settling of certain lands in St. Christopher's on our College, so as to render the said thoughts abortive. I have now my hands full of that business, and hope to see it soon settled to my wish. In the mean time, my attendance on this business renders it impossible for me to mind my private affairs. Your assistance, therefore, in them, will not only be a kind service to me, but also to the public weal of our College ; which would very much suffer if I were obliged to leave this kingdom before I saw an endowment settled on it. For this reason I must depend upon you. So hoping to hear from you upon this article by the first post,

I conclude, dear Tom,
                                            Yours affectionately,
                                                    GEOR. BERKELEY.
London, March 15, 1725/26

I need not tell you the time for setting my Deanery to farm is now so nigh that it is necessary something be done out of hand.

108   TO PRIOR

Dear Tom,

Last Saturday I sent you the instrument empowering you to set my Deanery. It is at present my opinion that matter had better be deferred till the Charter of St Paul's College hath got through the House of Commons, who are now considering it. In ten days at farthest I hope to let you know the event hereof ; which, as it possibly may affect some circumstance in the farming my said Deanery, is the occasion of giving you this trouble for the present, when I am in the greatest hurry of business I ever knew in my life ; and have only time to add that

I am,

Yours,

April 19, 1726   G. B.

109   TO PRIOR

Dear Tom,

After six weeks' struggle against an earnest opposition from different interests and motives, I have yesterday carried my point just as I desired in the House of Commons, by an extraordinary majority, none having the confidence to speak against it, and not above two giving their negative ; which was done in so low a voice as if they themselves were ashamed of it. They were both considerable men in stocks, in trade, and in the city : and in truth I have had more opposition from that sort of men, and from the governors and traders to America, than from any others. But, God be praised, there is an end of all their narrow and mercantile views and endeavours, as well as of the jealousies and suspicions of others (some whereof were very great men), who apprehended this College may produce an independency in America, or at least lessen its dependency upon England.

Now I must tell you, that you have nothing to do but go on with farming my Deanery, &c., according to the tenor of my former letter, which I suspended by a subsequent one till I should see the event of yesterday. By this time you have received the letters of attorney for Partinton's signing, in which I presume there will be no delay. Dear Tom,

Yours, &c.

G. BERKELEY.

London, May 12, 1726

What more easy than to cast an eye on the draught of the two sisters' debts as stated by Clarke ? What more unaccountable than that this is not yet done ?

London, 17th May 1726

My Lord,

Your Lordship hath every way been so good a friend to St. Paul's College in Bermuda, that I think it my duty to acquaint you with the success which hath of late attended it, the Commons of Great Britain having last Wednesday voted an address to His Majesty that he would be pleased to make such grant out of the lands of St. Christopher's for the endowment thereof as to him shall seem proper. This point was carried in a full house with but two negatives, and those pronounced in so low a voice as shewed that the persons who gave them were ashamed of what they were doing. I am heartily tired of soliciting for many weeks this point with all the diligence, patience, and skill, that I was master of ; and am not less pleased to see it carried contrary to all men's expectations, who thought it a hopeless affair, first, because the like step had never been taken in any reign for any college before, and secondly, because great interest and opposition had been made against it from several quarters and upon different principles, motives, and surmises, some whereof had got into the heads of very considerable persons.

I am exceedingly pleased at the good effects which the change of air hath had upon my Lady, not only as it hath bettered her health, but likewise as it must have improved her disposition towards Bermuda, by giving her Ladyship to understand what may be expected from the best air in the world. Let what will happen I am resolved not to quit the pleasing hopes that I shall one day see you both in that happy Island. In the meantime it would be a great credit and ornament to our College, as well as a particular pleasure to myself, if we had a youth of such an excellent genius as your eldest son to begin with ; but if this may not be hoped for, I put in an early claim to Master George and beg and insist upon it, that you will not refuse me the pleasure and the joy of assisting and forwarding the fine parts which already shine forth in him, and the rather because he seems to be of a constitution that should be likely to improve much in that climate.

I am (with my best respects and service to you all), My Lord,
Your Lordship's most obedt and most obliged Servant,
GEO. BERKELEY.

This is my third since I had the honour to receive a letter from your Lordship.

I had almost forgot to tell your Lordship that yesterday a Report was made of his Majesty's answer to the Commons Address. It is very gracious.

III   TO PRIOR

London, June 9, 1726

Dear Tom,

I am surprised to find there are any debts left unpaid in Ireland, having thought that debt of Henry's which you mention long since discharged. I am sure I concluded that, with what money was left with you, and what I laid out here (in discharge of debts whereof I acquainted you), my share of the remaining Irish debts would have been reduced to nothing. You formerly told me Marshal did not keep pace with me. I hoped you would not think of paying anything more until he had brought himself up to equality with me. I am also very much surprised at your proposing to me to pay money for Marshal there, which you say I may reimburse myself here, when I already told you that I would never have been at the pains to administer here, if the effects on this side the water were not allotted to pay English debts (which you made me believe, in a former letter, should be done). And I have reason to think that, after the payment of such English debts, nothing will be left of these effects wherewith to reimburse myself any payment you shall make for Marshal out of my money there. To your question, therefore, whether you shall make such payment ? I do answer in the negative. I am at a loss to explain what you mean by promising to try to state the English debts from the materials you have before you. I ask two distinct questions : 1st, Is there not among Mrs. V. Homrigh's papers a catalogue of her debts clearly stated, as I am told by Mr. Clarke ? 2ndly, Why have I not a copy of such catalogue transmitted to me ? Had I foreseen the difficulties I am reduced to for want of it, I would have cast my eye on the papers myself, and have known what the debts were before I left Ireland ; but I left that matter wholly to you. You still do not stick to tell me that Marshal will do nothing ; nay (which is worse), that he will not allow any English debts at all, without telling me one of his reasons. You (for example) averred to me in Ireland, that Mrs. Perkins's appeared a just demand from Mrs. V. Homrigh's own papers ; and I have seen here a note of Mrs. Esther V. Homrigh, the younger, to Mr. Tooke, for fifty pounds, together with interest of five per cent. Now I would fain know why are not these debts to be paid and acknowledged as well as those in Ireland ? Moreover, I would fain know why book debts should not be paid here as well as in Ireland ? In a word, why in any case a difference should be made between English and Irish debts ? I grant we should distinguish between the mother's and the daughter's debts ; and it was to make this distinction that I so often (to no purpose) dunn'd you for a catalogue of the daughter's debts, drawn up by her order, in Clarke's hand. But I find it is to no purpose to write ; I long to talk to you by word of mouth, either there or here.

Pray let me know next post when you design coming for England, for I would go over to Derbyshire to meet you, in case you do not come to London. On the other hand, I am very loath to be dragged to Ireland before the grant to our College is settled and perfected. I write in great hurry ; but before I conclude must tell you, that the Dean of Raphoe hath informed me of his desire to live in Derry : now I had rather he should live in my house for nothing than a stranger for a paltry rent. It is therefore my desire, that a stop may be put to any disposition thereof till such time as the Dean can hear whether a house be (pursuant to his order) already taken for him in Derry.

Dear Tom, write me something satisfactory about the debts by next post, or send me a flat denial, that I may no longer expect it. Last autumn you promised me a full state of my whole accounts what hath been received and what disbursed : having not received it, I must now put you in mind again of it. In my last I desired that my money for the last year of the Deanery be put in the hands of Swift and Company.

I am,

Yours,

G. BERKELEY.

London, June 14, 1726

Dear Tom,

 I received Messrs. M'Manus's account, in which there are certain articles that I cannot approve of. First, The ferry Mr. M'Manus himself told me I should not pay ; that charge having been for the late Dean's household, and the curates' passage when they were to preach his turns. But as I have no household there, and as I have otherwise provided for having my turns preached, there is no colour or occasion for my paying it ; and I am the more surprised at his charging it, because it was against his own positive opinion as well as my orders. Secondly, I do not see why the repairing of the church windows should be charged to me. Thirdly, I should have been acquainted with the paving of the street, or any such matters, before he had laid out money on them.   Fourthly, I know not what those charges are which Mr. Maccasland is said to be at for schoolmasters.   I write not this as if I valued either repairing the church windows or allowing somewhat to schoolmasters, provided those things had been represented to me for my consent ; but to be taxed without my knowledge is what I do not understand.   It is my duty not to suffer the Dean to be taxed at will, nor to connive at the introducing new precedents to the wrong of my successors.   To be plain, Mr. M'Manus being desired by me to make a list of such constant charges as the Dean should be at, I subscribed and warranted him to pay the same.   Since that time, by letter to him, I made some addition to the charity children ; but what is not warranted by that list, or by some subsequent order or warrant of mine, should not be allowed by me.   However, for what is in the account you have sent me, I refer myself to you ; only must beg you to signify to them that I shall never allow anything for the time to come but what I am apprised of, and consent to beforehand.   So that no vouchers will do (without an order under my own hand) for expenses not included in the list made by Mr. M'Manus, and approved by me at Derry.   This I believe you will think a reasonable precaution, in order to prevent myself or successors being imposed on.

 I am of opinion that you should immediately write to Messrs. Wogan and Aspinwall, directing and impowering them to sell whenever, from the circumstance of affairs, we shall think it proper so to do. Sudden occasions happen which will not allow waiting for orders from Ireland. We have already been great losers by that, which I very well foreknew here, though you knew nothing of it there ; though by this time you are convinced the information I sent you last autumn was true. In short, intelligence may be had here, but it can never there, time enough to be of use.

Yours affectionately,
G. B.

113   TO PERCIVAL

London, 24th June 1726

My Lord,

 I was truly grieved on all accounts by the late sad but common accident in your family which by this time I hope your Lordship's christian temper and good sense have got the better of. I am nevertheless apprehensive that my Lady (considering her weak nerves) may be much affected by it, though I dare say you will omit no topic either from religion or reason to induce her to bear it with proper resignation.

 I have lately had the honour of a letter from your Lordship overflowing with that goodness which is so natural to you I have experienced too long to doubt of. My observing that I had writ two or three times without receiving any answer was not meant to upbraid your Lordship in any sort, but only to signify that I had not been unmindful of my duty in case my letters were not come to hand, as it sometimes happens in foreign posts. Your patronage of and concern for the Bermuda affair justified my troubling you now and then with some short account of its progress, which is at present at a stand, and likely to continue so till Sir Robert Walpole returns from Norfolk, soon after which I hope the grant addressed for by the Commons will be perfected.

 Several years since your Lordship was so good as to supply me with sixty guineas, which I am sensible should have been restored before this time, but the truth is, the effects of Mrs. Van Homrigh are not yet disposed of, nor all her debts paid, there being a suit depending with Mr. Partinton which puts a stop to that affair which will fall much short of what was expected. Moreover, I was obliged to pay about eight hundred pounds for my Deanery house, together with first fruits and other expences upon my coming into that preferment : all which as likewise my having been long engaged at law, and lying under a necessity of providing for some who are very near to me and depend upon me, hath sunk my affairs lower than people imagine.

Your Lordship will be so good as to accept this plea for my not returning your favour sooner. I am now I thank God in a capacity of doing it without any inconvenience ; and therefore beg a line from you to direct me where to pay the abovementioned sum, which I am ready to return with all acknowledgment, and thanks, from, my Lord,

Yr Lordship's most obedt and most obliged humble Servant,
G. BERKELEY.

I beg the favour of a line by next post being impatient to know how my Lady bears her misfortune. Pray present my humble Service to her Ladyship and to all your good family.

114 TO PRIOR

Dear Tom,

Yours of the 2nd and the 9th of July are come to my hands. What you say in your last of the receipts in full, and the caution to be used thereupon, had occurred to my own thoughts, and I acted accordingly. With respect to Mrs. Philips and Mrs. Wilton, I found the former a palpable cheat ; but the latter still stands out, that she never received, at any time, any of Mrs. Mary's money. I must therefore desire you to look a second time on the receipt you mention from her to Mrs. Mary ; for you might possibly have been mistaken. I thought, when in Ireland, that you owned Mrs. Parkins's to be a true debt. Pray give me your thoughts particularly upon it. The same I desire on the charges for the mother's funeral, which, if in right they are to be paid by us, I cannot understand what you mean by the creditor's abating one half of his demand. I am glad to find that you will take advice upon the dubious debts. Pray do it soon : and when that is done, I shall hope for one list from you, containing your own judgment upon the whole, of what debts are to be discharged by the money here. The exact sum of the annuities received by Messrs. Wogan and Aspinwall I do not remember, but it is about £190. The next time I write you may know exactly.

I have considered about the house, and am come to this

resolution : If Dr. Ward be in Dublin, pray give my service to him, and tell him my house is at his service, upon condition only that he keep it in repair, and rid me of all charges about it, as hearth-money or the like. I had some time since a letter from him, desiring the use of it on these terms ; but the offer I had made the Dean of Raphoe disabled me for that time from giving him the answer I now desire you to do, because I know not where to write to him myself, he having been about to leave Chester for Ireland when I received his letter. But at present I think myself at liberty, it being about six weeks since the Dean was with me, since which time I have not heard from him, though I then desired he would let me have his answer forthwith. As to setting it, I am less inclined that way, because Dr. Ward, being Subdean, is at some trouble on my account, and I would willingly oblige him. You may therefore drop it to him, that I prefer his having it rent-free to a rent of twenty pounds, which you think I may get from another.

As to the account you have sent me of receipts and disbursements, I must observe to you, with respect to one particular, that when I made you a proposal of being concerned in the affairs accruing to me by the death of Mrs. V. Homrigh, the terms which I proposed, and you agreed to, were these, viz. that if you would undertake the trouble of settling that whole matter, when it was settled I should allow you twelve pence in the pound out of the profits arising therefrom. I never designed, therefore, nor promised to allow any thing, till the whole was settled ; nor was it reasonable, or indeed possible that I should : Not reasonable, because the main reason for which I made such proposal of 1s. *per* pound, was the difficulty of disembrangling our affairs with Partinton ; which difficulty seems hardly to have been touched hitherto, at least I do not find that any thing to the purpose hath been done since I left Ireland :—Not possible, because, till the debts are paid, and affairs settled with Partinton, I cannot know what doth, or what doth not, come to my share. It was my desire to have things concluded as soon as possible ; and in order to this, I expected more would be done by you than by another. I chose therefore putting my affairs into your hands rather than into Mr. Dexter's or Mr. Donne's ; one of whom, if you had declined it, I was resolved on. I was also willing, for that end, to allow more than is commonly allowed to solicitors or agents.

For these reasons, and especially because I shall have, on many accounts, pressing occasion for what money I can raise against my departure (which I propose to be next Spring), I must desire you to desist for the present from paying yourself, and to pay the whole of my money into the hands of Swift and Company, by them to be transmitted to me in England upon demand ; and I shall leave a note behind me with you, which shall intitle you in the fullest and clearest manner to the said twelve pence in the pound. I must desire you to let me know whether you have obliged the farmers of my deanery to make all future payments to my order in Dublin, as I directed. I should be glad to see a copy of the articles you concluded with them, which you may send me *per* post. I am surprised at what you tell me of Mr. Synge's paying 111 pounds to Mr. Bindon on my account, which, on a second inquiry, you must find a mistake. I had received only one hundred English from Mr. Bindon, who (because he wanted it in Ireland) let me have it on the same terms that the banker was to supply him there, by which I saved about 30 shillings in the exchange ; and so I drew on Mr. Synge for one hundred and ten pounds odd money, Irish. I shall hope to hear from you next post, after the receipt hereof, and that you will then tell me your resolution about coming to England. For myself, I can resolve nothing at present, when or whether I shall see Ireland at all, being employed on much business here.

I am, dear Tom,

Your affectionate humble Servant,

G. BERKELEY.

London, July 19, 1726

I have heard from Mr. M'Manus ; and by this post have wrote an answer, insisting that I will not allow any thing for the ferry, it being a gross imposition, and contrary both to his own advice and my express orders.

115 TO PRIOR

Dear Tom,

The stocks being higher than they have been for this long time, and, as I am informed, not likely to rise higher, I have consented to their being sold, and have directed Messrs. Wogan and Aspinwall to write you word thereof as soon as they are disposed of, with an account of their amounts. I hoped you would have sent me a copy of the articles for farming my deanery, that I may see whether they are according to my mind ; particularly whether the money is made payable to my order in Dublin, as I directed, for special reasons. I likewise expected a copy of the last balance, the deductions being larger than I can account for. I have spoke with Mr. Binden, who tells me he received within a trifle, under or over, one hundred and eleven pounds from Ned Synge. I have wrote to Ned Synge to let him know his mistake. I have also wrote to him and Mr. Norman to pay the money in their hands to Swift and Company, in order to have it transmitted hither.

I desire to know whether you come to England, at what time, and to what place, that I may contrive to see you, for I may chance not to be in London, designing to pass some time in the country ; but I would steer my course so as to be in your way in case you came on this side the water.

Mrs. Wilton persists that she never gave a receipt to Mrs. Mary. I must therefore desire you to send me her receipt inclosed in your next. As to Mr. Tooke's bond or note, you desire to know whether it be sealed ; which particular I do not remember : but I remember that it mentions interest ; and I desire to know whether, in point of right, such interest should not be paid ; and whether it would not seem odd to propose defalcating any part of a man's right for want of form, when it plainly appeared to be intended ? In short, I would know upon what principles you proceed, when you say he may be contented with no interest, or with half interest. By this post I suppose you will receive from Mr. Aspinwall an account of the sum-total of the transfer, &c. I am plagued with duns, and tired with put-offs, and therefore long to see it applied to pay them : but, in order to this, must desire you to send me two distinct lists, one of the undoubted legal demands, another of the equitable, that so I may have your opinion, in distinct terms, of what should be paid in law, and what in conscience. This was not answered by your last letter's observations, which nevertheless show you may easily do it ; and it is no more than what you had promised to do before. I shall therefore expect such lists from you in a post or two.

I am, dear Tom,

Your affectionate humble Servant,
G. Berkeley.

London, Aug. 4, 1726

You mentioned a friend of Synge's who was desirous to be one of our Fellows. Pray let me know who he is, and the particulars of his character. There are many competitors ; more than vacancies ; and the fellowships are likely to be very good ones : so I would willingly see them well bestowed.

116   TO PRIOR

Dear Tom,

It is a long time since I have heard from you, and am willing to suppose that some of your letters are miscarried. I have quitted my old lodging, and desire you to direct your letters to be left for me with Mr. Smibert, painter, next door to the King's Arms tavern, in the little piazza, Covent Garden.

I desired a copy of the articles concluded on with the farmers of my deanery. I likewise desired the receipt of Mrs. Wilton, and the particular catalogues of the debts, in the manner you promised. I must now repeat the same desires. As for the articles and bonds, I have thought proper to lodge them with Mr. Synge, who hath a fixed abode in town, and will take care to place them securely among his own papers. You will therefore deliver them to him. As I have occasion for my money to be gathered in and placed with Mr. Swift and Company, in order to be transmitted hither, I have wrote to M'Manus and Mr. Norman ; to the former, to send me the balance of accounts for last year ; to the latter, to pay the money you told me lay in his hands to Swift and Company : but hitherto I do not find either done. Mr. Aspinwall hath some time since informed you that the total of the effects transferred by him amounts to eight hundred and forty pounds odd money, out of which charges are to be deducted. He hath shewed me the bill of these in Doctors' Commons, which amount to about fourteen pounds. Some other money laid out by him, together with the fees for his own trouble, I have not yet seen the account of. I think you had better write to him by the next post to transmit the third part of the overplus sum to Swift and Company, for the use of Partinton Van Homrigh ; who, when he hath got his share remitted, can have nothing to complain of ; and, as you have hitherto treated in his behalf with Messrs. Wogan and Aspinwall, your orders will be followed therein by them more properly than mine. I had almost forgot to repeat to you, that I want to know what reason there is for disputing any part of the interest on the note to Mr. Tooke, whether it be sealed or no.

Let me know in your next what you resolve about coming to England, and when. I shall trouble you with no more at present, from,

Dear Tom,

Yours affectionately,

G. Berkeley.

London, August 24, 1726

117   TO PRIOR

London, 7ber 3rd, 1726

Dear Tom,

I received your letter in which you send me a copy of Mrs. Wilton's receipt. I shou'd be glad of the receipt itself, she pretending it might be a forgery. I long for the lists you promised of certain and legal debts in the first place, of equitable in the second, with your reasons for docking any part of them. I shall not repeat what I said in my last which I suppose you might have received since you writ to me. Ned Synge I understand is in the country, I must therefore desire you to pay out of the mony in your hands the charges you tell me Dr. Helsham hath been at in my brother's tryal. Give my service to him and tell him I am obliged to him as he intended a service to me in advancing that mony, without my knowledge, but that if I had been aware of it I wou'd not have disbursed half the sum to have saved that villain from the gallows. I must at the same time desire you to pay the sum of nine pounds to my Brother Robin.

Mr. MacManus hath sent me the accounts as stated by him for the two last payments, in which I observe that you mistook the ballance of the first account making it only 227 odd mony (wch you informed me of in your last letter but one as paid into Swift etc. tho' I could not draw for it having no note of theirs or acknowledgment for the same) whereas MacManus makes it to be 312 pounds 10sh i.e. the full of Maccasland's moiety from which he tells me nothing was deducted he himself having made all the payments on my behalfe. In his second account he subducts not only for past payments but for future (a new method of accounting) whereby he reduces the ballance of his moiety to

87 : 8 : 9½ which he saies Mr. Curtis was to pay to you, and that
Maccasland's £312 : 10s : 00d is to be paid entire to me, so that
their whole ballance stands thus

$$
\begin{array}{llll}
312 : 10 : 00 & & = & \\
212 : 10 : 00 & & \text{et} & \\
& & 712 & \\
87 : 8 : 9\tfrac{1}{2} & & 8 : 9\tfrac{1}{2}
\end{array}
$$

which sum I must desire you to see paid to Swift and Company
for my use and direct them to send a note for the sum to their
correspondent here, because I shall have occasion to transfer what
mony I can raise to England.

I must desire you to send me in a letter a full state of the
particulars of our pretensions upon Partinton, that I may have
a view of the several emoluments expected from this suit and
the grounds of each expectation (these affairs being at present
a little out of my thoughts) that so having considered the whole
I may take advice here and write thereupon to Marshal in order
to terminate that affair this winter (if possible). It is worth while
to exert for once. If this be done the whole partition may be made
and your share distinctly known and paid you between this and
Christmas. But I know it cannot be done unless you exert. As
for Marshal I had from the beginning no opinion of him (no more
than you have) otherwise I sh'd not have troubled anybody else.

I am, Dr Tom,

Yrs affectly,

G. BERKELEY.

118   TO PRIOR

Dear Tom,

I received yours ; and accordingly went to Messrs. Wogan
and Aspinwall, who promised to transmit the money drawn for
by Partinton, which I suppose is due. I desired them to let me
have their bill of charges ; which they also promised against the
next time I saw them.

As for the clamour of the people of Derry, I have not, nor ever
shall have, the least regard for it, so long as I know it to be unjust
and groundless : it being so false to suggest that I am for allowing
less than my predecessors, that I am now actually at seventy-six
pound *per annum* constant expence more than any of them ever

were, having just now directed Dr. Ward to provide a new curate
for Coll. Sampson's island, and having formerly appointed another
additional curate in Derry to preach my turns, as likewise having
added to the number of charity children, which are annual
expences, not to mention repairing the chancel, &c. ; nothing
of which kind I ever was against. I did not indeed like (nor would
any man in his senses) that people should make articles of expence
without acquainting me, or dispose of my money (though it were
to good uses) without my consent previously obtained. But all
this while I have gainsaid nothing but the ferry, and that for
reasons I formerly gave you ; not that I valued the expence,
which was a trifle, but that I would not be imposed on myself,
nor entail an imposition on my successor : for there is no man
so unknowing or negligent in affairs as not to be sensible that
little impositions lead to great ones. But as to that matter,
M'Manus having informed me that Dr. Ward had engaged I
would pay the ferry-money, I have wrote to Dr. Ward to know
the truth of that, and his judgment whether the same should be
continued, being resolved to comply therewith. As to what you
write about my making a difficulty of leaving 58 pounds in
M'Manus's hands for the curates, it is a mistake. The sum charged
in his account is about 140 pounds, not for charges paid, but to
be paid ; and not only to curates, but for several other purposes.
I never meant but the curates should be punctually paid ; nobody
need be at any pain about that : but I thought, as they were paid
the first year (when the farmers had no money of mine in their
hands), so they might have been paid the subsequent years out
of the running income. I thought likewise, and still think, that
the rents of the glebe, and the dues formerly farmed to the clerk,
are sufficient to make the November payment, without M'Manus's
advancing one penny, and without his retaining my income of
the preceding year, especially when the tithes of the current
become payable a little after. As my money is not at interest,
it is much the same whether these payments be stopt now or next
January ; but it was necessary to observe what I thought wrong,
to prevent people's growing upon me. I still want the lists you
promised me of the debts (legal and equitable), in order to make
the payments, that the business on this side the water (which
hath already cost me much trouble) may be at length dispatched.
In your next, I desire to be informed what the mistake is which
you observe in M'Manus's account, and likewise what you
say to his telling me there were no deductions made from the

650 pounds of Coll. Maccasland's moiety, as I observed to you already in my last.

As to what you say of matrimony, I can only answer, that as I have been often married by others, so I assure you I have never married myself.

I am, dear Tom,
Your affectionate humble Servant,
G. Berkeley.

London, Sept. 13, 1726

Before you went to the country, you told me about eight hundred pounds of the last year's income would be paid to Swift, & Co. I desire to know whether it be so, or what it is. In my last I sent you what appeared in M'Manus's letter to me ; but you are of opinion he mistook in my prejudice.

119 TO PRIOR

London, Oct. 14, 1726

Dr Tom,

It is now a long time since I have had a line from you so long that I apprehend you have forgot the purport of my last letters. I shall therefore repeat part of them. I desired you would send me one full letter containing an explicit particular account of what profits remain to be made in Ireland by the sales which Partinton puts a stop to and by the demands we have upon him, also what state the lawsuit is in i.e. what has been done these three years passed and what remains to be done in it. I desired to know what mony hath been paid in to Swift etc. on my account, and what mistake you observed in MacManus : I suppose it must be in his charging what Mac-casland had charged before, for by his account the latter sh'd have charged nothing and consequently paid more to you than by yours it appears he has done. I desired therefore to have that matter cleared but your answer, if any, has miscarried. I do therefore repeat these requests to you. I likewise once more desire to know whether the yearly income of my Deanry be by the bonds stipulated to be paid to my order in Dublin. This I desired you to stipulate at the making the agreement for particular reasons but find nothing of it in the articles. I desire you to send me enclosed the original receipt of Mrs. Wilton in her own hand, for she denies she ever gave any. I likewise desire you to send me yr particular thoughts of Mrs. Dupee the milliner's demands. In yr observations on it you say that what she furnished Mrs. Mary with was on the mother's credit who charged the daughter with it. I ask does it appear that the daughter in any account was charged therewith by the mother and paid the mother? Yr other observations are expressed in such ambiguous terms that in very few of them I can know what your judgment is or what mine should be. As to the ferry-mony I consulted Dr. Ward who writes me word that I ought in his opinion to pay nothing but for the curate's passage on holidaies, this he thinks the outside and is clear in it. He likewise affirms that he knew nothing of the matter nor ever gave any advice about it. Tho' McManus wrote to me that Dr. Ward had advised his paying that mony [he] promised to make it good himself if I wd not allow it. Dr Tom let me have a satisfactory letter on the above points by the first opportunity directed to Smibert's as yr last.

Yrs.

G. B.

120   TO PRIOR

Dear Tom,

  I have received your letter, and write you this in haste. I am much importuned by the creditors, and at a loss how to deal with them. Why should not Comyng's debt for the funeral be wholly paid? I have seen a letter under Mrs. Esther's hand promising to pay it : this was wrote to one Lancaster. What you say of paying half of this and other debts I cannot comprehend : Either they are due and should be all paid, or not due and none paid. I have seen a promissory note of Mrs. Esther's to Mrs. Hill, whereof I send you subjoined a copy. Let me know your opinion, and take advice of others on the nature of a note so worded ; and whether it obligeth absolutely, or only as far as the mother's assets will go. What shall I do with Mr. Fisher, who claims twenty-three pounds odd money from Mrs. Mary, and about six pounds for Mrs. Esther, all for goods delivered since the mother's death. A day or two before I received your letter, I had paid three pound odd money to Mrs. Wilton, being no longer able to withstand her importunity, and despairing of seeing her receipt. The truth is, she showed me a letter wrote several months after the date of that receipt from Mrs. Mary, acknowledging herself indebted, but mentioning no sum.   I therefore paid that bill, which was dated after the day of clearing, and no more.   What must be done with Farmer ?   and, above all, what must be done with the milliner Mrs. Du Puis or Du Pee ?   I before mentioned her to you :   She gives me great trouble.   It would be endless to go through all.   I desire a word in particular to each of these. To put them off till your coming in the spring, is utterly impracticable ;   they having been amused with hopes of seeing you all last summer :   and it being rumoured that I intend to leave Europe next spring, what would such a put-off look like.   In the account of demands you formerly sent me, you, or rather in your notes upon the demands, you often mentioned Mr. Clarke's catalogue, without signifying what catalogue that is, whether one sent from hence, or one wrote there for the use of Mrs. Esther, or Mrs. Mary in her lifetime.   If the latter, pray let me know it ; such a catalogue would be of great use to prevent impositions. I should be glad of a copy of it.   You observe it differs frequently from accounts sent from hence ;   for instance, it contains about half of Fisher's demand from Mrs. Mary, if I take you right. It should follow therefore, that Fisher should be paid, at least so much—should it not ?   Send a copy of that catalogue, with the time when it was drawn up.   You often mention an act of Parliament to prevent frauds, which you say makes for us.   Pray send me a distinct abstract of that act, or at least of the substance and purport of it.   The note shewed me by Mrs. Hill is in the following words :

' *London, January* 28, 1713–14.—I Esther Van Homrigh, junior, do promise to pay to Katharine Hill the sum of thirty-three pounds eleven shillings and sixpence, on the 28th day of April next, for my mother Mrs. Esther Van Homrigh, being her sole executrix, as witness my hand,

E. VAN. HOMRIGH

Witness present
Wm. Brunley.
Anne Kindon.'

I desire you will give me your opinion clearly upon this note. I likewise desire you to satisfy me in these three points ;   1*st*,

Whether Mrs. Mary was minor during the whole time of her living with her mother? 2*dly*, Whether the mother died indebted to Mrs. Mary, or had spent part of her fortune? 3*dly*, Whether the things which Mrs. Mary had during her minority were charged by the mother, and the mother satisfied for the same?

I entreat you satisfy me instantly as to the points contained in this letter; after which, I shall speedily expect an answer to the matters in my former letters, which now I have not time to repeat, or say any more but that

I am, dear Tom,

Yours affectionately,

G. BERKELEY.

London, Nov. 5, 1726

121   TO PRIOR

Dear Tom,

I have wrote to you often for certain eclaircissements which are absolutely necessary to settle matters with the creditors, who importune me to death. You have no notion of the misery I have undergone, and do daily undergo, on that account. I do therefore earnestly entreat you to answer all that I have queried on that head without delay, and at the same time resolve me in what follows.

Have you any letter or entry that takes notice of Mr. Collins as a creditor to Mrs. Esther, junior? He hath produced to me two notes of hers, one for ten, the other for four pound odd money. Mrs. Farmer demands, for hosiers goods, near six pound from Mrs. Mary, and one pound nineteen from Mrs. Esther. I have seen her books, and by them it appears something is due; but in some places it looks as if they had transferred the mother's debts to the daughter. Pray tell me distinctly and intelligibly what appears to you from the papers of this. You have told me that this, with many other demands, are only the mother's debts. Pray tell me withal your reasons for this, that the creditors themselves may be satisfied hereof, for they will not take your word or mine for it. *First*, Let me know what appears to you to have been supplied by each creditor for Mrs. Mary's use. 2*dly*, Let me know upon what grounds you conceive that and no more to have been so supplied. 3*dly*, Be distinct in giving your opinion, whether a minor be not chargeable for eatables and wearables supplied on the credit of another, or on their own credit, during the minority ? Whether it appears that Mrs. Mary was ever charged by her mother for those things ? *Lastly,* Let me know what you think was distinctly supplied for Mrs. Mary's use, used by her, and never paid for ; it being my opinion such debts should be discharged *in foro conscientiæ*, though perhaps the law might not require it, on score of minority or length of time.

For God's sake disembrangle these matters, that I may once be at ease to mind my other affairs of the College, which are enough to employ ten persons. You promised a distinct tripartite list, which I never got. The observations you have sent are all of them either so ambiguous and indecisive as to puzzle only, or else precarious ; that is, unsupported by reasons to convince me or others. Now, I suppose where you give a positive opinion you have reasons for it ; and it would have been right to have sent these reasons distinctly and particularly. I will not repeat what I have said in my former letters, but hope for your answer to all the points contained in them, and immediately to what relates to dispatching the creditors. I propose to make a purchase of land (which is very dear) in Bermuda, upon my first going thither ; for which, and for other occasions, I shall want all the money I can possibly raise against my voyage. For this purpose, it would be a mighty service to me if the affair with Partinton were adjusted this winter, by reference or compromise The state of all that business, which I desired you to send me, I do now again earnestly desire. What is doing or has been done in that matter ? Can you contrive no way for bringing Partinton to an immediate sale of the remaining lands ? What is your opinion and advice upon the whole ? What prospect can I have if I leave things at sixes and sevens when I go to another world, seeing all my remonstrances even now that I am near at hand, are to no purpose ? I know money is at present on a very high foot of exchange : I shall therefore wait a little, in hopes it may become lower ; but it will at all events be necessary to draw over my money. I have spent here a matter of six hundred pounds more than you know of, for which I have not yet drawn over.

As to what you write of Robin, I am glad to find that others think he behaves well : I am best judge of his behaviour to me. There is a way of resenting past favours, and there is a way of asking future ones ; and in both cases a right and a wrong. I had some other points to speak to, but am cut short, and have only time to add, that

I am,

Yours affectionately,

G. BERKELEY.

London, Nov. 12, 1726

122   TO PRIOR

December 1, 1726

Dear Tom,

    I have lately received several letters of yours, which have given me a good deal of light with respect to Mrs. V. Homrigh's affairs ; but I am so much employed on the business of Bermuda, that I have hardly time to mind any thing else. I shall nevertheless snatch the present moment to write you short answers to the questions you propose.

    As to Bermuda, it is now on a better and surer foot than ever. After the address of the Commons, and his Majesty's most gracious answer, one would have thought all difficulties had been got over : but much opposition hath been since raised (and that by very great men) to the design. As for the obstacles thrown in my way by interested men, though there hath been much of that, I never regarded it, no more than the clamours and calumnies of ignorant mistaken people : but in good truth it was with much difficulty, and the peculiar blessing of God, that the point was carried maugre the strong opposition in the cabinet council ; wherein, nevertheless, it hath of late been determined to go on with the grant, pursuant to the address of the House of Commons, and to give it all possible dispatch. Accordingly his Majesty hath ordered the warrant for passing the said grant to be drawn. The persons appointed to contrive the draught of the warrant are the Solicitor-General, Baron Scroop of the Treasury, and (my very good friend) Mr. Hutchenson. You must know that in July last the Lords of the Treasury had named commissioners for taking an estimate of the value and quantity of the crown lands in St Christophers, and for receiving proposals either for selling or farming the same for the benefit of the public. Their report is not yet made ; and the Treasury were of opinion they could not make a grant to us till such time as the whole were sold or farmed pursuant to such report. But the point I am now labouring is to have it done, without delay ; and how this may be done without embarrassing the Treasury in their after disposal of the whole lands was this day the subject of a conference between the Solicitor-General, Mr. Hutchenson, and myself. The method agreed on is by a rent-charge on the whole crown lands, redeemable upon the crown's paying twenty thousand pounds, for the use of the President and Fellows of St Paul's, and their successors. Sir Robert Walpole hath signified that he hath no objection to this method ; and I doubt not Baron Scroop will agree to it ; by which means the grant may be passed before the meeting of Parliament, after which we may prepare to set out on our voyage in April. I have unawares run into this long account because you desired to know how the affair of Bermuda stood at present.

You also desire I would speak to Ned. You must know Ned hath parted from me ever since the beginning of last July. I allowed him six shillings a week besides his annual wages ; and beside an entire livery, I gave him old clothes, which he made a penny of ; but the creature grew idle and worthless to a pro-digious degree. He was almost constantly out of the way ; and when I told him of it he used to give me warning. I bore with this behaviour about nine months, and let him know I did it in compassion to him, and in hopes he would mend ; but finding no hopes of this, I was forced at last to discharge him, and take another, who is as diligent as he was negligent. When he parted from me, I paid him between six and seven pounds which was due to him, and likewise gave him money to bear his charges to Ireland, whither he said he was going. I met him t'other day in the street ; and asking why he was not gone to Ireland to his wife and child, he made answer that he had neither wife nor child. He got, it seems, into another service since he left me, but continued only a fortnight in it. The fellow is silly to an incredible degree, and spoiled by good usage.

I shall take care the pictures be sold in an auction. Mr. Smibert, whom I know to be a very honest, skilful person in his profession, will see them put into an auction at the proper time, which he tells me is not till the town fills with company, about the meeting of parliament.

As to Bacon, I know not what to do with him. I spoke often to Messrs. Wogan and Aspinwall about him. Mr. Aspinwall also spoke to him, and threatened him with bringing the affair into court ; and he still promised, and always broke his promise.

I always, for my part, insisted they should prosecute him ; and, since your mentioning him in your letter, have done it in stronger terms than ever, but to no purpose ; for, upon the whole, I find they decline meddling with it. They say the fellow is a knave, and skilful in delays of law and attorneys' tricks, and that he may keep us employed for several years ; that it is a matter out of their sphere ; in short, they do not care to be employed in this affair. When I saw the man, I did not like his looks nor manner, and am now quite at a loss what to do with him. The whole expense they charge for management in South Sea House, and at Doctors' Commons, together with their own trouble, amounts to thirty-nine pounds ten shillings and sixpence. I have bills of the particulars. Some of the creditors I have paid ; but there are many more un-paid, whose demands I could not yet adjust. The first leisure I have I shall try to do it, by the help of the lights I have now got. As to M'Manus, I am content to favour him so far as to forbear his paying that part of my income on the first of January which was stipulated to be then paid ; but then the whole must be paid punctually on the first of February. I say I shall have necessary occasion for the whole income of the present year to be paid, without fail, on the first of February next ; and I wish he may have timely notice from you of this. I formerly gave him warning myself ; but since he has wrote to you, it is fit he know this answer. My affairs absolutely require this ; and I expect that he will not, upon any pretext, disappoint me. You tell me what is to be done with Mr. Tooke's note, in case it be a bond in form, or a simple promissory note, or a promissory note with interest sealed ; but still you omit what (to the best of my remembrance) is the true case, *to wit*, a promissory note unsealed, to pay the principal with interest. Before I closed this letter, the bond was brought me, sealed, witnessed, and bearing interest, making, with the principal, eighty pound, which I have paid this moment ; so that I was mistaken in thinking it a note, being a bond in form. In your last but one, you sent two opposite opinions of Howard and Marshal concerning Mrs. Hill's note, but promised to give your own, and to be more clear in the point in your next, which it seems you forgot to do. I have in a former letter desired you to send me over an abstract of the state of our case in dispute with Partinton, and a full account of our demands upon him. You have told me indeed where the point sticks at present ; but you may see that this does not fully answer my desire. I want to know (as if I had never heard anything of the matter) a full account of that

whole affair stated, what our demands amount to in each particular, and what expectations there are of succeeding, and grounds
for prosecuting, the said demands respectively. I remember to
have told you I could know more of matters here than perhaps
people generally do. You thought we did wrong to sell ; but the
stocks are fallen, and depend upon it they will fall lower. In a
former letter, I acquainted you that I desired the bonds may be
lodged with Ned Synge, who will call for them.

Yours,

G. BERKELEY.

123   TO PRIOR

London, Feb. 27, 1726/27

Dear Tom,

The packets you speak of you may direct, under cover, to
the right honourable Thomas, Earl of Pomfret, in Hanover Square;
but then you must take care that no one packet be above a certain
quantity or weight, and thereby exceed the limits of franking :
in which case the frank I know will not be regarded, and the papers
may miscarry. What the precise limits are I know not ; any
body there can inform you.

I send you herewith an account of our affairs transacted by
Wogan and Aspinwall. You may observe in the account of Mr.
Gyles (employed by them) a half guinea blotted out, which I paid
separately for an extract of a Will relating to Bermuda, and which
by mistake was inserted in this account, to which it had no relation.

The pictures were all sold for forty-five pounds, at an auction
which was held last week in Covent Garden, at the house of
one Mr. Russel, a painter. They were sold publicly and fairly
among several other pictures. The truth of it is, that of late
years the taste lies so much towards Italian pictures, many of
which are daily imported, that Dutch pictures go off but heavily.
Mr. Smibert did not think they would have brought so much.

I have taken the utmost care to keep myself within the limits
of your directions in the payments I have hitherto made, and
shall continue to act with the same caution. Mr. Marshal cannot
long more than I do to put an end to this matter of my administration, which I was willing to have declined, if he had thought good
to accept it. But the constant hurry of business I have on my
hands, together with my not being able to find out some of the

creditors, hath hitherto unavoidably delayed it. However, I have
paid between two and three hundred pounds, and shall finish all
as soon as possible. Mr. Clarke I have not seen this long time.
I suppose he is ashamed for my having found out that he was to
receive a sum of money from Mrs. Philips, whose unjust debt he
had undertaken to get paid. This, and his not giving me the notice
Alderman Barber said he desired him to give before the sale of the
jewels, makes me think very indifferently of him. Besides, there
is no sort of consistency between the accounts of creditors, as
given in by him, and their own demands, which still strengthens
my suspicion of him. As to the sum to be paid into Swift and
Company, and the deductions to be made for curates, &c., I only
desire that all may be done on the foot you told me you had agreed
with Mr. M'Manus, and whereof you stated the account in a letter
I have by me, and which I need not transcribe, because I suppose
you remember it. As to the sale of the reversionary lands, I desire
it may be done as soon as possible ; and not to stand out, but to
take the best terms you can. As to the rest, I long to see it all
finished by arbitration.

My going to Bermuda I cannot positively say when it will be.
I have to do with very busy people at a very busy time. I hope
nevertheless to have all that business completely finished in a few
weeks.

I am, dear Tom,
Yours,
G. B.

124   TO PRIOR

London, April 11, 1727

Dear Tom,

In my last I made no mention of any sums of my money
applied to the payment of debts, or other purposes common to
Mr. Marshal and me, because I suppose you have taken care that
he keep equal pace with me : if he be deficient, this is the only
time to right myself. As to those you call dubious debts, and
those which, being contracted in the mother's lifetime, are payable
by Partinton, I should be glad to hear your opinion in a line or
two, since I am not allowed to act otherwise than by strict legal
justice. Thus much I think Mr. Marshal and myself are obliged

to, viz. to pay those debts if nothing be stopt for them by Partinton ; and if there be, to advertise the creditors thereof. Since my last, I paid what you allowed to be due to Mrs. Farmer (now Mrs. Reed). For this and all other payments I have receipts or notes which I propose bringing with me to Ireland.

And now I mention my coming to Ireland, I must earnestly desire you, by all means, to keep this a secret from every individual creature. I cannot justly say what time (probably some time next month) I shall be there, or how long ; but find it necessary to be there to transact matters with one or two of my associates (who yet I would not have know of my coming till I am on the spot), and, for several reasons, am determined to keep myself as secret and concealed as possible all the time I am in Ireland. In order to this, I make it my request that you will hire for me an entire house, as neat and convenient as you can get, somewhere within a mile of Dublin, for half a year. But what I principally desire is, that it be in no town or village, but in some quiet private place, out of the way of roads, or street, or observation. I would have it hired with necessary furniture for kitchen, a couple of chambers, and a parlour. As the same time, I must desire you to hire an honest maid servant, who can keep it clean, and dress a plain bit of meat : a man servant I shall bring with me. You may do all this either in your own name, or as for a friend of yours, one Mr. Brown (for that is the name I shall assume), and let me know it as soon as possible. There are several little scattered houses with gardens about Clantarfe, Rathfarnum, &c. I remember particularly the old castle of Ramines, and a little white house upon the hills by itself, beyond the Old Men's Hospital, likewise in the outgoings or fields about St Kevin's, &c. In short, in any snug private place within half a mile or a mile of town. I would have a bit of a garden to it, no matter what sort. Mind this, and you'll oblige

Your affectionate humble Servant,
G. BERKELEY.

125 TO PRIOR

Dear Tom,

Things being as you say, I think you were in the right to pay only 100 pounds to Mr. Marshal at present. I have drawn on you for 12 pounds, which my B. Robin will call for.

I would by all means have a place secured for me by the end of June : it may be taken only for three months. I hope you will not have left Ireland before my arrival.

I take it for granted you have paid what I directed for Mr. Partinton Van Homrigh's share of the pictures. I sent the answer to his bill engrossed by post, and shall be glad to hear you have got it. I long to hear the sale of lands (reversionary) perfected to Mr. Conolly.

I am (God be praised) very near concluding the crown grant to our College, having got over all difficulties and obstructions, which were not a few.

I conclude, in great haste, dear Tom,

Yours,
G. BERKELEY.

London, May 20, 1727

126 TO PRIOR

Dear Tom,

Poor Caldwell's death I had heard of two or three posts before I received your letter. Had he lived, his life would not have been agreeable. He was formed for retreat and study ; but of late was grown fond of the world, and getting into business.

A house between Dublin and Drumcondra I can by no means approve of : the situation is too public ; and what I chiefly regard is privacy. I like the situation of Lord's house much better, and have only one objection to it, which is your saying he intends to use some part of it himself ; for this would be inconsistent with my view of being quite concealed ; and the more so because Lord knows me, which of all things is what I would avoid. His house and price would suit me. If you can get such another, quite to myself, snug, private, and clean, with a stable, I shall not matter whether it be painted or no, or how it is furnished, provided it be clean and warm. I aim at nothing magnificent or grand (as you term it), which might probably defeat my purpose of continuing concealed.

You have more than once talked of coming to England without coming : perhaps you may alter your mind now as well as heretofore ; but you are best judge of that. I desire to know when your business requires your being in England ?—whether you come to London ?—and how long you propose staying on this side of the water ? I am sure it will be at least a full month before I can reach Dublin. If you come over immediately, and make but a very short stay, possibly I might defer my going, to attend you in your return. At all events, I should be sorry we missed of each other by setting out at the same time, which may occasion my seeing you neither there nor here.

The bell-man calls for my letter, so I shall add no more but that

I am your affectionate humble Servant,
G. BERKELEY.

London, June 13, 1727.

Pray let me hear from you next post.

127   TO PRIOR

Dear Tom,

Yesterday we had an account of King George's death. This day King George II was proclaimed. All the world here are in a hurry, and I as much as any body ; our grant being defeated by the King's dying before the broad seal was annexed to it, in order to which it was passing through the offices. I have *la mer à boire* again. You shall hear from me when I know more. At present I am at a loss what course to take. Pray answer my last speedily.

Yours,
G. B.

London, June 15, 1727

London, June 27, 1727

Dear Tom,

    Yesterday I received your letter, containing an account of your design about coming to England. In a former letter, I gave you to know that my affairs were ravell'd [1] by the death of his Majesty. I am now beginning on a new foot, and with good hopes of success. The warrant for our grant had been signed by the King, countersigned by the Lords of the Treasury, and passed the Attorney General. Here it stood when the express came of the King's death. A new warrant is now preparing, which must be signed by his present Majesty, in order to a patent passing the broad seal.

    As soon as this affair is finished, I propose going to Ireland. I cannot certainly say when that will be ; but sure I am it will not be time enough to find you there, if you continue your scheme of coming over the next month. It is unlucky that we should both think of crossing the sea at the same time. But as you seem to talk doubtfully of your design, I hope it may suit with your conveniency to alter it ; in which case we may probably come together to England.

    The changes of ministry you talk of are at present but guessed at ; a little time will show.

Yours, &c.
G. BERKELEY.

Dear Tom,

    This is to inform you, that I have obtained a new warrant for a grant, signed by his present Majesty, contrary to the expectations of my friends, who thought nothing could be expected of that kind in this great hurry of business. As soon as this grant (which is of the same import with that begun by his late Majesty) hath passed the offices and seals, I purpose to execute my design of going to Ireland. In case, therefore, you continue your purpose of coming to England this summer, I must desire you to leave all papers relating to my affairs with Mr. Synge, sealed up in a bag

---

[1] So Lit. Rel. ; Stock reads ' unravelled.'

as things belonging to me, put into his hands for fear of accidents ; but to say nothing to him of my going to Dublin, which I would have by all means kept secret from every one ; my design being, in case I find you are absent, to make my arrival, after I am come, known to Synge ; to look into the papers myself, and try if I can state matters so as to bring them to a conclusion with Partinton. It would assist me much in this affair if you would do what I have long and often desired, viz. draw up a paper containing an account of my demands on Partinton or others in virtue of my executorship, with the several reasons supporting the said demands, and an account of the proceedings thereupon at law ; what hath been done, and what remains to be done. I hoped to have heard of the sale of the reversion by this time. Let me hear by next post.

I am yours,
G. BERKELEY.

London, July 6, 1727

130 TO PRIOR

Dear Tom,

In answer to your last letter, this is to let you know, that my grant is now got farther than where it was at the time of the King's death. I am in hopes the broad seal will soon be affixed to it, what remains to be done in order thereto being only matter of form ; so that I propose setting out from hence in a fortnight's time. When I set out, I shall write at the same time to tell you of it.

I know not whether I shall stay longer than a month on that side of the water. I am sure I shall not want the country lodging (I desired you to procure) for a longer time. Do not therefore take it for more than a month, if that can be done. I remember certain remote suburbs called Pimlico and Dolphin's Barn, but know not whereabout they lie. If either of them be situate in a private pleasant place, and airy, near the fields, I should therein like a first floor in a clean house (I desire no more) ; and it would be better if there was a bit of a garden where I had the liberty to walk. This I mention in case my former desire cannot be conveniently answered for so short a time as a month ; and, if I may judge at this distance, these places seem as private as a house in the country : for you must know, what I chiefly aim at is secrecy.

This makes me uneasy to find that there hath been a report spread among some of my friends in Dublin of my designing to go over. I cannot account for this, believing, after the precautions I had given you, that you would not mention it directly or indirectly to any mortal. For the present, I have no more to add, but only to repeat my request that you will leave all papers relating to my executorship with Mr. Synge sealed up in a bag, with directions to deliver them to my order. This I desired you to perform in my last, in case you leave Ireland before I arrive there. If with them you likewise leave what I formerly desired, it will save me some trouble.

I am, dear Tom,

Your affectionate humble Servant,

G. BERKELEY.

July 21, 1727

I observe you take no notice of what I said about selling the reversionary lands, though you formerly encouraged me to think I should have heard of their being sold before this time.

In case you do not make use of the power I gave you by letter of attorney to make sale of the reversionary lands before you come for England, I desire you would leave that said letter of attorney among the papers with Mr. Synge.

131   TO PRIOR

Dear Tom,

I agree that M'Manus should retain for payment of the curates to the first of May. After so many delays from Partinton, I was fully convinced the only way to sell the reversionary lands must be by compelling him to join in the sale by law, or by making a separate sale. This I proposed to you by word of mouth, and by letter, as much as I could ; and I now most earnestly repeat it, intreating you to do the one or the other out of hand if it be not done already, as I have hopes it is by what you say in your last. Dear Tom, fail me not in this particular ; but by all means order matters so that the purchase-money may be paid in to Swift, & Co. on the first of April, or at farthest ten days after ; which ten days I am willing to allow to M'Manus as desired. I need not repeat to you what I told you here of the necessity there is for my raising all the money possible against my voyage, which, God willing, I shall begin in May, whatever you may hear suggested to the contrary ; though you need not mention this.

I propose to set out for Dublin about a month hence ; but of this you must not give the least intimation to any body. I beg the favour of you to look out at leisure a convenient lodging for me in or about Church-street, or such other place as you shall think the most retired. Mr. Petit Rose writes me from Portarlington about renewing his lease, which he desires I would empower you to do. He mentions a promise I made on the last renewal, that I would another time allow him one year gratis. For my part, I absolutely deny that I know any thing of any such promise. If you remember any thing of it, pray let me know ; for if there was such a thing, it must have been made by you, to whom I referred the management of that affair. As I do not design to be known when I am in Ireland, I shall comply with his desire in sending you a letter of attorney to perfect the renewal, agreeable to such draught as you transmit hither ; provided still, that his proposal (which I have by this post directed him to send to you) be approved by you ; to whom I leave it, to do what to you shall seem fair and reasonable in that matter.

I am,
Your affectionate humble Servant,
GEOR. BERKELEY.

London, Feb. 20, 1727/28

132   TO PRIOR

London, April 6, 1728

Dear Tom,

I send you herewith the letter of Attorney and that to Dr. Ward. Four Irish pacquets are now due, one of which I expect brings an account of your having finished the sale of those lands which I have been pressing for these four years.

I have been detained from my journey partly in expectation of Dr. Clayton's coming, who was doing business in Lancashire, and partly in respect to the excessive rains. The Doctor hath been several days in town, and we have had so much rain that probably it will be soon over. I am therefore daily expecting to set out, all things being provided.

13

Now it is of all things my earnest desire (and for very good reasons) not to have it known that I am in Dublin. Speak not, therefore, one syllable of it to any mortal whatsover. When I formerly desired you to take a place for me near the town, you gave out that you were looking for a retired lodging for a friend of yours ; upon which everybody surmised me to be the person. I must beg you not to act in the like manner now, but to take for me an entire house in your own name, and as for yourself : for, all things considered, I am determined upon a whole house, with no mortal in it but a maid of your own putting, who is to look on herself as your servant. Let there be two bed-chambers, one for you, another for me ; and, as you like, you may ever and anon lie there. I would have the house, with necessary furniture, taken by the month (or otherwise, as you can), for I purpose staying not beyond that time : and yet perhaps I may. Take it as soon as possible, and never think of saving a week's hire by leaving it to do when I am there. Dr. Clayton thinks (and I am of the same opinion) that a convenient place may be found in the further end of Great Britain Street, or Ballibough-bridge— by all means beyond Thomson's the Fellow's. Let me entreat you to say nothing of this to anybody, but to do the thing directly. In this affair I consider convenience more than expense, and would of all things (cost what it will) have a proper place in a retired situation, where I may have access to fields and sweet air, provided against the moment I arrive. I am inclined to think, one may be better concealed in the outermost skirt of the suburbs than in the country, or within the town. Wherefore, if you cannot be accommodated where I mention, inquire in some other skirt or remote suburb. A house quite detached in the country I should have no objection to ; provided you judge that I shall not be liable to discovery in it. The place called Bermuda I am utterly against. Dear Tom, do this matter cleanly and cleverly, without waiting for further advice. You see I am willing to run the risk of the expence. To the person from whom you hire it (whom alone I would have you speak of it to) it will not seem strange you should at this time of the year be desirous, for your own convenience or health, to have a place in a free and open air. If you cannot get a house without taking it for a longer time than a month, take it at such the shortest time it can be let for, with agreement for further continuing in case there be occasion.

Mr. Madden, who witnesses the letter of attorney, is now going

to Ireland.   He is a clergyman, and man of estate in the north
of Ireland.   I am,

Your affectionate humble Servant,

GEORGE BERKELEY.

Divide this letter from that of Attorney.

133   TO FAIRFAX

Sir,
        When I waited on you I took the liberty to inform you that
my library was to be sent from Dublin to London in order to lie
there till it might be conveniently shipped off again and I now
give you this trouble to let you know that it is actually put on
board the ship called William & James and consigned to the
bearer hereof.   The whole parcel amounts to fifty eight boxes,
whereof fifty five contain only books ; the other three beside books
contain papers and Mathematical instruments, all old except
a water level which I take to be the only instrument made in this
kingdom.   The books printed here are very inconsiderable though
I cannot punctually tell the number.   I do verily think they are
not worth ten pds.   The others which were either printed in
England or came from thence (as all our books constantly used
to do) may be presumed liable to no duty upon their return into
England.   But this is submitted to the Honourable board of
Commissioners to whom I beg the favour of you to set forth this
case, and that you will be pleased to give orders accordingly
which will much oblige.

Sir,

Your most obedient humble Servt,

GEOR. BERKELEY.

Dublin, June 7, 1728

134   TO PERCIVAL

Greenwich, 3rd Sept. 1728

My Lord,

I think myself obliged before I set sail from Europe to take leave of your Lordship and express my sincere gratitude for all your favours, my being withheld from doing this in person is no small mortification to me though perhaps it would have been greater to have done it, taking leave being in my opinion the most disagreeable instance of good manners that custom obliges us to. To-morrow we sail down the river. Mr. James and Mr. Dalton go with me. So doth my wife, a daughter of the late Chief Justice Forster, whom I married since I saw your Lordship. I chose her for the qualities of her mind and her unaffected inclination to books. She goes with great cheerfulness to live a plain farmer's life, and wear stuff of her own spinning. I have presented her with a spinning wheel, and for her encouragement have assured her that from henceforward there shall never be one yard of silk bought for the use of myself, herself, or any of our family. Her fortune was two thousand pounds originally, but travelling and exchange have reduced it to less than fifteen hundred English money. I have placed that, and about six hundred pounds of my own, in the South Sea Annuities, as your Lordship will perceive by the enclosed letter of Attorney which I take the liberty to send you. I design to give your Lordship no farther trouble by it than one journey in a year into the City ; and that only to such time as I can find means of laying it out to advantage where I am going. Your Lordship's goodness and readiness to serve your friends which I have so frequently experienced have drawn this trouble upon you and prevent any further apology.

My most humble respects and best wishes attend my Lady, your whole family, and the good company at your house. That God may preserve your Lordship in health and happiness is the sincere hearty prayer of

Your Lordship's
Most obedient humble Servant,
G. Berkeley.

If your Lordship should at any time favour me with a line please direct to Dean Berkeley at Rhode Island, near Boston, and enclose the letter in a cover to Thomas Corbett, Esq. at the Admiralty Office in London, who will further it by the first opportunity.

135   TO PRIOR

Gravesend, Sept. 5, 1728

Dear Tom,

To-morrow, with God's blessing, I set sail for Rhode Island, with my wife and a friend of hers, my lady Hancock's daughter, who bears us company. I am married since I saw you to Miss Forster, daughter of the late Chief Justice, whose humour and turn of mind pleases me beyond any thing that I know in her whole sex. Mr. James, Mr. Dalton, and Mr. Smibert, go with us on this voyage. We are now all together at Gravesend, and are engaged in one view.

When my next rents are paid, I must desire you to inquire for my cousin Richard Berkeley, who was bred a public notary (I suppose he may by that time be out of his apprenticeship), and give him twenty moidores as a present from me, towards helping him on his beginning the world.

I believe I shall have occasion to draw for six hundred pounds English before this year's income is paid by the farmers of my Deanery. I must therefore desire you to speak to Messrs. Swift, &c., to give me credit for said sum in London about three months hence, in case I have occasion to draw for it ; and I shall willingly pay their customary interest for the same till the farmers pay it to them, which I hope you will order punctually to be done by the first of June. Give me advice of your success in this affair, viz. whether they will answer such draught of mine in London, on what interest, and on whom, and how I am to draw ?

Direct for me in Rhode Island, and inclose your letter in a cover to Thomas Corbet, Esq., at the Admiralty office in London, who will always forward my letters by the first opportunity. Adieu. I write in great haste,

Yours,

G. B.

I wrote by this post to M'Manus to comply with all the points proposed in Dr. Ward's memorial. A copy of my Charter was sent to Dr. Ward by Dr. Clayton.   If it be not arrived when you go to London, write out of the Charter the clause relating to my absence.   Adieu once more.

136   TO PERCIVAL

Newport in Rhode Island, 7th Feby 1728/29

My Lord,

Though I am at present in no small hurry and have been so ever since my landing with visits and business of several kinds, yet I would not omit the first opportunity of paying my duty to your Lordship, and acquainting you with our safe arrival in this Island.   We came last from Virginia, where I received many unexpected as well as undeserved honours from the Governour and principal inhabitants.   The same civil kind treatment attends us here.   We were a long time blundering about the ocean before we reached Virginia, but our voyage from thence hither was as speedy and prosperous as could be wished.   Mr. James who proposeth to continue in Virginia till spring, and Mr. Dalton who pursued his journey to this place by land, will both repent of their choice, when they find us arrived so long before them.   I shall soon (I hope) be able to give your Lordship a more particular account of things.   For the present I shall only say that this Island wants only your Lordship's family and a few more of my friends to make it the most agreeable place I ever saw.   And (that which pleases me beyond all things) there is a more probable prospect of doing good here than in any other part of the world.   I am so fully convinced of this, that (were it in my power) I should not demur one moment about situating our College here.   But no step can be taken herein without consent of the Crown, and I shall not apply for that till his Majesty's bounty from St Christopher's is paid to Dr. Clayton, till which time this design should be kept private.

I took the liberty to trouble your Lordship with a Letter of Attorney which Dr. Clayton was to put into your hands relating to my stock in the South Sea Annuities.   It occurs to me that it is possible you may once more travel abroad into France or Italy, in which case I beg the favour of you to sell my said Annuities and receive the dividend due thereupon at that time, and place the whole in some known banker's hands making it payable to my order. Mr. Hoare, of all others, I should choose ; but as the contributors' money belonging to our College of Bermuda is in his hands, and as I would have my private stock entered into the banker's books under a distinct article as my own money, in order to prevent any confusion, I must request your Lordship to be particular with him on that head, if the money be put into his hands. And you will be pleased to let me know his partner's names that I may draw in form, for I intend to purchase land in this country. Your Lordship's usual goodness will pardon this trouble.

The post is just going out so I conclude with my best wishes and respects to my Lady Percival and your whole family in which I include Mr. Dering.

> My Lord,
> Yr most obedt and obliged humble Servt,
> G. BERKELEY.

I shall hope for a line from your Lordship.

Since I wrote and sealed the enclosed I have heard something which makes it highly expedient for me to draw for the money which I left in the South Sea Annuities, and must therefore request the favour of your Lordship to sell the same out of hand and place it together with dividend due thereupon in a sure banker's hand, and to send me as soon as possible directions how to draw for it. I shall ever acknowledge this with the many other obligations I owe your Lordship. If your Lordship will be so good as to send a duplicate of the said directions, one by the Admiralty and the other by Mr. Newman's conveyance (to whom my humble service), it will be the likelier to come to my hands.

137   TO PERCIVAL

Newport, 28th March 1729

My Lord,

Sometime I wrote to your Lordship requesting the favour of you to sell my South Sea Annuities and place the money in a banker's hand making it payable to my order, and if in Mr. Hoare's to see it put into a distinct article from the Bermuda accounts, to prevent confounding my private money with that of the College. I know not whether my letter arrived, and therefore repeat the same request by the opportunity of a gentleman, who I am just told is going from Boston to be ordained in England. As he intends to return I shall hope for a line from your Lordship by him with directions how to draw for my money. You see my Lordship the genuine effects of your great goodness is trouble to yourself and benefit to your friends ; though if I had known what I now do, I should have avoided trespassing on your Lordship's good nature and brought my money in specie with me, which would have been more to my advantage.

I have now some experience of this place, and can tell your Lordship the climate is like that of Italy north of Rome, and in my opinion not quite so cold, though this season has been reckoned colder than ordinary. The land is pleasantly diversified with hills, vales, and rising grounds. Here are also some amusing rocky scenes. There are not wanting several fine rivulets and groves. The sea, too, mixed with capes and adjacent islands, makes very delightful prospects. But I forget myself and am running the risk of being thought romantic, though I assure you I write much below the truth. The town is prettily built, contains about five thousand souls, and hath a very fine harbour. The people industrious, and though less orthodox, I cannot say they have less virtue (I am sure they have more regularity) than those I left in Europe. They are indeed a strange medley of different persuasions, which nevertheless all agree in one point, viz. that the Church of England is the second best. Mr. Honyman, the only Episcopal clergyman in this Island, in whose house I now am, is a person of very good sense and merit on all accounts, much more than I expected to have found in this place.

I must send my letter by this morning's post to Boston, so have time to say no more but that I am and ever shall be,
　　　My Lord,
Your Lordship's most obliged and most obedt humble Servant,
　　　　　Geo. Berkeley.

My best respects to my Lady and all your family. I long to know how you all do, Mr. Dering, &c. and what is become of Père Courayer, to whom pray my humble service.

Newport, Avril 9, 1729

Monsieur,

J'aurois repondu plutôt a la lettre dont vous m'avez honoré
si je n'etois empeché tantôt par des affaires tantôt par un indisposition laquelle me travailloit de tems en tems, mais ni l'un ni
l'autre m'auroit detourné d'avoir rendue cette service a l'eglise
de Dieu que vous attendez de moy si j'avois quelque pouvoir de
juger ou de decider sur cet affaire malheureuse dont vous m'avoit
fait un recit si touchant & si pleine de zele pour la gloire de Dieu.

Il faut avouer, Monsieur, que je ne suis qu'un simple passager
dans ce pais sans etre revetûe d'aucune autorité ni jurisdiction sur
les Eglises de cette colonie & que toute ma petite jurisdiction
(telle qu'elle soit) est bornée par la diocese de London-derry en
Irlande. Vous voyez donc qu'il e[s]t impossible que j'apportasse
aucune remede a votres inconveniens les quelles neanmoins me
touchant au fond du coeur. Je puis cependant vous assurer que
je ne doute gueres que Monseigneur l'Evêque de Londres &
l'honorable Societé prendront des mesures tres justes & tres sages
pour y remedier. C'est donc de leur conduite qu'il faut attendre
la remede que vous souhatez. Je ne laisseroy pas pourtant de
supplier le Bon Dieu de secourir & de proteger votre Eglise de
Providence la quelle est si rudement secouée par cet triste evene-
ment dont vous m'avez fait part & de vous consoler dans votre
venerable viellesse par la decouverte de cette verité pour la quelle
vous faites des voeus si ardens. Vous aurois la bonte Monsieur
de me pardonner ce que j'ecris dans une langue que je n'ay
pratiqué que tres rarement & de croire que je suis avec beaucoup de respect Monsieur votre tres humble & tres obeissant
serviteur.

GEOR. BERKELEY.

Newport in Rhode Island, April 11, 1729

Dr Sir,

In compliance with your own desire I delay'd writing till
such time as I could say something from my own experience of

this place and people. The inhabitants are a mixed kind containing many sects and subdivisions of sects. Here are four sorts of Anabaptists besides Independents, Quakers and many of no profession at all. These several sects do all agree in one point viz: that each thinks our church the second best.

The climate is like that of Italy, tho' not quite so cold in the winter as I have known it in many places north of Rome. But the spring is later. The fields are now green and the trees budded but the leaves are not yet shot forth. To make amends I am told on all hands that they have the pleasantest summer and the longest and most delicious autumn in the world. The great plenty of melons, standard peaches, and wild vines etc. are a proof of this. The face of the country is pleasantly laid out in hills vales woods and rising grounds, watered with several rivulets. Here are also in some parts very amusing rocky scenes, and fine landschapes of the sea intermixed with capes and islands. But I forbear for fear of being thought Romantic. Give me leave only to add that the town of Newport is exceeding pretty and hath the advantage of a very fine situation both for prospect and access, the harbour being very commodious. The people are industrious and not given to quarrel about Religious matters. Mr. Honeyman the only Episcopal clergyman of this island is a Scholar and every way a man of considerable merit. James is not yet arrived from Virginia. Dalton hath been here some time, he and Smibert are now at Boston where they propose passing a few daies. Your little friend hath been much embarrassed in dealing with a Quaker of this island for the hire of his farm. This affair is one of the greatest eclat and importance that for many years hath been transacted in this Rhodian Government the principal persons of the State having all interposed therein. I have purchased a pleasant farm of about one hundred acres with two fine groves and winding rivulet upon it. Till such time as I hear of my associates having arrived with his Majesty's bounty money at Bermuda I do not think I cou'd be so useful in any part of the world as in this place. The subject of our last conversation I am now convinced of more than ever. God keep it warm in your heart. I intended to have wrote by this same opportunity to Dr. Rundle, but think it will do better to wait for another, not to overcharge you with two letters at once. I doubt not you have made the proper apologies to my friends which I desired. You will be so good as to make my humble service & best respects accepted of all our common friends : To mention particulars would be endless. Those in Hannover Square & Dover Street are always especially to be understood. Sir Philip York & Mr. Talbot who had been so useful in furthering our College patents and so very obliging to me might well have expected I shou'd not have left the Kingdom without waiting on them. But you know the reason. I have all the gratitude imaginable towards these Gentlemen & a most particular respect for my Lady York whom I look upon to be one of the most reasonable and valuable women in Europe. God protect & preserve you Dear Archdeacon to the joy of all your friends among whom I am sure you will never forget those in this new world, who are most sincerely yours, but no body is or can be more than

Dr Sir,

Yr most affect. humble Servt,

GEOR. BERKELEY.

I have not had a line from Europe (but one from Mr. Newman) since my arrival. Nothing can be more welcome than a letter from you. enclose in a cover to Thomas Corbet Esqe at the Admiralty office.

His majesties instructions meet with great opposition in the neighbouring government of New England. The church of England men as many as are in the assembly or the council are all unanimous for complying in the most respectful manner with the Governor. Every impartial statesman who knows how things are carried in these parts must conclude it wou'd be the most effectual, the cheapest, & on all accounts the most desirable way to promote and secure his majesties interests in these parts by planting an Episcopal Seminary in Rhode Island which I doubt not wou'd greatly lessen that party which at present gives uneasiness in New England. You will know the proper use to be made of this hint, or whether any use shou'd be made of it, before the St Christopher's money be paid or the mind of the court be declared further on that matter. I long to hear what people say or mean to do.

Newport, in Rhode Island, April 24, 1729

Dear Tom,

I can by this time say something to you, from my own experience, of this place and people.

The inhabitants are of a mixed kind, consisting of many sects and subdivisions of sects. Here are four sorts of Anabaptists, besides Presbyterians, Quakers, Independents, and many of no profession at all. Notwithstanding so many differences, here are fewer quarrels about religion than elsewhere, the people living peaceably with their neighbours, of whatever profession. They all agree in one point, that the Church of England is the second best. The climate is like that of Italy, and not at all colder in the winter than I have known it every where north of Rome. The spring is late ; but, to make amends, they assure me the autumns are the finest and longest in the world, and the summers are much pleasanter than those of Italy by all acounts, forasmuch as the grass continues green, which it doth not there. This island is pleasantly laid out in hills and vales and rising grounds ; hath plenty of excellent springs and fine rivulets, and many delightful landscapes of rocks and promontories and adjacent islands. The provisions are very good ; so are the fruits, which are quite neglected, tho' vines sprout up of themselves to an extraordinary size, and seem as natural to this soil as to any I ever saw. The town of Newport contains about six thousand souls, and is the most thriving flourishing place in all America for its bigness. It is very pretty and pleasantly situated. I was never more agreeably surprised than at the first sight of the town and its harbour. I could give you some hints that may be of use to you if you were disposed to take advice ; but of all men in the world, I never found encouragement to give you any.

By this opportunity I have drawn on Messrs. Wogan and Aspinwall for ninety-seven pounds, and shall soon draw for about five hundred pounds more. I depend on your taking care that my bills be duly paid. I hope you have well concerted that matter with Swift and Company, as I desired you. My draughts shall always be within my income ; and if at any time they should be made before payment thereof into their hands, I will pay interest. I doubt not you keep my farmers punctual.

I have heard nothing from you or any of my friends in England or Ireland, which makes me suspect my letters were in one of the vessels that wreck'd. I write in great haste, and have no time to say a word to my brother Robin. Let him know we are in good health. Once more take care that my draughts are duly honoured (which is of the greatest importance to my credit here) ; and if I can serve you in these parts, you may command

Your affectionate humble Servant,
GEOR. BERKELEY.

Send the state of my accounts and affairs, directed and enclosed to Thomas Corbet, Esq., at the Admiralty Office in London. Direct all your letters the same way. I long to hear from you.

141　TO BERNON

Monsieur,

Le promt retour du messager qui m'apportât la lettre dont vous m'aves honoré ne me permet pas de vous ecrire une response digne de votre belle prose & belle poesie : je vous remercie pour l'une & l'autre.

Vos reflexions sur les evenemens de ce monde montrent une zele tres louable pour la religion & pour la gloire de Dieu, qui dans le tems que bon semblera a sa sagesse infinie mettera fin aux schismes aux heresies a la tyrannie du Pape & aux scandales de tous façons. Pour ce qui regarde le Monsieur qui se trouve chez vous permettez moy de vous dire que comme je n'ay aucun droit de decider sur son affaire je ne trouve pas a propos de m'y meler du tout. Je prie le bon Dieu de vous conduire & tous autres la dessus en sorte que tout scandale se puisse passer. On croit qu'il feroit bien de ne pas venir a Newport pour rencontrer le Clergé jusque a ce qu'une response vien de la part de Monseigneur l'Eveque de Londres sur son sujet.

Je vous prie de me croire avec beaucoup de respect
　　Monsieur,
Votre tres humble & tres obeissant Serviteur,
GEOR. BERKELEY.

May 30 eme 1729

Newport in Rhode Island, June 12, 1729

Dear Tom,

Being informed that an inhabitant of this country is on the point of going for Ireland, I would not omit writing to you, and acquainting you that I received two of yours, dated September 23 and December 21, wherein you repeat what you formerly told me about Finney's legacy. The case of Marshall's death I had not before considered. I leave it to you to act in this matter for me as you would for yourself if it was your own case. I depend on your diligence about finishing what remains to be done, and your punctuality in seeing my money duly paid in to Swift and Company, and sending me accounts thereof.

If you have any service to be done in these parts, or if you would know any particulars, you need only send me your questions, and direct me how I may be serviceable to you. The winter, it must be allowed, was much sharper than the usual winters in Ireland, but not at all sharper than I have known them in Italy. To make amends, the summer is exceedingly delightful ; and if the spring begins late, the autumn ends proportionably later than with you, and is said to be the finest in the world.

I snatch this moment to write ; and have time only to add, that I have got a son, who, I thank God, is likely to live. My wife joins with me in her service to you.

I am, dear Tom,

Your affectionate humble Servant,

G. BERKELEY.

I find it hath been reported in Ireland that we propose settling here. I must desire you to discountenance any such report. The truth is, if the King's bounty were paid in, and the charter could be removed hither, I should like it better than Bermuda : but if this were mentioned before the payment of said money, it may perhaps hinder it, and defeat all our designs.

As to what you say of Hamilton's proposal, I can only answer at present by a question, viz. Whether it be possible for me, in my absence, to be put in possession of the Deanery of Dromore ? Desire him to make that point clear, and you shall hear farther from me.

Newport in Rhode Island, 27th June 1729

My Lord,

As I had reason to believe that before this time the St.
Christopher's money would have been returned into the exchequer,
and as we were alarmed in these parts with speedy expectation
of a war, I intended to have drawn my money out of the South
Sea Annuities into this part of the world, which in that case
would have been more convenient for my affairs. But the rumour
of a war daily decreasing and no account being come that the
St. Christopher money is yet paid into the Treasury, I think it
more advisable to let my money remain where it was.   In case
therefore it is not already taken out, I desire it may remain in
the South Sea Annuities.   The trouble I give your Lordship on
this subject is I am confident more uneasy to myself than it is to
you whose ready and obliging goodness I have so often experienced.

I am here in no small anxiety waiting the event of things.
I understand that in Ireland they have been told it is my resolution to settle here at all events.   This report I am concerned at
and would have it by all means discouraged, for it may give a
handle to the Treasury for withholding the £20,000, and at the
same time disgust my associates.   The truth is, I am not in my
own power, not being at liberty to act without the concurrence
as well of the Ministry as of my associates.   I cannot therefore
place the College where I please ; and though on some accounts
I did and do still think it would more probably be attended with
success if placed here than in Bermuda, yet if the Government
and the gentlemen engaged with me should persist in the old
scheme, I am ready to go thither, and with God's blessing actually
shall do so as soon as I hear the money is received and my associates
are arrived.   This is the truth and I beg the favour of your Lordship to mention it as often as occasion offers.   Before I left England
I was reduced to a difficult situation.   Had I continued there,
the report would have obtained (which I found beginning to
spread) that I had dropped the design after it had cost me and
my friends so much trouble and expense.   On the other hand,
if I had taken leave of my friends, even those who assisted and
approved my undertaking would have condemned my coming
abroad before the King's bounty was received.   This obliged me
to come away in the private manner that I did, and to run the

risk of a tedious winter voyage. Nothing less would have convinced the world that I was in earnest, after the report I knew
was growing to the contrary.

For my amusement in this new world I have got a little son
whom my wife nurses.

I shall trouble your Lordship no farther than with my best
wishes for yourself and family to whom
> I am,
> > A most devoted and most humble Servant,
> > GEO. BERKELEY.

Under cover to your Lordship's most humble Servant,
> HENRY NEWMAN.

144   TO NEWMAN

Rhode Island, Newport, 27th June 1729

Sir,

Since my arrival in this island I received the favour of a
packet from you, which I long since acknowledged in a letter
consigned to Mr. Marshal, who I doubt not hath forwarded the
same to you. It is needless to send you any account of this place
or climate, which you are so well acquainted with. I shall only
observe that upon the whole it seems to me a proper situation for
a college, though it must be owned that provisions are neither
so plenty nor so cheap as I apprehended. And as to the inhabitants, I find them divided in their opinions, those in the country,
or (as they are termed here) the men in the woods, being grossly
ignorant and uneducated, are not a little alarmed at the coming
of strangers, and form many fears and ridiculous conclusions thereupon. The inhabitants of the town of Newport, particularly the
Churchmen, are much better disposed towards us.

I have wrote to some friends in England to take the proper
steps for procuring a translation of the College from Bermuda to
Rhode Island as soon as the £20,000 arising by sale of lands in
St. Christopher's is paid to our order, and I have furnished them
with the weightiest reasons that occured for so doing, but I don't
think it advisable to make this proposition, or say anything about
it before the money is received. In the meantime I am understood to remain here till I hear of the said payment, and the arrival
of my associates in Bermuda where I am to join them, which

indeed is the truth of the case, supposing I should not be able to bring about the translation before-mentioned.

Believing your packets are taken particular care of, I have enclosed some letters under your cover, which I beg the favour of you to forward as directed, which will be an obligation upon,

Sir,

Your most obedt humble Servt,
GEO. BERKELEY.

145   TO PERCIVAL

Rhode Island, 30th Aug. 1729

My Lord,

I congratulate your Lordship in the share you had in redressing the villanies in the Fleet Prison, and was much pleased to find you recorded in the monthly Register, (which with us supplies the place of all other newspapers), as a principal agent in that most laudable piece of justice and charity. At the same time I return my humble thanks to your Lordship for the favour of your letter and your goodness in taking my money out of the fund and placing it in Mr. Hoare's hands : mine which I wrote to prevent your Lordship's giving yourself that trouble having it seems been sent too late. I am ashamed to desire your Lordship to put it again into the Annuities, but if this were done I should think it a great favour and be very cautious how I gave you any further trouble.

The truth is we were alarmed here by accounts of a war with Spain and that the stocks would fall, which alarm being since abated I have altered my design, so that I am now desirous to have interest for my money, and the rather because I have been at great expense since I saw you. And I know no other way of laying out my money but in the public fund, which I am told will be as secure at least as any private bankers. Rather than to break the sum of £2000 (which I would have secured for my family) I have got credit for 600 pounds at the legal interest, which Mr. Prior is to pay out of my Deanery. This enables me to perfect the purchase of my land and house in this Island, which purchase in case the College should not go on will be much to my loss. For lands within this Island being very well cleared and near an excellent harbour are very dear, at an average about

14

ten pounds sterling an acre, and it was expedient I should buy lands fit to produce provisions, and near a good seaport where they may be easily exported to Bermuda for the supply of our College. True it is that on the continent within this government uncleared lands may be bought very cheap, even for a twentieth part of the above-mentioned price ; but the clearing of them would be very expensive, and require much time, and in the interim they produce nothing. Though if they were left to lie till the colony fills, without any pains or any expense bestowed upon them, they would in time grow very valuable, and I should think this the best way of laying out my money in case the College were settled in these parts. But where it will be settled, or when is a point still in the dark, nor by what I can find likely to be cleared during the present uncertainty of public affairs. I doubt not the Treasury is backward in all payments ; but I cannot, I will not, understand that they can form any resolve to withhold a grant conveyed in such legal and authentic manner by His Majesty's patent under the broad seal, though it may possibly be postponed for some time. In the interim I must patiently wait the event and endeavour to be of some use where I am.

For the first three months I resided at Newport and preached regularly every Sunday, and many Quakers and other sectaries heard my sermons in which I treated only those general points agreed by all Christians. But on Whit-Sunday (the occasion being so proper) I could not omit speaking against that spirit of delusion and enthusiasm which misleads those people : and though I did it in the softest manner and with the greatest caution, yet I found it gave some offence, so bigoted are they to their prejudices. Till then they almost took me for one of their own, to which my everyday dress, being only a strait-bodied black-coat without plaits on the sides, or superfluous buttons, did not a little contribute.

I live now in the country and preach occasionally sometimes at Newport, sometimes in the adjacent parts of the continent. Mr. James and Mr. Dalton have taken a house at Boston ; in which town I have not yet been, though I have had several invitations and been visited in this Island by many of the principal inhabitants thereof. My family I bless God are well. My little son thrives, and we are already flattered by the neighbours upon his parts and person.

I heartily wish to your Lordship, and all that belong to you, increase of health and joy. My wife, who has a very sincere respect for your Lordship and my good Lady joins with me in these wishes, and her humble service with mine to both of you. I am with the greatest truth, My Lord,

> Your Lordship's most obliged and most obedt Servant,
> G. BERKELEY.

What might have been formerly an inconvenience is now none at all. I must therefore desire your Lordship, before my money is replaced in the funds, to take sixty guineas out of it, which money I had long since from your Lordship, and for which with many other favours I shall always hold myself obliged to you.

146   TO PRIOR

Rhode Island, March 9, 1730

Dear Tom,

My situation hath been so uncertain, and is like to continue so till I am clear about the receipt of his Majesty's bounty, and, in consequence thereof, of the determination of my associates, that you are not to wonder at my having given no categorical answer to the proposal you made in relation to Hamilton's Deanery, which his death hath put an end to. If I had returned, I should perhaps have been under some temptation to have changed ; but as my design still continues to wait the event, and go to Bermuda as soon as I can get associates and money (which my friends are now soliciting in London), I shall in such case persist in my first resolution of not holding any Deanery beyond the limited time.

I long to hear what success you have had in the law-suit. Your account of the income of the Deanery last paid in is come to my hands. I remember that one of Mrs. Van Homrigh's creditors (I think a stay-maker) was in France, and so missed of payment. I should be glad you could find some way of paying him, and any others if you find anything still due, even during the minorities of the young ladies, if in books of account charged to their credit. I suppose Mr. Marshall will agree to this ; but whether he doth or no, I think it should be done. I do therefore leave that matter to be fully accomplished by you as you can find opportunity, as perhaps some affair might call you to London, or you may have some friend there : for, in the hurry of things, I should be sorry to have overlooked any, or that any should suffer who should make out their pretensions since. I now call to mind that for this reason I withheld that forty pounds which was paid Mr. Marshall when I was in Dublin ; but this was then out of my thoughts, or I should not have ordered the payment thereof. I agree to what you propose about paying Finny's son, since it is agreeable to Mr. Marshall.

I live here upon land that I have purchased, and in a farm-house that I have built in this island. It is fit for cows and sheep, and may be of good use for supplying our College at Bermuda.

Among my delays and disappointments, I thank God I have two domestic comforts that are very agreeable, my wife and my little son ; both which exceed my expectations, and fully answer all my wishes. My wife gives her service to you ; and, at her request, I must desire you to pay, on my account, two guineas yearly to her brother's wife, towards the support of a young girl, child of my wife's nurse. The girl's name is Betty Smith. Mrs. Forster lives in Henry-street. As this is a piece of charity, I am sure you will not neglect it.

I must also desire that out of the next payment made by M'Manus, you give one hundred pounds to brother Robin, to be disposed of by him as I have directed, in pursuance of a letter I had from him ; and that the rest be paid into Swift and Company.

Messrs. James, Dalton, and Smibert, &c., are at Boston, and have been there these four months. My wife and I abide by Rhode Island, preferring quiet and solitude to the noise of a great town, notwithstanding all the solicitations that have been used to draw us thither. No more at present but that
        I am, dear Tom,
                Your affectionate humble Servant,
                  GEOR. BERKELEY.

As to what you ask about my companions, they are all at Boston, and have been there these four months, preferring that noisy town to this peaceful retreat which my wife and I enjoy in Rhode Island. Being in a hurry, I have writ the same thing twice.

I have desired M'Manus, in a letter to Dr. Ward, to allow twenty pounds *per annum* for me, towards the poor-house now on foot for clergymen's widows, in the diocese of Derry.

Rhode Island, 29th March 1730

My Lord,

About three weeks ago I had the honour of receiving one of your Lordship's of an old date. I am glad the public affairs go on so well, but sorry that the private account of your family is not equally agreeable. I long to hear that my good Lady Percival and Mrs. Dering get rid of their ailments, which I doubt will never be done but by change of air and exercise. If I should pretend to advise them to a long voyage my advice may be suspected, I can nevertheless affirm sincerely that I believe it would be the best remedy for them in the world. My wife, whose constitution had been much hurt and weakened by a long ague, found wonderful relief from sea sickness and even from the hardships and distresses of the voyage, and is now in health better than she had been for several years before.

We have passed the winter in a profound solitude on my farm in this Island, all my companions having been allured five or six months ago to Boston, the great place of pleasure and resort in these parts, where they still continue. After my long fatigue of business this retirement is very agreeable to me ; and my wife loves a country life and books so well as to pass her time contentedly and cheerfully without any other conversation than her husband and the dead.

There is no truth in what your Lordship heard of Mrs. Handcock's being married, or about to marry.

I wait here with all the anxiety that attends suspense till I know what I can depend upon or what course I am to take. On the one hand I have no notion that the Court would put what men call a bite upon poor clergymen, who depended upon charters, grants, votes, and the like encouragements. On the other hand, I see nothing done towards payment of the money. All I can do is to continue to recommend it to those who are most likely and able to push this matter, and I could do no more if I were on the spot, which makes me not follow the advice of some who have lately wrote to me to return home and solicit myself. When the Charter and grant were verified in legal form I thought all solicitation was at an end. One thing I am sure of, that if the Treasury will not issue the money in regard to his Majesty's command, subscribed by his own hand and sealed with the broad seal (which is in Dr. Clayton's custody), they will not be likely to pay it in regard to anything I can say or do. I have therefore hinted (in a letter I sent by this same opportunity) to Dr. Clayton that it would be right to go in form with his Majesty's Letter patent in his hands to the Treasury and there make his demand that we may obtain at least a public and direct answer from the proper persons. My views are still the same with regard to Bermuda, whither I am ready to set sail as soon as the money is paid.

I have many thanks to return your Lordship for your kind and friendly care in the concerns I presume to trouble you with, and hope the letter which I wrote several months ago containing my request that your Lordship will be pleased to replace my money in the South Sea Annuities is arrived safe to your hands. Wherever I am I find my self always increasing my debt of obligations to your Lordship, a grateful sense of which I shall ever preserve, and on all occasions be glad to shew how truly and faithfully,

I am, My Lord,
Yr Lordship's most obedt and most humble Servt,
GEO. BERKELEY.

My wife joins in our best respects and humble service to your Lordship and good Lady Percival. I am glad to hear that P. Courayer is taken care of. Pray my humble service to him and Mr. Dering, &c.

148 TO NEWMAN

Rhode Island, March 29, 1730

Sir,

I thank you for the favour of yours with the box of books which arrived some time ago. I gave what was directed to Mr. Honeyman and may venture to assure you that whatever you send of that kind to him will be committed to the hands of a man of sense & merit who will not fail to make the best use thereof & distribute them where they may be of most service. If there remains any thing of the money you get from Mr. Hoare please to remit it in those two small pamphlets you sent for a specimen, the one an abstract of the bible, the other a small catechetical piece.

The delay that our affair depending in the Treasury hath met with is no small discouragement & I very much apprehend it may cause an alteration in the minds of my associates. I have not failed to set this matter in its proper light & recommend it in the most earnest manner to such friends in England as I judged most able and willing to sollicit at Court. But the same reasons which determined me to come away without taking leave of my friends or waiting on men in power are still as prevalent to hinder me from soliciting in person which shou'd be my last shift and forelorn hope, being at present altogether of opinion that it may be solicited to better purpose by others than by myself.

What you observe of the growth of Atheism and Irreligion hath a fatal aspect upon England but it is no more than hath been carrying on for many years past by a set of men who under the notion of liberty are for introducing Licence and a general contempt of all laws Divine or Humane. Political societies have their diseases as well as natural bodies and this seems that which will be the death of Great Brittain. God governs the world and knows his own times and seasons : it is our duty to endeavour not be unserviceable in this our day and patiently leave the event to Providence. My wife is obliged to you for yr. kind compliment & joins with me in her respects to you.

I am Sir,

Yr most obedient Servt,
GEOR. BERKELEY.

149 TO PRIOR

Dear Tom,

Last week I received a packet from you by the way of Philadelphia, the postage whereof amounted to above four pounds of this country money. I thank you for the enclosed pamphlet, which in the main I think very seasonable and useful. It seems to me, that in computing the sum-total of the loss by absentees, you have extended some articles beyond the due proportion ; *e.g.* when you charge the *whole* income of occasional absentees in the third class : and that you have charged some articles twice ; *e.g.* when you make distinct articles for law-suits £9,000 and for attendance for employments £8,000, both which seem already charged in the third class. The tax you propose seems very reasonable, and I wish it may take effect, for the good of the kingdom, which will be obliged to you whenever it is brought about. That it would be the interest of England to allow a free trade to Ireland, I have been thoroughly convinced ever since my being in Italy, and have upon all occasions endeavoured to convince English gentlemen thereof, and have convinced some, both in and out of Parliament ; and I remember to have discoursed with you at large upon this subject when I was last in Ireland. Your hints for setting up new manufactures seem reasonable ; but the spirit of projecting is low in Ireland.

Now, as to my own affair, I must tell you that I have no intention of continuing in these parts but in order to settle the College his Majesty hath been pleased to found at Bermuda ; and I wait only the payment of the king's grant to transport myself and family thither. I am now employing the interest of my friends in England for that purpose ; and have wrote in the most pressing manner either to get the money paid, or at least to get a positive answer that may direct me what course I am to take. Doctor Clayton indeed hath wrote me word, that he hath been informed by a good friend of mine (who had it from a very great man), that the money will not be paid. But I cannot look upon a hearsay, at second or third hand, to be a proper answer for me to act upon. I have therefore suggested to the Doctor, that he ought to go himself with the letters-patent containing the grant in his hands, to the Treasury, and there make his demand in form. I have also wrote to others to use their interest at Court ; though indeed one would have thought all solicitation at an end when once I had obtained a grant under his Majesty's hand and the broad seal of England. As to going to London and soliciting in person, I think it reasonable first to see what my friends can do ; and the rather because I cannot suppose my own solicitations will be more regarded than theirs. Be assured I long to know the upshot of this matter ; and that, upon an explicit refusal, I am determined to return home ; and that it is not the least in my thoughts to continue abroad and hold my Deanery. It is well known to many considerable persons in England, that I might have had a dispensation for holding it for life ; and that I was much pressed to it, but I resolutely declined it : and if our design of a College had taken place as soon as I once hoped it would, I should have resigned before this time. A little after my first coming to this island, I entertained some thoughts of applying to his Majesty (when Dr. Clayton had received the 20,000 pounds, the patent for which I left with him), to translate our College hither ; but have since seen cause to lay aside all thoughts of that

matter. I do assure you, *bona fide,* that I have not the least intention
to stay here longer than I can get a clear answer from the Government ; for, upon all private accounts, I should like Derry better
than New England. As to the reason of my coming to this island,
I think I have already informed you that I have been at great
expence in purchasing land and stock here, which might supply
the defects of Bermuda, and so obviate a principal objection that
was made to placing a College there. To conclude, as I am here
in order to execute a design addressed for by Parliament, and set
on foot by his Majesty's royal Charter, I think myself obliged to
wait the event, whatever course is taken in Ireland about my
Deanery. I had wrote to both the bishops of Raphoe and Derry ;
but letters are of uncertain passage. Yours was half a year in
coming ; and I have had some a year after their date, though
often in two months, and sometimes less. I must desire you to
present my duty to both their Lordships, and acquaint them with
what I have now wrote to you in answer to the kind message from
my Lord of Derry, conveyed by your hands ; for which I return
my humble thanks to his Lordship.

I long to hear the success of our law-suit with Partinton. What
I hear from England about our college-grant you shall know.

My wife gives her service to you. She hath been lately ill of
a miscarriage ; but is now, I thank God, recovered. Our little
son is great joy to us. We are such fools as to think him the
most perfect thing we ever saw in its kind. I wish you all happiness ; and remain,

Dear Tom,
Yours affectionately,
G. BERKELEY.

Rhode Island, May 7, 1730

P.S. [Sent with duplicate]

This is a duplicate of a letter I sent you several months ago.
I have not since had one line from the persons I had wrote to,
to make the last instances for the 20,000 pounds. This I impute
to an accident that we hear happened to a man of war, as it was
coming down the river, bound for Boston, where it was expected
some months ago, and is now daily looked for, with the new
governor.

The newspapers of last February mentioned Dr. Clayton's
being made bishop. I wish him joy of his preferment, since I
doubt we are not likely to see him in this part of the world.

I know not how to account for my not hearing that the dispute with Partinton is finished one way or other before this time.

Newport in Rhode Island, July 20, 1730

150   TO PERCIVAL

                                        Rhode Island, July 20th, 1730
My Lord,
        Your Lordship is entitled to more thanks than I know how to express for your kind care about my money. I waited this opportunity of a vessel going from hence, whereby I send the enclosed authorities drawn in the most authentic manner, and which I suppose will enable your Lordship to do what you are so good to take upon you.
        I must beg leave to repeat and insist upon your Lordship's paying yourself out of the first money that shall become due on my South Sea Annuities, and am concerned this was not done sooner. Be pleased therefore my good Lord to put your humble servant (who hath a thousand other favours to acknowledge) to no further confusion on this head.
        I have not heard from Dr. Clayton since he was made Bishop. I take him to be a man of worthy views and heartily wish success to his endeavours of being useful in that station since we are not likely to see him in this part of the world.
        The enclosed letter to Mr. Archdeacon Benson I entreat your Lordship to send by a careful hand as directed. I appoint him to take care of our College affairs instead of the Bishop of Killala, and to take into his custody the Patents and the College seal, and papers that were left with his Lordship. He is a true friend to me and the undertaking, and nobody hath better inclinations or more opportunity to do it service. I long to know the issue of his endeavour, and what course I am to take, or what to expect.
        I already informed your Lordship that I hold myself in readiness to go to Bermuda, and I beg that you will take occasion to do me justice in that particular, because I understand the contrary hath been given out, though without any truth or foundation, since I have for this year past taken all possible pains to undeceive the people and contradict that report. Bermuda after all is the proper place, for, besides that the £20,000 were addressed for

by Parliament and granted by the Crown for that individual spot, there are other reasons which lie against placing the College here, particularly the extreme dearness of labour and the difficulty of getting Indians, the number whereof is very inconsiderable in this part of America, having been consumed by wars and strong liquors, not to mention some other particulars wherein I take Bermuda to have the advantage.

As for the raillery of European wits, I should not mind it if I saw my College go on and prosper ; but I must own the disappointments I have met with in this particular have nearly touched me, not without affecting my health and spirits. If the founding of a College for the spreading of religion and learning in America had been a foolish project, it cannot be supposed the Court, the Ministers, and the Parliament, would have given such public encouragement to it ; and if, after all that encouragement, they who engaged to endow and protect it, let it drop, the disappointment indeed may be to me, but the censure, I think, will light elsewhere.

My best wishes wait on your Lordship, my good Lady Percival, and all your family. I wrote to Mr. Dering but have not heard from him. I shall ever be glad to hear that good health and prosperity attend you all.

I am sorry that I live in a country that resembles England so much in its produce of every kind, that here is not any one curiosity worth sending, otherwise I would not have been unmindful of my duty to my Lady. Be pleased to accept of mine and of my wife's respects and believe that I am with the greatest truth and gratitude,

Your Lordship's most obedient and most humble Servant,
G. BERKELEY.

151   TO PERCIVAL

Rhode Island, 2nd March 1730/31

My Lord,

I was very much concerned at an account I met with not long since in the public papers of Dan Dering's death and the disposal of his employments. His good qualities and long intimate acquaintance (things that I myself shared in and was long a witness of) I doubt not endeared him to your Lordship as much as the nearness of relation. I am sincerely touched with everything that affects your Lordship and your family, but on this occasion I was sensibly affected on my own account.

I have received such accounts on all hands both from England and Ireland that I now give up all hopes of executing the design which brought me into these parts. I am fairly given to understand that the money will never be paid. And this long continued delay and discountenance hath (as I am informed by several letters) made those persons who engaged with me entirely give up all thoughts of the College and turn themselves to other views. So that I am absolutely abandoned by every one of them. This disappointment which long lay heavy upon my spirits I endeavour to make myself easy under, by considering that we even know not what would be eventually good or bad, and that no events are in our power. Upon the whole my thoughts are now set towards Europe, where I shall endeavour to be useful some other way.

What they foolishly call free thinking seems to me the principal root or source not only of opposition to our College but of most other evils in this age, and as long as that frenzy subsists and spreads, it is in vain to hope for any good either to the mother country or colonies, which always follow the fashions of Old England. I am credibly informed that great numbers of all sorts of blasphemous books published in London are sent to Philadelphia, New York, and other places, where they produce a plentiful crop of atheists and infidels, I am to think more from an affectation of imitating English customs (which is very prevalent in America) than from any other motive.

My wife and child are both I thank God very well, and very much, together with myself, humble servants to your Lordship and my good Lady. My wife is big with child and so far gone that we cannot safely put to sea least she should be brought to bed on shipboard. As soon as this event is over and that she and her infant can put to sea, I propose with God's blessing to return. I pray God preserve your Lordship and good family and remain with sincere affection and respect,

My Lord,
Your Lordship's most obedt and most obliged humble Servant,
G. BERKELEY.

213

152 TO JOHNSON

Rev. Sir,

I am now upon the point of setting out for Boston, in order to embark for England. But the hurry I am in could not excuse my neglecting to acknowledge the favour of your letter. In answer to the obliging things in it, I can only say I wish I might deserve them.

My endeavours shall not be wanting, some way or other, to be useful ; and I should be very glad to be so in particular to the College at Newhaven, and the more as you were once a member of it, and have still an influence there. Pray return my service to those gentlemen who sent their complements by you.

I have left a box of books with Mr. Kay, to be given away by you—the small English books where they may be most serviceable among the people, the others as we agreed together. The Greek and Latin books I would have given to such lads as you think will make the best use of them in the College, or to the School at Newhaven.

I pray God to bless you, and your endeavours to promote religion and learning in this uncultivated part of the world, and desire you to accept mine and my wife's best wishes and services, being very truly,

Rev. Sir,
Your most humble Servant,
GEORGE BERKELEY.

Rhode Island, Sep. 7, 1731

153 TO JOHNSON

London, July 25, 1732

Rev. Sir,

Some part of the benefactions to the College of Bermuda, which I could not return, the benefactors being deceased, joined with the assistance of some living friends, has enabled me without any great loss to myself, to dispose of my farm in Rhode Island in favor of the College in Connecticut. It is my opinion that as human learning and the improvements of Reason are of no small use in religion, so it would very much forward those ends, if some of your students were enabled to subsist longer at their studies, and if by a public tryal and premium an emulation were inspired into all. This method of encouragement hath been found useful in other learned societies, and I think it cannot fail of being so in one where a person so well qualified as yourself has such influence, and will bear a share in the elections. I have been a long time indisposed with a great disorder in my head ; this makes any application hurtful to me, which must excuse my not writing a longer letter on this occasion.

The letter you sent by Mr. Beach I received, and did him all the service I could with the Bishop of London and the Society. He promised to call on me before his return, but have not heard of him, so am obliged to recommend this pacquet to Mr. Newman's care. It contains the instrument of conveyance in form of law, together with a letter for Mr. President Williams, which you will deliver to him. I shall make it my endeavor to procure a benefaction of books for the College library, and am not without hopes of success. There hath of late been published here a treatise against those who are called Free Thinkers, which I intended to have sent to you and some other friends in those parts, but on second thoughts suspect it might do mischief to have it known in that part of the world what pernicious opinions are boldly espoused here at home. My little family, I thank God, are well. My best wishes attend you and yours. My wife joins her services with mine. I shall be glad to hear from you by the first opportunity after this hath come to your hands. Direct your letter to Lord Percival at his house in Pall Mall, London, and it will be sure to find me wherever I am. On all occasions I shall be glad to show that

I am very truly, Rev. Sir,

Your faithful humble Servt,
GEOR. BERKELEY.

154   TO PRIOR

Dear Tom,

I thank you for the good account you sent me of the house, &c., in Arbor Hill. I approve of that and the terms ; so you will fix the agreement for this year to come (according to the tenor of your letter) with Mr. Lesly, to whom my humble service. I remember one of that name, a good sort of man, a class or two below me in the College.   I am willing to pay for the whole year commencing from the 25th instant ; but cannot take the furniture, &c., into my charge till I go over, which I truly propose to do as soon as my wife is able to travel.   But, as I told you in my last, my wife expects to be brought to bed in two months ; and having had two miscarriages, one of which she was extremely ill of in Rhode Island, she cannot venture to stir before she is delivered. This circumstance not foreseen, occasions an unexpected delay, putting off to summer the journey I proposed to take in spring. Mr. Lesly, therefore, or whoever is at present in it, may continue there gratis for about three months to come.

I hope our affair with Partinton will be finished this term.   We are here on the eve of great events, to-morrow being the day appointed for a pitched battle in the House of Commons.   I hope to hear from you speedily, particularly on the subject of my two last letters.   I have no objection to you setting the Deanery to Messrs. Skipton and Crookshanks for two years, as you propose, provided the security be good.   My wife gives her service to you ; and my son, who (I thank God) is very well, desires me to send his love and service to Mr. *Puddleya.*

I am,
Your affectionate humble Servant,
G. BERKELEY.

Green-street, March 13, 1732/33

155   TO PRIOR

London, March 27, 1733

Dear Tom,

This comes to desire you'll exert yourself on a public account, which you know is acting in your proper sphere.   It has been represented here, that in certain parts of the kingdom of Ireland, justice is much obstructed for the want of justices of the peace, which is only to be remedied by taking in dissenters.   A great man hath spoke to me on this point.   I told him the view of this was plain ; and that, in order to facilitate this view, I suspected the account was invented, for that I did not think it true.   Depend upon it, better service cannot be done at present than by putting this matter as soon as possible in a fair light, and that supported by such proofs as may be convincing here. I therefore recommend it to you to make the speediest and exactest inquiry that you can into the truth of this fact ; the result whereof send to me. Send me also the best estimate you can get of the number of papists, dissenters, and churchmen, throughout the kingdom ; an estimate also of dissenters considerable for rank, figure, and estate ; an estimate also of the papists in Ulster. Be as clear in these points as you can. When the above-mentioned point was put to me, I said that in my apprehension there was no such lack of justices or magistrates except in Kerry and Connaught, where the dissenters were not considerable enough to be of any use in redressing the evil. Let me know particularly whether there be any such want of justices of the peace in the county of Londonderry ; or whether men are aggrieved there by being obliged to repair to them at too great distances. The prime serjeant, Singleton, may probably be a means of assisting you to get light in these particulars. The dispatch you give this affair will be doing the best service to your country. Enable me to clear up the truth, and to support it, by such reasons and testimonies as may be felt or credited here. Facts I am myself too much a stranger to, though I promise to make the best use I can of those you furnish me with, towards taking off an impression which I fear is already deep. If I succeed, I shall congratulate my being here at this juncture.

Yours,

G. Berkeley.

156   TO PRIOR

Green-street, April 14, 1733

Dear Tom,

I thank you for your last, particularly for that part of it wherein you promise the numbers of the justices of the peace, of the Papists also, and of the Protestants, throughout the kingdom, taken out of proper offices. I did not know such inventories had been taken by public authority, and am glad to find it so. Your argument for proving Papists but three to one, I had before made use of ; but some of the premises are not clear to Englishmen. Nothing can do so well as the estimate you speak of, to be taken from a public office ; which therefore I impatiently expect.

As to the design I hinted, whether it is to be set on foot there or here I cannot say. I hope it will take effect nowhere. It is yet a secret. I may nevertheless discover something of it in a little time ; and you may then hear more.

The political state of things on this side the water I need say nothing of. The public papers probably say too much ; though it cannot be denied much may be said.

I would have Petit Rose's fine, and the deficiencies of the last payments of the Deanery farms, paid into Swift and Company to answer my demand. As soon as this is done, pray let me know, that I may draw accordingly.

I must desire you, in your next, to let me know what premium there is for getting into the public fund, which allows five *per cent.* in Ireland ; and whether a considerable sum might easily be purchased therein ? Also, what is the present legal interest in Ireland ? and whether it be easy to lay out money on a secure mortgage where the interest should be punctually paid ?

I shall be also glad to hear a word about the law-suit.

I am, dear Tom,

Your affectionate humble Servant,

G. BERKELEY.

My wife and child's service to you.

157   TO PRIOR

April 19, 1733

Dear Tom,

Not finding Mr. Percival at home, I got his valet-de-chambre and another Irish servant to witness to the letter of attorney ; which herewith I send you back. You may farm the Deanery to the persons mentioned, since you find their security to be good, for two years. I thank you for your last advices, and the catalogue of justices particularly ; of all which the proper use shall be made. The number of Protestants and Papists throughout the kingdom, which in your last but one you said had been lately and accurately taken by the collectors of hearth-money, you promised, but have omitted to send. I shall hope for it in your next. The enclosed subpœna (as I take it to be) was left two days ago at my lodging by an unknown person. As I am a stranger to what hath been done or is doing in the suit with Partinton, I thought proper to transmit it unto you; who, upon perusal thereof, will know or take advice what is to be done, without delay, to avoid further expence or trouble, which may be incurred by neglect of this *billet doux*. In your next let me know your thoughts on this and the whole affair. My wife and child give their service. We are all glad to hear of your welfare.

I am, dear Tom,

Yours sincerely,

GEOR. BERKELEY.

158   TO PRIOR

Dear Tom,

I long for the numeration of Protestant and Popish families, which you tell me has been taken by the collectors. A certain person now here hath represented the Papists as seven to one; which, I have ventured to affirm, is wide of the truth. What lights you gave me I have imparted to those who will make the proper use of them. I do not find that any thing was intended to be done by act of parliament here. As to that, your information seems right. I hope they will be able to do nothing anywhere.

I give my consent to your setting the Deanery for three years, and for postponing the later payment to the first of July in consideration that it will, as you say, produce punctual payment. As to a gardener, I do not design to hire one into my service, but only employ him by the job. Your letter of attorney I sent back to you, signed and witnessed, the following post after I had received it.

The approaching Act at Oxford is much spoken of. The entertainments of music, &c., in the theatre, will be the finest that ever were known. For other public news, I reckon you know as much as

Your affectionate humble Servant,

GEOR. BERKELEY.

My wife sends her service. She is well for one in her circumstances; so is my little boy. Your letter came not to my hands before yesterday. Let me hear if you know any fair man, of a clear estate, that wants two or three thousand pounds at $5\frac{1}{2}$ per cent. on mortgage.

London, May 1, 1733

London, May 31, 1733

Revd Sir,

    I thought I could not better apply the benefactions of certain persons who left them to my disposal than in purchasing a collection of usefull books for the publick Library of your College, which books are contained in eight cases & accompany this letter. I earnestly hope that the pious intentions of the benefactors may be answer'd in the use of this Gift for the increase of Religion and Learning.   These cases of books are consigned by Mr. Henry Newman to Mr. Belcher (son of the Govr) merchant at Boston who will deliver them to your order ; the freight to Boston hath been paid here.   I wrote to you last summer by the same Vessel wch brought a deed for conveying the farm I formerly possessed in Rhode Island to the use of your College ; but have not since heard from you.   I remain with sincere wishes that true learning and Piety may ever grow and flourish among you,

                Sir,

                    Your obedient humble Servt,
                    GEORGE BERKELEY.

London, 31 May 1733

Revd Sir,

    being desirous so far as in me lies to promote sound learning and true religion in your part of the world I judged that the purchasing a good collection of books for the library of Yale College might be a proper application of the liberality of certain publick spirited persons who left it to my disposal accordingly I have sent herewith 8 cases of books, I think well chosen which I heartily wish may shed a copious light in that remote wilderness, and answer the worthy intentions of the benefactors.   The aforementioned cases of books are consigned by Mr. Hen Newman to Mr. Belcher son of the Govr at Boston.   I had a letter from you dated in last December wherein you intimate some defect in the expression of the instrumt conveying the farm in Rhode Island to the use of Yale College in wch benefaction, as I told you before.

I had but a small share. I know not particularly wherein that defect consists ; and as I have heard nothing from the Presidt or College, I must desire you to place this matter in a clear light and shew how it may be rectified. If you think a (Lre) of Attorney empowering certain persons there to make a conveyance in such terms as shall best answer the design would be the proper means, let me know ; and name the persons you would have joyned with yourself (for there should be 2 or 3 to provide in case of mortality or accidents) and I will send you such (Lre) of Attorney. In order to which it might be proper to send me a patern thereof conformable to the advice of your own Lawyers. Though I should be gone to Ireland, Mr. Henry Newman will forward any letters to me. This Gentleman is I doubt not by reputation, if not by person, known to you and to all New England for the service of which as he is very zealous ; so letters directed to him will be very safe. In order to preserve the books I doubt not the College [doubt not] will think fit to make proper statutes and regulations ; particularly in lending them out, it would seem convenient that the full price (if not the double) of the book lent should be lodg'd in the hands of the Prsident by way of caution or security. I hope this will find you and your family well. My wife and I join our services to you. I thank God my health seems on the mending hand. I write by this same opportunity to Mr. Williams Rector of the Colledge. Pray give my service to any friends in your Colony not forgetting Mr. Elliot in particular.

I am, Revd Sir, with great truth,

Your most faithfull humble Servt,
GEORGE BERKELEY.

161   TO WADSWORTH

London, May 31st, 1733

Revd Sir,

With this letter I take the liberty to introduce a box of books containing all the Latin Classick Authors in quarto being of the fairest editions and the best comments for the use of your Society. This is owing to certain well disposed who having made me the steward of their liberality I thot it might in part answer their views for the encouragement of usefull Learning if I shoud send to your Colledge at new Cambridge the fore-mentioned books which as they seemed to me wanting in your Publick Library so I am persuaded there are not wanting those in your Society who will make the proper use of them. I remain with sincere wishes that piety and learning may flourish among you,

Sir,

Your obedient humble Servt,

GEORGE BERKELEY.

The box is markt CC and consign'd by Mr. Henry Newman to Mr. Belcher the Governor's son at Boston.

162   TO WILLIAMS

London, August 27, 1733

Revd Sir,

I am to thank you for the favour of your letter with the copy of a printed poem wherein the ingenious author has made me undue compliments. I am in good hopes that the Donation to Yale College, in procuring whereof I was instrumental, will under the management of a person of your prudence and abilities be found to answer its end, to wit the encouragement of useful learning. In the former deed transmitted to you, containing that Donation, I understand that there was some mistake in the titles or naming of the Grantees : which mistake I have endeavor'd to correct, and also made some small additions in another deed, that will be convey'd to you with this letter. It will be in your option which deed to abide by, and to cancel the other. I have sent herewith all the titles and papers relating to the estate which I had upon my purchase thereof. The library of books for your college is, I hope, safely arrived : the catalogue of them is sent by this conveyance. The disorder in my head and the short warning on which I write will permit me only to add my best respects to your self and the rest of yr learned Society, and to assure you that

I remain,

Your faithful humble Servant,

G. BERKELEY.

163 TO PERCIVAL

London, Thursday noon [c. 6 November 1733]

My Lord,

This morning I endeavoured to have waited on your Lordship at your house in Pall Mall, but was told there that you intend going tomorrow from Charlton to Bath, I therefore take this opportunity of congratulating your Lordship on your new honour, which I most heartily wish yourself and your posterity may long enjoy with the greatest prosperity. How just a title you have to it, I endeavoured to say in the preamble, a rough draught whereof I had some time since put into my young Lord Percival's hands to be perused by you, intending nevertheless when I had your Lordship's thoughts thereupon to have reviewed and corrected it. The theme was ample, but I was straitened by your Lordship's commands which I shall always think it my duty to obey. Whatever defects you observe in it I beg you to impute not to want of care or zeal, but to the disorder in my head which is very great and renders me more unfit for things of that kind than I have formerly been. I thank your Lordship for the American pacquet you have pleased to forward my wife, which she is still hourly expecting.

I conclude with both our humble services, and best wishes of health and happiness to your self, and the good countess of Egmont.

My Lord,

Yr Lordship's most obedient and most humble Servant,

G. BERKELEY.

164 TO PRIOR

Green-street, London, Jan. 7, 1733/34

Dear Tom,

I did not intend you should have made the proposal to the B. of D.; but since you did, am well enough pleased with his answer. Only I would have the matter understood as proposed and transacted by yourself, without my privity, as indeed it was. I had myself thought of a preferment, a sinecure in the North, formerly possessed by old Charles Lesly. I took it to be the chancellorship of Connor, and imagined it might have been in the gift of the Crown ; but do now believe it to be that you mention, possessed by Dr. Wetherby, and in the Bishop's disposal. I must desire that your next step may be to inform yourself precisely what the Deanery and that Chancellorship are each at this present time actually set for ; and not to say a word of the notion I have conceived (which is indeed an hypothetical one) to any mortal : but only, as soon as you have informed yourself, to send me an account of the foresaid values.

My family are, I thank God, all well at present ; but it will be impossible for us to travel before the spring. As to myself, by regular living, and rising very early (which I find the best thing in the world), I am very much mended ; insomuch, that though I cannot read, yet my thoughts seem as distinct as ever. I do therefore, for amusement, pass my early hours in thinking of certain mathematical matters, which may possibly produce something.

I doubt not you have done as I advised in settling accounts with M'Manus ; at least that you have his bonds till he pay what is due. You say nothing of the law-suit ; I hope it is to surprise me in your next with an account of its being finished.

Perhaps the house and garden on Montpelier-hill may be got a good pennyworth ; in which case, I should not be averse to buying it, as also the furniture of the bed-chambers and kitchen, if they may be had cheap. It is probable a tenement in so remote a part may be purchased at an easy rate. I must, therefore, entreat you not to omit inquiring in the properest manner about it, and sending me the result of your inquiry. You'll be so good as to take care of the inclosed letter. My wife's and son's services wait on you.

I am, dear Tom,

Your affectionate humble Servant,

G. BERKELEY.

165   TO PRIOR

London, Jan. 15, 1733/34

Dear Tom,

I received last post your three letters together ; for which advices I give you thanks. I had at the same time two from Baron Wainwright on the same account.

That, without my intermeddling, I may have the offer of somewhat, I am apt to think, which may make me easy in point of
situation and income, though I question whether the dignity will
much contribute to make me so.   Those who imagine (as you
write) that I may pick and choose, to be sure think that I have
been making my court here all this time, and would never believe
(what is most true), that I have not been at the Court or at the
Minister's but once these seven years.   The care of my health,
and the love of retirement, have prevailed over whatsoever
ambition might have come to my share.

I approve of the proposal you make from Mr. Nichols for my
continuing the tenement upon Arbor Hill, at the same rent, till
I go over and can make a judgment thereupon.   As soon as any
thing is done here, you shall be sure to hear from me ; and if
any thing occurs there (or even if there doth not), I should be
glad to hear from you.   We are all well at your service.

I am, dear Tom,

Your affectionate humble Servant,
G. BERKELEY.

It was something odd that yours of January 1st should not
come to my hands till the 13th at night.

Pray send me as particular an account as you can get of the
country, the situation, the house, the circumstances of the bishopric
of Cloyne ; and let me know the charges of coming into a bishopric
i.e. the amount of the fees and first-fruits.

I remain,
Yours, &c.

166   TO PRIOR

Dear Tom,

Since my last I have kissed their Majestys hands for the
Bishopric of Cloyne, having first received an account from the
Duke of Newcastle's office, setting forth that his Grace had laid
before the King the Duke of Dorset's recommendation, which was
readily complied with by his Majesty.   The condition of my own
health, and that of my family, will not suffer me to travel in this
season of the year.   I must therefore intreat you to take care of
the fees and patent, which Mr. Delafoy tells me will be perfected
there in consequence of the King's warrant sent to Mr. Cary.   Let

me know what the fees amount to. There is some proper person who does business of that kind to whom you need only pay the fees ; which I will draw for as soon as you let me know the sum. I shall be glad to hear from you what particulars you can learn about this Bishopric of Cloyne. I am obliged to conclude in haste,

Dear Tom,

Your affectionate humble Servant,

G. BERKELEY.

London Jan. 19, 1733/34

167   TO PRIOR

Dear Tom,

On the sixth instant the Duke sent over his plan, wherein I was recommended to the Bishopric of Cloyne. On the fourteenth I received a letter from the secretary's office, signifying his Majesty's having immediately complied therewith, and containing the Duke of Newcastle's very obliging compliments thereupon. In all this I was nothing surprised ; his Grace the Lord Lieutenant having declared, on this side the water, that he intended to serve me the first opportunity, though at the same time he desired me to say nothing of it. As to the A. B. D. I readily believe he gave no opposition. He knew it would be to no purpose ; and the Queen herself had expressly enjoined him not to oppose me. This I certainly knew when the A. B. was here, though I never saw him. Notwithstanding all which I had a strong *penchant* to be Dean of Dromore, and not to take the charge of a Bishopric upon me. Those who formerly opposed my being Dean of Downe, have thereby made me a Bishop ; which rank, how desirable soever it may seem, I had before absolutely determined to keep out of.

The situation of my own and my family's health will not suffer me to think of travelling before April. However, as on that side it may be thought proper that I should vacate the Deanery of Derry, I am ready, as soon as I hear the Bishopric of Cloyne is void, by Dr. Synge's being legally possessed of the See of Ferns, to send over a resignation of my Deanery ; and I authorize you to signify as much where you think proper. I should be glad you sent me a rude plan of the house from Bishop Synge's description, that I may forecast the furniture. The great man whom you mention as my opponent concerted his measures but ill ; for it appears by your letter, that at the very time when my brother informed the Speaker of his soliciting against me there, the Duke's plan had already taken place here, and the resolution was passed in my favour at St. James's. I am nevertheless pleased, as it gave me an opportunity of being obliged to the Speaker, which I shall not fail to acknowledge when I see him, which will probably be very soon, for he is expected here as soon as the Session is up. My family are well, though I myself have gotten a cold this sharp foggy weather, having been obliged, contrary to my wonted custom, to be much abroad paying compliments and returning visits. We are all at your service ; and

I remain, dear Tom,

Yours affectionately,

GEOR. BERKELEY.

London, Jan. 22, 1733/34

168   TO PRIOR

London, Jan. 28, 1733/34

Dear Tom,

In a late letter you told me the Bishopric of Cloyne is let for 1,200 pounds *per annum*, out of which there is a small rent-charge of interest to be paid. I am informed by a letter of yours which I received this day, that there is also a domain of 800 acres adjoining to the episcopal house. I desire to be informed by your next whether these 800 acres are understood to be over and above the 1,200 pounds *per annum*, and whether they were kept by former bishops in their own hands ?

In my last, I mentioned to you the impossibility of my going to Ireland before spring, and that I would send a resignation of my Deanery, if need was, immediately upon the vacancy of the See of Cloyne. I have been since told that this would be a step of some hazard, viz. in case of the King's death, which I hope is far off. However, one would not care to do a thing which may seem incautious and imprudent in the eye of the world ; not but that I would rather do it than be obliged to go over at this season. But, as the bulk of the Deanery is in tithes, and a very inconsiderable part in land, the damage to my successor would be but a trifle upon my keeping it to the end of March. I would know what you advise on this matter.

My wife and children are, I thank God, all well at present, and join in service to you.

> I am, dear Tom,
>> Your affectionate humble Servant,
>>> G. BERKELEY.

Not long since I sent you inclosed a letter for my brother Robin, which I desired you to deliver to him. It contained a bill of forty pounds upon Swift and Company, to be received and disposed of by him. But as you make no mention of this letter, and I have had no account of its coming to hand, I begin to apprehend it might have miscarried ; in which case I desire you to inquire at Swift's, &c., to give warning. Pray let me hear next post.

169 TO PRIOR

Dear Tom,

The post is just going out, so I have time only to tell you that I have altered my mind about the house on Monpelier hill. To have two houses to furnish at once would be an indiscreet expence. If therefore you have not yet given my last answer to the landlord, I would have you say that I have no further thoughts of it. But if you have already told him that I will continue till I see it, I must abide by what I authorised you to say. However I hope and wish it may not be too late.

> I am, Dr Tom,
>> Yrs affectionately,
>>> G. BERKELEY.

London, Feb. 1st, 1733/34

170 TO PRIOR

Dear Tom,

This comes to tell you that I have been for several days laid up with the gout. When I last wrote to you I was confined ; but at first knew not whether it might not be a sprain or hurt from the shoe : but it soon shewed itself a genuine fit of the gout in both my feet, by the pain, inflammation, swelling, &c., attended with a fever and restless nights. With my feet lapp'd up in flannels, and raised on a cushion, I receive the visits of my friends, who congratulate me on this occasion as much as on my preferment.

As to Bishop Synge's furniture, we shall be able to judge upon seeing it, which will be as soon as possible. His stock and his overseer will, I think, suit my purpose, especially if I keep the lands in my own hands ; concerning which I would know your opinion ; as also, whether that domain be reckoned in the income of 1,200 pounds *per annum*. I conclude with my wife and son's compliments to you.

Dear Tom,

Your affectionate humble Servant,

G. BERKELEY.

London, Feb. 7, 1733/34

171   TO PRIOR

London, Feb. 19, 1734

Dear Tom,

Now I have been confined three weeks by the gout, an unusual length for the first fit ; but my friends and physician think it will be of so much the more service to me in carrying off the dregs of my long indisposition, and clearing my head. I have had it successively in my feet, head, stomach, and one knee. It is now got into my feet again, but is comparatively very gentle. I hope to get soon abroad : but I shall have some business to do beside the taking leave of my friends, and pre-paring things for my departure for Ireland ; where, I am sure, I long to be more than any one there can long to see me. I must, however, neither hurt my health, after the tenderness of a long confinement, nor neglect things absolutely necessary. And to make people concerned as easy as I am able, I by this post send inclosed to Baron Wainwright a formal resignation of my deanery.

Yours,

GEOR. BERKELEY.

London, Feb. 23, 1733/34

Dear Tom,

In a late letter, you told me that the wardenship of Tuam, to which I had no title, was inserted in my patent. But some time since I received a letter from one Mr. Rugge, a class-fellow of mine in the College, dated from Youghall, of which town he tells me I am Warden. Now, it comes into my head that there may be a mistake in the patent of Tuam for Youghall, which mistake may deprive me of a considerable part of the Bishop's income. I must therefore desire you to look into the patent in order to clear up this point, and let me know how to rectify it. Bishop Synge (from whom I have not yet heard) and Mr. Lingen can tell how this matter stands, and what is to be done. Pray send me the favour of a line by next post on this head.

I have not yet received M'Manus's account for the last year of his farming ; so I cannot justly say, but I expected a much greater balance in his hands than 50 pounds. You perceive, by the 20 pounds overcharged for the widows, how requisite it is that his accounts be sharply looked after, especially in the great article of paying the curates, concerning which I already wrote you my thoughts. As I confide that affair to your care, I trust you will look sharp, and not suffer me to be imposed on. I need not mention that no deductions are to be made by Mr. Skipton for cures, since, in pursuance to your letter, I agreed they should be paid out of the profits of the foregoing year. Pray, in your next, let me know when I may expect Mr. Skipton's payments, that I may order my affairs accordingly ; and whether my brother be gone to Cloyne. I have sent a resignation of the Deanery to Baron Wainwright, witnessed by Dr. King, and in full form. I hope to get abroad in two days, and to be able to put on my gouty shoes. My family is well, and give their service.

Yours,

G. BERKELEY.

London, March 2, 1734

Dear Tom,

As to what you write of the prospect of new vacancies, and your advising that I should apply for a better bishopric, I thank you for your advice.   But, if it pleased God the Bishop of Derry were actually dead, and there were ever so many promotions thereupon, I would not apply, or so much as open my mouth to any one friend to make an interest for getting any of them.   To be so very hasty for a removal, even before I had seen Cloyne, would argue a greater greediness for lucre than I hope I shall ever have.   Not but that, all things considered, I have a fair demand upon the Government for expence of time and pains and money, on the faith of public charters : as likewise because I find the income of Cloyne considerably less than was at first represented. I had no notion that I should, over and above the charge of patents and first fruits, be obliged to pay between £400 and £500, for which I shall never see a farthing in return ; besides interest I am to pay for upwards of £300, which principal devolves upon my successor.   No more was I apprized of three curates, viz. two at Youghal and one at Aghada, to be paid by me.   And, after all, the certain value of the income I have not yet learned.   My predecessor writes that he doth not know the true value himself, but believes it may be about £1,200 *per annum*, including the fines, and striking them at a medium for seven years.   The uncertainty, I believe, must proceed from the fines ; but it may be supposed that he knows exactly what the rents are, and what the tithes, and what the payments to the curates ; of which particulars you may probably get an account from him.   Sure I am, that if I had gone to Derry, and taken my affairs into my own hands, I might have made considerably above £1,000 a year, after paying the curates' salaries.   And as for charities, such as school-boys, widows, &c. those ought not to be reckoned, because all sorts of charities, as well as contingent expences, must be much higher on a bishop than a dean.   But in all appearance, subducting the money that I must advance, and all expence of the curates in Youghal and Aghada, I shall not have remaining £1,000 per ann. ; not even though the whole income was worth £1,200, of which I doubt, by Bishop Synge's uncertainty, that it will be found to fall short.   I thank you for the information you gave me of a house to be hired in Stephen's Green. I should like the Green very well for situation : but I have no thoughts of taking a house in town, suddenly ; nor would it be convenient for my affairs so to do considering the great expence I must be at on coming into a small bishopric. My gout has left me. I have nevertheless a weakness remaining in my feet, and, what is worse, an extreme tenderness, the effect of my long confinement. I was abroad the beginning of this week to take a little air in the park, which gave me a cold, and obliged me to physic and two or three days' confinement. I have several things to prepare in order to my journey, and shall make all the dispatch I can. But why I should endanger my health by too much hurry, or why I should precipitate myself, in this convalescent state, into doubtful weather and cold lodgings on the road, I do not see. There is but one reason that I can comprehend why the great men there should be so urgent ; viz. for fear that I should make an interest here in case of vacancies ; which I have already assured you I do not intend to do ; so they may be perfectly easy on that score.

I am, dear Tom,

Your affectionate humble Servant,

G. BERKELEY.

174   TO PRIOR

London, March 9, 1733/34

Dear Tom,

I think what my brother and you write about the impropriety and uselessness of his going now to Cloyne very reasonable, and must intreat you to give him the inclosed letter with your own hands. I have not yet seen Mr. Roberts, but am willing to do all the service I can in relation to the affair you mention ; though I apprehend I am not likely to do much, for two reasons : *first,* because I can hardly stir abroad without catching cold, such is my tenderness after so long confinement ; *secondly,* because I apprehend there will be council heard, which makes it a judicial case, in which there is no room for favour. I shall, however, endeavour to speak for it in the best manner I can to the Lord Chancellor, Lord President, Lord Chief Justice, and to the Master of the Rolls ; which four I take to be persons of the most weight,

at least that I know, in the Privy Council. I shall attempt to
find them at home ; though in this busy time it is very difficult
to come at them there : and as for going to the Parliament House
in my present condition, I should run too great a risk to think of
it. On Monday I shall have a useful servant, whom I shall employ
in hastening things for my departure as soon as possible ; for I
sincerely long to be with you. My wife's service and mine.

I am, dear Tom,

Your affectionate humble Servant,
G. Berkeley.

175   TO PRIOR

Dear Tom,

        I received your letter, containing M'Manus's account for
the last year. I have not leisure to examine it at present ; but,
at first sight, it strikes me that he charges 20 pounds where he
should have charged but ten, i.e. to the clergymen's widows.
You'll inquire how this comes to pass.

        I am *bonâ fide* making all the haste I can. My library is to be
embarked on board the first ship bound to Cork, of which I am
in daily expectation. I suppose it will be no difficult matter to
obtain an order from the commissioners to the custom-house
officers there to let it pass duty-free, which, at first word, was
granted here on my coming from America. I wish you would
mention this, with my respects, to Dr. Coghill. After my journey,
I trust that I shall find my health much better, though at present
I am obliged to guard against the east wind, with which we have
been annoyed of late, and which never fails to disorder my head.
I am in hopes, however, by what I hear, that I shall be able to
reach Dublin before my Lord-Lieutenant leaves it. I shall reckon
it my misfortune if I do not. I am sure it shall not be for want
of doing all that lies in my power. I am in a hurry. I am obliged
to manage my health, and I have many things to do.

        I must desire you, at your leisure, to look out a lodging for us,
to be taken only by the week ; for I shall stay no longer in Dublin
than needs must. I shall want three beds for men-servants, one
bed for maid-servants, two convenient bed-chambers, a dining-
room and parlour, utensils for the kitchen and table ; for though

I believe my wife and I shall dine seldom at home, yet my family must. I imagine the house in St. Mary's parish, where I first lodged in my solitude, when I was last in Dublin, might do, if it might be had. There was only a woman and a maid in it ; and I should be glad to have as few of the people in the house as may be. Baron Wainwright I should like to be near ; but in Stephen's Green I should not like to be. But, if the aforesaid conveniences are not easily to be had in William-street, you may probably find them on the other side the water without difficulty ; and a coach soon carries me wherever I have a mind to visit. I would have the lodging taken for the 10th of April. But say nothing of this providing a lodging, nor of the time, except to my brother, who perhaps may be helpful in looking out for it.

You may remember that, upon my being made Dean of Derry, I paid the curates for the current year. The reason assigned why I should do this, will hold good for my successor, viz. because I was to have the whole tithes of the year. Pray be mindful of this.

I am, dear Tom,
Your affectionate humble Servant,
G. BERKELEY.

London, March 17, 1733/34

You will also remember to take bonds for the money, to be reimbursed for the Deanery-house.

176   TO PRIOR

Dear Tom,
Last post I received one from you, wherein you mention orders sent to clear the curates till the 5th instant. I hope you will recollect, and see that I am done by as I myself did by my predecessor on first coming into the Deanery. The same reason that was then assigned for my paying the curates for the year, though I came in so late as May, will surely hold for my successor's doing the same thing.

Your account of my income I should be glad to find true. It widely differs from what Bishop Synge writes ; and both of your accounts differ from my brother's. I would fain know what I might depend on. There may be some uncertainty in the fines

16

or tythes ; but the rents regularly and annually paid must surely be known to the bishop. By this post I inform Bishop Synge of my design to employ the person recommended by him. As for the distance, I shall know by experience how far that is inconvenient. I wish you could get money from Skipton to make up what was wanting in your hands towards paying for the patents ; for I have largely drawn of late, and shall draw again before I set out, on Swift and Company ; so that there will be little left in their hands. I shall have time to receive another letter from you before I leave this.

The agent you mentioned for the bill against the heirs of Burton and Harrison never came to me to state the case ; so I have little to say : and by what I find, it is to no purpose, for the bill is not likely to pass. I reasoned as well as I could on the little and wrong lights which I had with my Lord President ; but I found by him, that the Committee of Council have weighty reasons against passing it. I spoke also to another privy counsellor, but I doubt to no effect. There will be pleadings probably, as well as petitions, on both sides, which must determine, and in the mean time procrastinate, the fate of this bill.

There is one Mr. Cox a clergyman, son to the late Dr. Cox near Drogheda, who I understand is under the patronage of Dr. Coghill. Pray inform yourself of his character, whether he be a good man, one of parts and learning, and how he is provided for. This you may possibly do without my being named. Perhaps my brother may know something of him. I would be glad to be apprized of his character on my coming to Dublin. No one has recommended him to me ; but his father was an ingenious man, and I saw two sensible women, his sisters, at Rhode Island, which inclines me to think him a man of merit, and such only I would prefer. I have had certain persons recommended to me ; but I shall consider their merits preferably to all recommendation. If you can answer for the ingenuity, learning, and good qualities of the person you mentioned, preferably to that of others in competition, I should be very glad to serve him.

I must put you in mind of what I mentioned long since, viz. getting Dr. Helsham's note for 200 pounds under my hand, which I allowed to you, and you had allowed to Bishop Synge, who paid that sum out of my money long ago. You promised when you were here to see it cancelled, but I suppose you might have forgot it. I think the more of it at present, because I have, for want of exactness, paid the sum of sixteen pounds twice over ; and a burnt child, you know, dreads the fire.   My wife makes you her compliments.

I am, dear Tom,

Yours affectionately,

G. BERKELEY.

March 20, 1733/34

177   TO PRIOR

London, April 2, 1734

Dear Tom,

The other day Mr. Roberts called at my lodging ; where, not meeting with myself, he left your letter, a full month after its date.   I wish I had seen him, to have known more particulars of the case ; though, on second thoughts, I imagine it was not needful, for all these points will be opened by lawyers before the Attorney-General and before the Committee of Council.   I have, in compliance with your desire, talked of this affair with the Lord President, Lord Chancellor, and Master of the Rolls ; to all whom I recommended it, as far as was decent to recommend a judicial affair wherein private property is concerned.   I spoke also to one or two more of the privy council ; all the members whereof I thought equally judges of the bill.   But I find that the committee for Irish bills consists only of the Lords of the Cabinet and the Law Lords of the Council.   I tried to find my Lord Hardwicke, the Chief Justice of the King's Bench, and shall try again. To-morrow I propose to speak on the same subject to the Duke of Newcastle.   I am in no small hurry, have many things to do, and many things to think of ; but would not neglect or omit to throw in my mite towards forwarding an affair which you represent to be of national concern.

I hear of a ship going to Cork, on board of which I design to have my things embarked next week.   But it will be impossible for me to go till after Easter ; and if it was possible, would not be decent.   I propose, therefore, without fail, to set out from hence either on the Tuesday or at farthest on the Wednesday after Easter-day ; and if the lodging in Dublin be secured against that day se'ennight it will be time enough.   We would either have a furnished house to ourselves by the week, or else a house with as few inhabitants as may be.   I wrote to my brother Robin last week ; which letter I directed to the College. Let him know this when you see him. I thank you for thinking of my library's passing easily through the custom-house. It is to be sent to Messrs. Harper and Morris, as Bishop Synge directed ; who, I hope, hath apprised them of it, and recommended it to their care. I shall have occasion to draw for about a hundred pounds. I hope you'll urge Mr. Skipton to be early in his payment. My wife and son give their service to you.

I am, dear Tom,

Your affectionate humble Servant,

G. BERKELEY.

178   TO JOHNSON

London, April 4, 1734

Reverend Sir,

Your ordering matters so that every year one Scholar of the House be chosen, is quite agreeable to my intentions. As to lending out the books of your library, I think there should be made some public statute by the proper authority, which same authority may alter it, if it prove upon trial to be so inconvenient. But this rests on the trustees or governors of the College. My private opinion is, that you may, for the present, lend out books to any persons residing in the Colony, who have studied either in that or any other College, but always under the caution mentioned in my former letter—upon forfeiture whereof the book is to be returned within a limited time.

As to the Bishop of Cork's book, and the other book you allude to, the author whereof is one Baxter, they are both very little read or considered here ; for which reason I have taken no public notice of them. To answer objections already answered, and repeat the same things, is a needless as well as disagreeable task. Nor should I have taken notice of that Letter about Vision, had it not been printed in a newspaper which gave it course, and spread it through the kingdom. Beside, the Theory of Vision I found was somewhat obscure to most people ; for which reason I was not displeased at an opportunity to explain it.

Of late I have been laid up with the gout, which hath hindered me hitherto from going to Ireland to be consecrated

Bishop of Cloyne, to which his Majesty nominated me near three months ago.

The hurry I am now in, providing for my journey to Ireland, doth not allow me time to add any more than my service and best wishes to yourself, Mr. Williams, Mr. Elliot, &c.

I am, Rev. Sir,

Your faithful humble Servant,

G. BERKELEY.

When you write next, direct for me at Cloyne in Ireland.

179   TO PRIOR

London, April 16, 1734

Dear Tom,

Last Friday evening I saw Mr. Roberts for the first time. He told me he apprehended opposition from Lord Hardwicke. Next day I attempted to find my Lord, but could not. This day I saw his Lordship, but to no purpose ; for he told me the affair of the Banker's bill was finished last night. I then said nothing, but only asked him how it had gone. He told me they had made Harrison's estate liable to one moiety of the demands on the Bank, and that this was just : so the bill is passed, but with alteration ; yet such as it is hoped will not defeat the intention of it. It is very late ; and I have time only to add, that

I am,

Your affectionate humble Servant,

G. BERKELEY.

I thought I should have set out to-morrow ; but it is impossible before Monday. You shall soon hear again from me. My wife and son make their compliments.

St. Alban's, April 30, 1734

Dear Tom,

I was deceived by the assurance given me of two ships going for Cork. In the event, one could not take in my goods, and the other took freight for another port. So that, after all their delays and prevarications, I have been obliged to ship off my things for Dublin on board of Captain Leach. From this involuntary cause, I have been detained here so long beyond my intentions, which really were to have got to Dublin before the Parliament, which now I much question whether I shall be able to do ; considering that, as I have two young children with me, I cannot make such dispatch on the road as otherwise I might.

I hope Skipton's first payment hath been made ; so that you have got the money you returned, and that the rest is lodged with Swift and Company to answer my draughts ; otherwise I have overdrawn.

The lodging in Gervais-street, which you formerly procured for me, will, I think, do very well. I shall want, beside the conveniences I before mentioned, a private stable for six coach-horses ; for so many I bring with me. I shall hope for a letter from you at the post-office in Chester, giving an account of the lodging, where and what it is, &c. My wife thinks that on breaking up of the Duke's kitchen, one of his under-cooks may be got ; and that a man-cook would be a great convenience to us. If you can procure a sober young man, who is a good cook, and understands pickling and preserving, at a reasonable price, we shall be much obliged. The landlady of the lodging must, in your agreement, be obliged to furnish linen and necessaries for the table, as also to dress our meat. This is to be included in the price that we pay by the week for the lodgings. In your last, you mentioned black cattle and sheep of Bishop Synge's, which I am resolved to purchase, and had long ago signified the same to my brother, if I remember rightly. If I meet with a good ship at Chester, I propose going from thence. As for sending a ship, I doubt this will not come time enough ; and write sooner I could not, because of my uncertain situation. However, you can tell what passage-ships are on this side the water, and what is proper to be done. If a ship be sent, you will take care it is the best can be got. I have a coach and six to embark. We propose being at Chester

on Saturday evening. I write this on Tuesday morning from
St. Alban's. We are on the point of taking coach. So with my
little family's compliments and my own,

I remain

Your affectionate humble Servant,

George Berkeley.

I hope to find a letter at the post-office in Chester, informing
where the lodging is taken.

181   TO ARCHBISHOP HOADLY

My Lord,

Though upon receipt of your Grace's letter, I had ordered
the proper inquiries to be made, yet I was not enabled before
yesterday to return a satisfactory answer to it. But I believe the
following account may be depended on. As for Ballihay, there
is a Prebend so called in my Diocese, but no part thereof is impropriated : So here is a mistake in the gentlemen of the Choir.
There is a like mistake, as I am informed, with regard to the
parish of Temple-Robin, no part of which belongs to them. But
the tythes of Temple-Bodane (wch is not mentioned in your
Grace's letter) are half in the Vicar and half in the impropriater
(? tor) holding under the choir of St. Patrick's. The former share
amounts from 25 to 30 pds pannum and the impropriated share
is set at 23 pds pannum. The tythes of Killalay are equally
divided between the vicar and the impropriater. The former
share communibus annis is set for 20 pounds : the impropriater sets his for 16 pds pannum. The impropriated tythes of
Carigleamleary were set to Mr. Causabon for sixteen pds pannum.
The Vicar's moiety never exceeded twenty pds pannum. This is
the best information that could be procured by,

My Lord, yr Grace's

most obedient humble servant

Geor: Cloyne.

Cloyne March 17, 1734-5

Cloyne, 31st of May 1735

Dear Mr. Smibert,

A great variety and hurry of affairs, joined with ill state of health, hath deprived me of the pleasure of corresponding with you for this good while past, and indeed I am very sensible that the task of answering a letter is so disagreeable to you, that you can well dispense with receiving one of mere compliment, or which doth not bring something pertinent and useful. You are the proper judge whether the following suggestions may be so or no. I do not pretend to give advice ; I only offer a few hints for your own reflection.

What if there be in my neighbourhood a great trading city ? What if this city be four times as populous as Boston, and a hundred times as rich ? What if there be more faces to paint, and better pay for painting, and yet nobody to paint them ? Whether it would be disagreeable to you to receive gold instead of paper ? Whether it might be worth your while to embark with your busts, your prints, your drawings, and once more cross the Atlantic ? Whether you might not find full business at Cork, and live there much cheaper than in London ? Whether all these things put together might not be worth a serious thought ? I have one more question to ask, and that is, whether myrtles grow in or near Boston, without pots, stones, or greenhouses, in the open air ? I assure you they do in my garden. So much for the climate. Think of what hath been said, and God direct you for the best.

I am, good Mr. Smibert,

Your affectionate humble Servant,

G. CLOYNE.

P.S.—My wife is exceedingly your humble servant and joins in compliments both to you and yours. We should be glad to hear the state of your health and family. We have now three boys, doubtful which is the prettiest. My two eldest past well through the small-pox last winter. I have my own health better in Cloyne than I have either in Old England or New.

Cloyne, June 11, 1735

Reverend Sir,

It is very agreeable to find that the public examinations appointed in your College have not failed of their design in encouraging the studies of the youth educated therein. And I am particularly pleased that they have given to some of your own family an opportunity of distinguishing themselves. One principal end proposed by me was to promote a better understanding with the Dissenters, and so by degrees to lessen their dislike to our communion ; to which methought the improving their minds with liberal studies might greatly conduce, as I am very sensible that your own discreet behaviour and manner of living towards them hath very much forwarded the same effect. The employing young men, though not in orders, to read a sermon, and some part of the Liturgy, in those places where they are unprovided with churches and ministers, I always thought a reasonable and useful institution ; and though some among you were prejudiced against it, yet I doubt not their prejudices will wear off when they see the good effects of it. I should imagine it might be some encouragement to well disposed students to reflect that by employing themselves in that manner they not only do useful service to the Church, but also thereby recommend themselves in the properest manner to Holy Orders, and consequently to missions, whenever vacancies shall make way for them, or when the Society shall be enabled to found new ones.

My wife is obliged to you for your kind remembrance, and sends her compliments to you. Our little family is increased to three boys, whereof the two eldest past the small pox last winter.

I wish you and yours all happiness, and pray God to forward your good endeavours for the advancement of true religion and learning, being very truly,

Reverend Sir,

Your faithful Brother and humble Servant,

GEORGE CLOYNE.

When any from your College have encouragement to pass over to England in expectation of Holy Orders and a mission, I would have them, now I am absent myself, to apply to Dr. Benson, the bishop of Gloucester, as they were used to do to me.

He is a most worthy prelate, and attends the meetings of the Society ; and in my present situation I cannot do better service than by recommending your candidates to his protection.

184   TO TAYLOR

Cloyne, 9th October 1735

D/Sr,

I shou'd be very glad there was a Chapple of Ease established at the place you mention in your letter. But how to endow it I am at a loss. The thing I shall readily agree to but the means I doubt are not in my power—at present I am confined by my disorder but in the Spring purpose to visit those parts when I may have an opportunity of talking with you at large on this subject. In the meantime I question whether my Authority extends so far as to set out a Sinecure for the Service of such Chapple.

I am, Sir
Your most faithfull humble Servant,
GEO. CLOYNE.

185   TO JOHNSON

Cloyne, March 12, 1735/36

Reverend Sir,

My remote distance from London deprives me of those opportunities which I might otherwise have of being serviceable to your missionaries, though my inclinations are still the same. I am very glad to find persons of Mr. Arnold's character disposed to come over to our Church, which, it is to be hoped, will sooner or later prevail over all their prejudices. It were indeed to be wished that the Society was able to establish new missionaries as often as candidates offer themselves ; but I persuade myself that what their funds will allow them to do will not be wanting in favour of your natives. I have wrote to my friend the Bishop of Gloucester, desiring an allowance from the Society may be obtained for Mr. Arnold towards defraying the expenses of his voyage. But for a salary he must wait till provision can be made, or till a vacancy occurs.

It is no small satisfaction to me to hear that a spirit of emulation is raised in our scholars at Newhaven, and that learning and good sense are gaining ground among them. I do not wonder that these things should create some jealousy in such as are bigotted to a narrow way of thinking, and that this should produce uneasiness to you and other well-wishers of our Church. But I trust in God that the prudence and temper of yourself and your associates will, with God's blessing, get the better of misguided and unruly zeal, which will never be a match for the wisdom from above.

I have passed this winter at Cloyne, having been detained from Parliament by my ill-health, which is now pretty well re-established. My family are all well, and concur with me in best wishes to you and yours.
I am, Reverend Sir,

> Your most faithful, humble Servant and Brother,
> George Cloyne.

As to your postscript, I can only say that Ireland contains ten times more objects of charity, whether we consider the souls or bodies of men, than are to be met with in New England. And indeed there is so much to be done (and so few that care to do it) here at home, that there can be no expectations from hence.

186 TO JAMES

Cloyne, 30th of June 1736

Dear Sir,

In this remote corner of Imokilly, where I hear only the rumours and echoes of things, I know not whether you are still sailing on the ocean, or already arrived to take possession of your new dignity and estate. In the former case I wish you a good voyage ; in the latter I welcome you, and wish you joy. I have a letter written and lying by me these three years, which I knew not whither or how to send you. But now you are returned to our hemisphere, I promise myself the pleasure of being able to correspond with you. You who live to be a spectator of odd scenes are come into a world much madder and odder than that you left. We also in this island are growing an odd and mad people. We were odd before, but I was not sure of our having the genius necessary to become mad. But some late steps of a public nature give sufficient proof thereof.

Who knows but when you have settled your affairs, and looked about and laughed enough in England, you may have leisure and curiosity enough to visit this side of the water? You may land within two miles of my house, and find that from Bristol to Cloyne is a shorter and much easier journey than from London to Bristol. I would go about with you, and show you some scenes perhaps as beautiful as you have seen in all your travels. My own garden is not without its curiosity, having a number of myrtles, several of which are seven or eight feet high. They grow naturally, with no more trouble or art than gooseberry bushes. This is literally true. Of this part of the world it may truly be said that it is—

> ' Ver ubi longum, tepidasque præbet
> Jupiter brumas.'

My wife most sincerely salutes you. We should without compliment be overjoyed to see you. I am in hopes soon to hear of your welfare, and remain,
> Dear Sir,
> > Your most obedient and affectionate Servant,
> > > G. CLOYNE.

187   TO PRIOR

Cloyne, March 5, 1736/37

Dear Tom,
I here send you what you desire. If you approve of it, publish it in one or more of our newspapers; if you have any objection, let me know it by the next post. I mean, as you see, a brief abstract; which I could wish were spread through the nation, that men may think on the subject against next session.

But I would not have this letter made public sooner than a week after the publication of the Third Part of my *Querist*, which I have ordered to be sent to you. I believe you may receive it about the time that this comes to your hands; for, as I told you in a late letter, I have hastened it as much as possible. I have

used the same editor (Dr. Madden) for this as for the foregoing
two Parts.

I must desire you to purchase for me six copies of the Third
Part of the *Querist*, which I would have stitched in six pamphlets ;
so that each pamphlet shall contain the First, Second, and Third
Parts of the *Querist*. I would have these pamphlets covered with
marbled paper pasted on white paper, and the leaves cut and
gilt on the edges ; and you will let me know when they are done
—the sooner the better.

Our spinning-school is in a thriving way. The children begin
to find a pleasure in being paid in hard money ; which I understand they will not give to their parents, but keep to buy clothes
for themselves. Indeed I found it difficult and tedious to bring
them to this ; but I believe it will now do. I am building a work-
house for sturdy vagrants, and design to raise about two acres
of hemp for employing them. Can you put me in a way of getting
hemp-seed ; or does your Society distribute any ? It is hoped
your flax-seed will come in time.

Last post a letter from an English bishop tells me, a difference
between the king and prince is got into parliament, and that it
seems to be big with mischief, if a speedy expedient be not found
to heal the breach. It relates to the provision for his Royal
Highness's family.

My three children have been ill. The eldest and youngest
are recovered ; but George is still unwell. We are all yours truly.

Your affectionate humble Servant,
GEOR. CLOYNE.

188   TO ECLES

Cloyne, 7ber 1, 1737

Sir,

As I hold my visitation next week I shall have occasion for
a Buck out of my Lord Burlington's park : I must therefore use
the privilege his Lordship has given me, and desire you'll please
to order it to be sent on Monday next, which will oblige,

Sir,
Your very humble Servt,
GEOR. CLOYNE.

Cloyne, 7br 14, 1737

Revd. Sir,

Your letter found me confined to my bed by the cholic.
A few daies after I ordered the surveyor who is usually employed
in these parts to be sent for. He happened to be absent from the
country. Soon after I procured another from the county of
Lymeric, who set about the work ; but was interrupted and
hinderd by Mr. Smyth, from making an inward survey in small
divisions, with the quality and value of each parcel distinctly
noted, as I had ordered him to do in compliance with the desire
of your board. Beside my illness I had several lets and delaies
thrown in my way, perhaps by some who are under Mr. Smyth's
influence. Even my own agent is, I find, his tenant for two farms.
The business I perceive is somewhat odious. However you have
here enclosed what I could get done. If it be not as compleat
as I could wish, I assure you it is not for want of zeal for the
interest of your Society, which I shall alwaies be ready to serve
to the utmost of my power, being very truly their and your,

Revd. Sir,

Most faithful humble Servt,

GEOR. CLOYNE.

I have given Mr. Kelly twenty five shillings. He hath measured
the entire contents and the outline anew, and pretends his survey
to be more accurate than the former. As I desire to live well
with my neighbours, the *less* I am mentioned in this affair, the
better.

190 TO JOHNSON

Dublin, May 11, 1738

Reverend Sir,

I should not have been thus long in arrear in regard to my
correspondence with you, had I not been prevented by ill health,
multiplicity of business, and want of opportunities. When I last
heard from you I was at Cloyne, and am returning thither now
with my family, who, I bless God, are all well except myself, who
for a long time past have been troubled with an habitual colic,

nor am I yet freed from it   My wife sends you her compliments, and we both join in good wishes to you and your family.   The accounts you sent me from the College at Newhaven were very agreeable, and I shall always be glad to hear from you on that or any other subject.   I am sensible you have to do with people of no very easy or tractable spirit.   But your own prudence will direct you when and how far to yield, and what is the proper way to manage with them.   I pray God preserve you and prosper your endeavours.   And I am,

> Reverend Sir,
>> Your very faithful Servant and Brother,
>> G. CLOYNE.

191   TO EVANS

Cloyne, 7ber 7, 1738

Sir,

Two nights ago I received the favour of your letter, but deferred answering it till I should have seen Dean Bruce at my visitation ; from which the Dean happened to be detained by the illness of his son.   I am very sorry there hath arisen any difference between you ; but, as you have been silent as to particulars, and as the Dean hath mentioned nothing of it to me, either by word of mouth, letter, or message, I can do no more than in general terms recommend peace and good neighbourhood, for the providing of which my best endeavours should not be wanting.   In the meantime give me leave to assure you that I have not the least reason to entertain ill thoughts of your conduct ; and that where no blame is imputed all apology is useless.   Upon the whole, since the Dean hath not stirred in this matter, I hope it may die and be forgotten.   My wife presents her compliments, and

> I remain, Sir,
>> Yr very obedient humble Servt,
>> G. CLOYNE.

Cloyne, November 25, 1738

Reverend Sir,

My wife sends her compliments to Mrs. Gervais and yourself for the receipt &c., and we both concur in thanks for your
venison. The rain hath so defaced your letter that I cannot read
some parts of it. But I can make a shift to see there is a compliment of so bright a strain, that if I knew how to read it I am sure
I should not know how to answer it. If there was anything agreeable in your entertainment at my house, it was chiefly owing to
yourself, and so requires my acknowledgment, which you have
very sincere. You give so much pleasure to others, and are so
easily pleased yourself, that I shall live in hopes of your making
my house your inn whenever you visit these parts, which will be
very agreeable to, etc.

193   TO PRIOR

Cloyne, Feb. 8, 1740/41

Dear Tom,

I should have complied with your desire sooner, but I was
not so well able to say what method I thought best to take in this
epidemical bloody flux, that distemper not having been rife in
this town till very lately, though it had made a great progress in
other parts of this county. But this week I have cured several
by the following course ; than which nothing is easier or cheaper.
I give to grown people a heaped spoonful of rosin powdered fine,
in a little broth ; and this is repeated at the distance of six or
eight hours till the blood is staunched. To children I give a bare
spoonful not heaped. A farthing's worth of rosin (if I may judge
by my own short experience) will never fail to stop the flux of
blood, with a regular diet. Broth seems to me the most proper
diet ; and that simple, of mutton or fowl, without salt, spice, or
onions. I doubt not clysters of the same broth and rosin would
likewise have a good effect ; but this I have not yet tried. In the
first place, make some private experiments of this as you have
opportunity. If, after the bloody flux is over, a looseness remain,
chalk in boiled milk and water may remove it. I have also known

tow, dipped in brandy and thrust into the fundament, to be effectual in strengthening that sphincter. What you call a felon is called in the books a phlegmon, and often is the crisis following a fever or other distemper. I believe tar-water might be useful to prevent (or to perfect the cure of) such an evil; there being, so far as I can judge, no more powerful corrector of putrid humours. But I am making a farther enquiry, and more experiments, concerning the virtues of that medicine, which I may impart to you before it be long.

I find what you say of the two plain looms to be true, you having allowed me for them. I desire you not to forget the wheels; and to procure what seed you can, if not what I wrote for. My wife and all here join in wishing you all happiness, and hoping to see you here in May.

Adieu, dear Tom,

Your most faithful humble Servant,
G. CLOYNE.

I thank you for thinking of the French book. Let me hear your success in using the rosin.

194   TO PRIOR

Cloyne, Feb. 15, 1740/41

Dear Tom,

I must desire you to take up what money I have in Henry's and Alderman Dawson's hands, and lodge it in the bank of Swift and Company. You have their notes, so I need not draw. Upon paying this money into Swift, you will send me his account balanced.

Our weather is grown fine and warm; but the bloody flux has increased in this neighbourhood, and raged most violently in other parts of this and the adjacent counties. By new trials, I am confirmed in the use of the rosin, and do therefore send you the following advertisement, which you will communicate to the printer. We are all yours, particularly

Your affectionate
G. CLOYNE.

Faulkner's *Dublin Journal*, 17 February 1741 contains the following
letter :

Mr Faulkner,

The following being a very safe and successful cure of the
bloody flux, which at this time is become so general, you will do
well to make it publick. Take a heaped spoonful of common
rosin, powdered, in a little fresh broath, every five or six hours,
till the bloody flux is stopt ; which I always found to have
happened before a farthing's worth of rosin was spent. If, after
the blood is staunched, there remain a little looseness, this is soon
carried off by milk and water boiled with a little chalk in it.
This cheap and easy method I have tried of late, and never knew
it fail. I am your humble servant,

A. B.]

195   TO PRIOR

Cloyne, Feb. 24, 1740/41

Dear Tom,

I find you have published my remedy in the newspaper
of this day. I now tell you that the patients must be careful of
their diet, and especially beware of taking cold. The best diet
I find to be plain broth of mutton or fowl, without seasoning of
any kind. Their drink should be, till they are freed both from
dysentery and diarrhœa, milk and water, or plain water boiled
with chalk, drunk warm, e.g. about a large heaped spoonful to
a quart. Sometimes I find it necessary to give it every four hours,
and to continue it for a dose or two after the blood hath been
stopped, to prevent relapses, which ill management has now and
then occasioned. Given in due time (the sooner the better), and
with proper care, I take it to be as sure a cure for a dysentery
as the bark for an ague. It has certainly, by the blessing of God,
saved many lives, and continues to save many lives in my neighbourhood. I shall be glad to know its success in any instances you
may have tried it in. We are all yours. Adieu,

G. CLOYNE.

196 TO CLARKE

Cloyne, April 16, 1741

Revd Sir,

I have been this week very unwell with my habituall Cholic, otherwise I shou'd have sent the enclosed letter sooner. My own acquaintance in the universities is very little. At Cambridge I have never passed above two daies. I passed as many months at Oxford, but so long ago as Queen Anne's reign. And all I then knew are since dead or gone.

If your curiosity shall lead you to Lambeth, you will go on one of the Archbishop's public daies, be present at Chapel, after that deliver your letter, and stay to dine with his Grace.

I am sensible how far I am obliged and honoured by you and the rest of those Gentlemen who think of me for Vice-Chancellor. But as my ill health and distance from the University would not permit me to serve it as I could wish, so to aim at the honour without discharging the duty is what I cannot think of.

I wish you good health and all the satisfaction you propose in your voyage, and am,

Rev. Sir,
Your obedient humble Servant,
GEOR. CLOYNE.

197 TO PRIOR

Cloyne, May 19, 1741

Dear Tom,

The Physico-Theology you mention of Dr. Morgan is not the book I want ; but I should nevertheless be glad to have it, and therefore desire you to get it, with the French book of Mr. Bouillet.

Though the flax-seed came in such quantity and so late, yet we have above one half ourselves in ground ; the rest, together with our own seed, has been given to our poor neighbours, and will, I doubt not, answer, the weather being very favourable.

The distresses of the sick and poor are endless. The havoc of mankind in the counties of Cork, Limerick, and some adjacent places, hath been incredible. The nation probably will not

recover this loss in a century. The other day I heard one from
the county of Limerick say that whole villages were entirely dispeopled. About two months since I heard Sir Richard Cox say
that five hundred were dead in the parish where he lives, though
in a country I believe not very populous.

It were to be wished people of condition were at their seats
in the country during these calamitous times, which might provide
relief and employment for the poor. Certainly if these perish,
the rich must be sufferers in the end.

Sir John Rawdon, you say, is canvassing for an English election.
If he doth not lose it, I doubt his country will lose him.

Your journey hither is, it seems, put off for some time. I wish
you would hasten : the sooner the better, both for your own
health and the pleasure of your friends in this family, where we
all expect you, and think we have an annual right in you.

You have not said a word this age about our suit with Partinton.
Pray how stands that matter ?

Adieu, dear Tom.

I am your affectionate humble Servant,
G. CLOYNE.

All here salute you.

We have tried in this neighbourhood the receipt of a decoction
of briar-roots for the bloody flux which you sent me, and in some
cases found it useful. But that which we find the most speedy,
sure, and effectual cure, above all others, is a heaped spoonful
of rosin dissolved and mixed over a fire with two or three spoonfuls
of oil, and added to a pint of broth for a clyster ; which, upon once
taking, hath never been known to fail stopping the bloody flux.
At first I mixed the rosin in the broth, but that was difficult, and
not so speedy a cure.

198   TO DALTON

[1741]

When I expected to have heard you were an exile at Rome
or Paris, I am agreeably surprised to hear you are the happiest
man in London, married to a young and beautiful nymph. O
terque quaterque beate, in this degenerate age ; when so many
are afraid to marry once, you dare to do it a third time. May
all happiness and success attend your courage. Were I a Dictator,
there should be a *Jus trium uxorum* for those who magnanimously

endeavour to repair the late breaches made upon the public by famine, sickness, and wars.

Without compliment, my wife and I do sincerely congratulate your nuptials, and wish your example may prevail with those worthy batchelors Sir John James and Mr. Wolfe, who have not much time to lose. A long continuance of ill health has weaned me from the world, and made me look with indifference on the most dazzling things in it. But, so long as I live, I shall retain good wishes for my friends, and a sense of their happiness.

I look upon you now as a man who may one day be my neighbour, and take it for granted that your roving spirit is fixed in your native land, which I was heartily sorry to think had been forsaken by you and Sir John James, and am as much pleased to think myself mistaken. Sir John tells me his health can stand the climate ; and for everything else I imagine he will give the preference to his country, which, with all its faults about it, I take to be the goodliest spot of Europe.

I hope all your family are well and thriving. My little ones are so, amidst a raging epidemic (fever and bloody flux)—three sons and a daughter. But such a daughter ! so bright a little gem ! that, to prevent her doing mischief among the illiterate squires, I am resolved to treat her like a boy and make her study eight hours a day !

199   TO [WOLFE]

Dear Sir,   [1741]
I have lived so long in this Irish nook, by ill health as well as situation cut off from the ways of men and sequestered from the rest of the world . . . which nevertheless hath not effaced the memory of my friends, and good wishes for them.

You will therefore pardon me if, having no news to send, I send you instead thereof a letter of advice. Our friend Mr. Dalton is, I hear, married the third time, which shews him to be a prudent man as well as a laudable patriot. Such an example is indeed a public benefit, when the nation is drained by war and hard times, and when our gentlemen conspire to put marriage out of countenance. It is to be wished you may profit by this example, not only for the public good but for your own. Though you are far from being an old man, I will take the freedom to say you are bordering on what we call an old batchelor, a character not the most useful to the public, nor the most agreeable to him that wears it. The former point needs no common-place to clear it. For the other, give me leave to say, Mr. Dalton and I are better judges than you. Health and affluence may bear you up for some years, but when age and infirmities come on, you will feel and bewail the want of a family of your own, and the comforts of domestic life. A wife and children are blessings invaluable, which as a man cannot purchase for money, so he would sell them for no price. The privation of those that orbitas the disgrace as well as disaster both to Jews and Pagans it is miraculous that it shou'd be fashionable or affected in a Christian country. Fear is unmanly I will not therefore suppose you are afraid of a woman of your own chusing. But how shall you chuse ? Chuse her by reputation. The quicksightedness and malice of the world will not keep the faults of a woman concealed from those eyes that are not already blinded by Love. Therefore chuse first and love after. But I fear you are already tired of this impertinent letter, which yet (odious as advice is) defends a good construction as it springs from a good will and is agreeable to the sincere opinion of &c.

Before I have done give me leave to add one hint, viz., that Plato (who you know was a wise man for a Gentile) sacrificed to nature as an atonement for his not having children. Your godson exceeds my hopes. I wish I had twenty [like] George. I assure you I would rather have them than twenty thousand pounds a year.

200   TO [JAMES]

[1741]

Your letter refreshed me like a shower after a drought. I thought you had been in foreign lands, but am glad to find you have been so long in England, and your health not the worse for it. Give me leave to reckon it at least among the possibilities, that you may sometime or other come to Bath, and from thence take it in your head to make a short trajet to our coast, where you will find me with a wife, three sons, and a daughter—of starlike beauty—rejoicing literally under our fig-trees.

Your patriots surely are the most profound or the most stupid of politicians. Why they should freely and with open eyes make such a step seems a most inexplicable riddle. I have long wished well to the public, but my wishes have been so often disappointed, that public affairs are grown more my amusement than concern. But news will alwaies be entertaining.

> ' Stultorum regum et populorum continet æstus.'

I thank you for what you told me. What you sent was very agreeable, as, indeed, a line from you always will be. Here we have no news ; but this, in all this province of Munster great devastations are made by bloody fluxes, fevers, and want, which carry off more than a civil war.

Our well-bred friend whom you call the Abbé acts a becoming part ; I wish we had many more such Abbés among his brethren. Mr. Dalton, who I expected was abroad with you, is, it seems, made happy the third time (O terque quaterque beatus) ; I wish you would once [marry to have that natural comfort of children] dare to do what he does so often. Without that expedient you will lose the comforts of domestic life, that natural refuge from solitude and years which is to be found in wife and children. Mine are to me a great joy [the chief of the good things of this world], and alone capable of making a life tolerable—so much embittered by sickness as mine has been for several years. I had many symptoms of the stone, and for a long time suspected my . . . cholic to be an effect thereof. But of late I am satisfied that it is a scorbutic cholic, and that my original disease is the scurvy.

201 TO [*addressee unknown*]

[1741]

My Register who puts this letter into your hands will make my compliments also to your colleague, with my request that you would both honour me with lodging at my house which will hardly be out of your way. I am at present confined by a gentle fit of the gout which is some relief to my cholic and your visit will put me in high spirits. I have many things to say to you tête à tête. And shall no further intrude on your busy hours at present than to add that I shall reckon the greatest favor if you give me what moments you possibly can at Cloyne which will alwaies be thankfully acknowledged by etc.

Let me know when you come and I will do myself the honour to go as far as I am able or can venture to meet you.

202   TO BENSON

[1741]

I had in my late desired yr Lordship to let me know wt
was become of [M] James & Dalton.   I received a letter from
Sir John James by which I found they are both in England that
Mr. Dalton is married a third time to a young and beautiful
damsel.   I cannot wish better to all my good unmarried friends
than that they should follow his example who is a delicate con-
noisseur as to the ease and comforts of life.   I will not throw away
my artillery on your Lordship who have the Church and the
State to take care of, [and beside your own way of thinking.   I
wou'd not give one of my sons] though in my humble opinion
the care of a family wou'd interfere with neither.   Besides Mr.
Dalton who is a better judge than your Lordship of that matter
can tell you marriage lessens and divides care.   I will only say
to you that my greatest want is children.   I have but three boys
and a daughter.   And even this little daughter I wou'd not give
for the Duke of Bedford's estate.   Wolfe is a grave regular man, I
endeavor to make him a proselyte to marriage.   I think he wd
educate his children well.   My friend Sir John applauds your and
the Bishop of Oxford's conduct in parliament.   I congratulate you
both upon it.   You cou'd not have the applause of a more sincere
and incorrupt heart.   At the same [sic] it was no surprise to me
who knew you that you behaved well.   I shou'd be surprised if it
were otherwise.   The malcontents were I think beside them selves
in this last step.   I beg the favor of yr Lordship to send the enclosed
letters not knowing where to direct them.

203   TO GERVAIS

Cloyne, Jan. 12, 1741–2

Revd. Sir,

You forgot to mention your address, else I shd. have
sooner acknowledged the favor of your letter, for which I am
much obliged, though the news it contained had nothing good but
the manner of telling it.

I had much rather write you a letter of congratulation than of
comfort ; and yet I must needs tell you for your comfort, that I
apprehend you miscarry by having too many friends.   We often
see a man with one only at his back pushed on and making his
way, while another is embarrassed in a croud of well-wishers.

The best of it is, your merits will not be measured by your success. It is an old remark that the race is not alwaies to the swift. But at present who wins it, matters little. For all Protestant Clergymen are like soon to be at par ; if that old priest your Countryman continues to carry on his schemes with the same policy and success he has hitherto done.

The accounts you send agree with what I hear from other parts. They are all alike dismal. Reserve your self however for future times, and mind the main chance. I wou'd say, shun late hours, drink tar-water, and bring back (I wish a good deanry at least) a good stock of health and spirits to grace our little parties in Imokilly, where we hope, 'ere it be long to see you and the sun returned together.

My wife, who values her self on being in the number of your friends, is extremely obliged for the Italian psalms you have procured, and desires me to tell you, that the more you can procure, the more she shall be obliged. We join in wishing you many happy new years, health, and success.

I am, Rev.d Sir,

Your most faithful & obedient Servt.

Geor: Cloyne.

204   TO GERVAIS

Cloyne, Jan. 19th, 1741/42

Rev. Sir,

The pleasure you take in serving your friends is apt to encourage their importunity. We address our selves to you as a virtuoso, a lover of music, and one who converses with musical men, in hopes it may fall in your way to hear of a great four-string bass violin with a fine sounding base, approved by a good master. Such a one if you meet with, be so good as to agree for at any price you shall think reasonable, and I have wrote to Mr. Prior in Bolton Street to pay for it and to send it hither. We are contriving a concert for your entertainment the next time you favour us at Cloyne, and in the mean time intreat you accept our compliments and excuse this trouble from,

Revd Sir,

Yr most faithful humble Servt,

G. Cloyne.

Not knowing yr address I enclosed my last as I do this to Mr. Prior.

205 TO PERCIVAL (*fils*)

Cloyne, Jan. 24, 1741/42

My Lord,

Though by the want of five pacquets I have not yet seen it certified from England, I venture on the credit of a general report to congratulate your Lordship on your late success.

I do not congratulate you merely from the long and intimate attachment I have to you and your family which claims and will alwaies be entitled to my best wishes, because I do not look on a place in Parliament as a private perquisite to a family.

Nor yet do I congratulate your Lordship on the prospect of an approaching change of hands, which God knows whether it will be for better or worse ; though worse I think our affairs can hardly be.

But what I congratulate you upon is the being nearer to execute your excellent scheme of an Agrarian law, for want of which we are undone by luxury and avarice.

If you suffer not your vertue to cool with years, but persist and succeed in that scheme which you imparted to me at Cloyne, you will do a thing at once most beneficial to the public and most glorious to your self, by cutting out the core of our evil, the very root of all corruption, which I fear will otherwise only change hands, but never be remedied.

That God would preserve you and yours and keep this generous spark alive in your breast, and conduct and prosper all your endeavours for the public good is the sincere wish and hearty prayer of my good Lord

Your Lordship's most obedient faithfull Servt,
GEO. CLOYNE.

206 TO GERVAIS

Cloyne, Feb. 2, 1742

I condole with you on your cold, a circumstance that a man of fashion who keeps late hours can hardly escape. We find here that a spoonful, half tar and half honey, taken morning, noon, and night, proves a most effectual remedy in that case. My wife, who values herself on being in your good graces, expresses great gratitude for your care in procuring the psalms, and is doubly pleased with the prospect of your being yourself the bearer. The instrument she desired to be provided was a large four-stringed bass violin : but, besides this, we shall also be extremely glad to get that excellent bass viol which came from France, be the number of strings what it will. I wrote indeed (not to overload you) to Dean Browne to look out for a six-stringed bass viol of an old make and mellow tone. But the more we have of good instruments, the better ; for I have got an excellent master, whom I have taken into my family, and all my children, not excepting my little daughter, learn to play, and are preparing to fill my house with harmony against all events : that if we have worse times, we may have better spirits. Our French woman is grown more attentive to her business, and so much altered for the better, that my wife is not now inclined to part with her, but is nevertheless very sensibly obliged by your kind offer to look out for another. What you say of a certain pamphlet is enigmatical ; I shall hope to have it explained *viva voce*.

As this corner furnishes nothing worth sending, you will pardon me if, instead of other news, I transcribe a paragraph of a letter I lately received from an English bishop. ' We are now shortly to meet again in parliament, and by the proceedings upon the state of the nation Sir Robert's fate will be determined. He is doing all he can to recover a majority in the House of Commons, and is said to have succeeded as to some particulars. But in his main attempt, which was that of uniting the Prince and his court to the King's, he has been foiled. The bishop of Oxford was employed to carry the proposal to the Prince, which was, that he should have the £100,000 a year he had demanded, and his debts paid. But the Prince, at the same time that he expressed the utmost respect and duty to his Majesty, declared so much dislike to his Minister, that without his removal he will hearken to no terms.' I have also had another piece in the following words, which is very agreeable. ' Lady Dorothy, whose good temper seems as great as her beauty, and who has gained on every one by her behaviour in these most unhappy circumstances, is said at last to have gained over Lord Euston, and to have entirely won his affection.'

I find by your letter, the reigning distemper at the Irish Court is disappointment. A man of less spirits and alacrity would be apt to cry out, *Spes et fortuna valete*, &c., but my advice is, never to quit your hopes. Hope is often better than enjoyment. Hope is often the cause as well as the effect of youth. It is certainly a very pleasant and healthy passion. A hopeless person is deserted by himself; and he who forsakes himself is soon forsaken by friends and fortune, both which are sincerely wished you by, &c.

207   TO PRIOR

Cloyne, Feb. 26, 1741/42

Dear Tom,

    I believe there is no relation that Mr. Sandys and Sir John Rushout have to Lord Wilmington other than what I myself made by marrying Sir John Rushout's sister to the late Earl of Northampton, who was brother to Lord Wilmington. Sandys is nephew to Sir John. As to kindred or affinity, I take it to have very little share in this matter ; nor do I think it possible to foretel whether the ministry will be whig or tory. The people are so generally and so much incensed, that (if I am rightly informed) both men and measures must be changed before we see things composed. Besides, in this disjointed state of things, the Prince's party will be more considered than ever. It is my opinion there will be no first minister in haste ; and it will be new to act without one. When I had wrote thus far, I received a letter from a considerable hand on the other side the water, wherein are the following words : ' Though the whigs and tories had gone hand in hand in their endeavours to demolish the late minstry, yet some true whigs, to shew themselves such, were for excluding all tories from the new ministry. Lord Wilmington and Duke of Dorset declared they would quit if they proceeded on so narrow a bottom ; and the Prince, Duke of Argyle, Duke of Bedford, and many others, refused to come in, except there was to be a coalition of parties. After many fruitless attempts to effect this, it was at last achieved between eleven and twelve on Tuesday night ; and the Prince went next morning to St James's. It had been that very evening quite despaired of ; and the meeting of the parliament came on so fast, that there was a prospect of nothing but great confusion.' There is, I hope, a prospect now of much better things. I much wanted to see this scheme prevail, which it has now done ; and will, I

trust, be followed by many happy consequences.   We are all yours.
Adieu.

Your affectionate humble Servant,
G. CLOYNE.

You say that Swift & Co., acquainted me by letter of their
receipt of Purcel's bill ; but I have got no such letter.

208   TO GERVAIS

March 5, 1742

Your last letter, containing an account of the Queen of
Hungary and her affairs, was all over agreeable.   My wife and I
are not a little pleased to find her situation so much better than
we expected, and greatly applaud your zeal for her interests,
though we are divided upon the motive of it,   She imagines you
would be less zealous were the Queen old and ugly ; and will
have it that her beauty has set you on fire even at this distance.
I, on the contrary, affirm, that you are not made of such combustible stuff ; that you are affected only by the love of justice,
and insensible to all other flames than those of patriotism.   We
hope soon for your presence at Cloyne to put an end to this
controversy.

Your care in providing the Italian psalms set to music, the
four-stringed bass violin, and the antique bass viol, require our
repeated thanks.   We have already a bass viol made in South-
wark, A.D. 1730, and reputed the best in England.   And through
your means we are possessed of the best in France.   So we have
a fair chance for having the two best in Europe.

Your letter gives me hopes of a new and prosperous scene.   We
live in an age of revolutions so sudden and surprising in all parts
of Europe, that I question whether the like has been ever known
before.   Hands are changed at home : it is well if measures are
so too.   If not, I shall be afraid of this change of hands ; for
hungry dogs bite deepest.   But let those in power look to this.
We behold these vicissitudes with an equal eye from the serene
corner of Cloyne, where we hope soon to have the perusal of your
budget of politics.   Mean time accept our service and good
wishes.

209   TO PERCIVAL (*fils*)

Cloyne, March 26, 1742

My good Lord,

It is with singular pleasure that I find your Lordship is
blessed with a third son, and your lady safe : two blessings natural
and domestic, which may in some degree soften though not extin-
guish the sense of whatever you find amiss in this public jumble
of affairs.   The hopes of the future age depend on nothing so much
as the education of the present.   Early habits of hardiness and
industry introduced into young children render their whole lives
easy and happy to themselves, and useful to their country.   And
as your views extend to posterity, I doubt not you will be delighted
to breed up a young race of patriots.

The letter you obliged me with (which was highly entertaining)
shou'd have been sooner acknowledged.   But I imagined a letter
from this corner to one at the fountain head, in the very center
of affairs, and at a juncture the most busy and critical that perhaps
ever happened, must seem unseasonable, and only to be excused
by the double motive of congratulating your happiness as well
as acknowledging your favour.

Utopian schemes (I grant) are not suited to the present times,
but a scheme the most perfect *in futuro* may take place in idea at
present.   The model or idea cannot be too perfect though perhaps
it may never be perfectly attained in fact.   Things though not
adequate to a rule, will yet be less crooked for being, even clumsily,
applied to it.   And though no man hits the mark, they who come
nearest merit applause.

As luxury seems the real original root of those evils under
which we groan, avarice, ambition & corruption ; must it not
seem at the same time that agrarian and sumptuary laws are
highly expedient if we wou'd cut out the core of the national evil.
To attempt or even mention such things now wou'd be madness,
but to have them in view is right : and to steer by that view may
be useful.   An excellent mathematician of the last age proposed
to square the circle.   He failed of his end, but by the way fell
upon many useful discoveries.   To grasp at more than we can hold
is the way to lose all.   But a man's aim may be immense though
his grasp be but a span.   And what cannot be seized at once may
be grasped successively.

Though we live among dregs worse perhaps than the dregs of

Romulus, yet Plato's republic may be kept in view, if not for a rule, yet for an incentive. There was something inhumanly rugged and austere in that iron virtue of the Spartans. We are in the other extreme. The more the bands of virtue and piety are loosed the coercive discipline of the laws shou'd be so much the harder tied. The worst thing in a monarchy is that a court debauches the people : the best thing in a republic are sumptuary laws. And why we may not have them without change of government I do not see. They have them in France as well as in Venice or Genoa. And if we are wise they may be by little and little introduced to far better purpose at home.

It wou'd be very impertinent to pretend to inform your Lordship, that without virtue liberty is precarious. There is now a noble field for bettering the manners of a people (the only way of mending their circumstances) opening itself to the young Senators of virtue and resolution. A few such may do something, but old men are generally wanting in vigour as well as virtue. I should be sorry to see Great Britain in labour and nothing brought forth but a mouse, a sorry scramble for Employments.

The commoner your Lordship mentioned is a frugal prudent man, and such as are vulgarly esteemed prudent are often found to be under the influence of mony. The Peer is too stately and too lazy for a premier ministre. To find one man of virtue and capacity fit for a minister in these times is no easy matter. How difficult then must it be to furnish out a Senate of such men ? This is sufficient to shew the madness of republican schemes. But whatever is amiss in our body politic may perhaps be remedied if not by a speedy purgation, yet by gentle alteratives.

I am sorry to find the Tories are quite excluded. I am not near enough to see the wisdom of this step. Certainly those Tories who are not Jacobites seem to me as good subjects and as deserving of favor as any others. Some men I suspect are for narrowing the public bottom that they may enlarge their private prospect. When I consider the wretched maxims that prevail both at home and abroad I am tempted to say with Cicero—*imbecillitate aliorum non nostra virtute valemus.* My good Lord you will pardon my day-dreams and believe me most sincerely

Yr Lordship's most obedient and affectionate Servant,
GEO. CLOYNE.

My wife and family were much honoured by yr remembrance. We all join in service. I pray God preserve you and yours.

[Cloyne, 1742]

My dear Lord,

I was very much obliged by the letter you favoured me with amidst such a hurry of business.   And I should have acknowledged the obligation sooner, if I had not been shy of breaking in upon your busy moments.   The scene of affairs on your side of the water is a very horrid one as your Lordship sketched it out, and I doubt not your sketch is a very just one.   Hard as it is to ride out such stormy weather your Lordship is embarked and must go through it, with the utmost caution not to make a wrong step at this critical conjuncture.   It is indeed very difficult not to make a censurable step on such tottering and unstable footing, especially whilst there are so many open and earnest eyes ready to remark.   In a state unsettled and factious as that of England, it must be owned, the honestest and prudentest man alive may be often at a loss how to act, with whom to act, or whether to act at all.   This was the circumstance of Cicero in the Roman State, and his letters contain many useful hints and parallels to our present time.

The modern patriots have to my mind shewn as little skill as honesty.   Their dividing from their body puts them absolutely in the power of the late ministers, who have baited them with present advantages, and in all appearance will soon have them out again.   For how is it possible they should long subsist without the favour either of Prince or People.   It seems therefore a clear case that the old ministry will bring in their old friends.

Much might be said for supporting the Queen of Hungary and demolishing the power of France.   But whether this might not be better and cheaper done by supplies of money than troops is a question your Lordship can better decide than I.   But I blame myself for pretending to speak of matters so much out of my sphere.   Thus much however may be said in general, and it holds true at all times : that it is politic to stand by one's friends and honest to abide by principles ; and that those two points of steadiness and honesty, where they meet, do constitute the surest basis for a great reputation, the most necessary of all engines for a man that would make a great and useful figure in public affairs.

Pardon, my good Lord, this political stuff that I write for want of news. This island is a region of dreams and trifles of so little consequence to the rest of the world, that I am sure you expect no important news from it. But I could tell you a very ridiculous piece of news I lately heard from Dublin, which I am sure would make you laugh, but as it would be at the expense of a prelate, I must be excused telling it.

My best wishes and respects attend you and yours.

I am, my dear Lord,

Yr most obedient and faithful Servt,

G. CLOYNE.

211   TO PERCIVAL (*fils*)

My Lord,

I was just now favoured with a letter of your Lordships by the hands of Mr. Brereton. You must not measure my inclination to serve you by my serving him this time, which I fear will not be in my power, though it alwaies will be in my wishes to do what is agreeable to your Lordship.

It was no small mortification to find you had been within four miles of Cloyne, without my hearing any thing of it till you were gone. If I were in travelling circumstances, the distance of Cloyne from your Castle shou'd not hinder my waiting on your Lordship and Lady Percival. But for above three years together I have not gone three miles off, being nailed down to Cloyne by a cholic and pain in my side which is irritated by the motion of a horse or a coach.

My wife joins with me in best respects to Lady Percival and your Lordship, and we shou'd reckon it a great good fortune, if you wou'd both be pleased to make our house your Inne while you wait for the going off of your ship, which may take you up within two miles of Cloyne. Be it daies, so much the better : or be it hours, this is better than nothing. Deny us not this favor, and count on my being ever

My good Lord,

Your most affectionate and obedient Servt,

G. CLOYNE.

Cloyne, July 2, 1742

18

212 TO PERCIVAL (*fils*)

My Lord,

I happened to hear you have a carriage but no horses. Please to let me know by the bearer what horses and harness you would have, and on what day, and I shall not fail to send them, with my Coachman and Postilion who are very safe drivers and will I hope bring my Lady Percival and your Lordship safely to Cloyne, which honour is expected with great pleasure by

My Lord,
Your Lordships most faithful & obedient Servant,
G. CLOYNE.

My wife joins with me in compliments to her ladyship.
Cloyne, July 9, 1742

213 TO PERCIVAL (*fils*)

Cloyne, 9ber 17, 1742

My Lord,

When you interested your self for Mr. Brereton I made, in answer to your letter, no promise choosing rather to be better than my word. I have now the pleasure to acquaint your Lordship that I have given him the vicarage of Kilbrin, being a benefice without cure, adjacent to that of Burton, and so lying most convenient for him. I am informed it set last year for fourscore pounds, and by increase of tillage is likely to grow more valuable. I need not tell your Lordship how much pleased I am with this opportunity of shewing my attachment to your family as well as the ready inclination & sincere regard with which I am,

My Lord,
Your L'ps most obedient and most faithful Servt,
GEORGE CLOYNE.

Our respects and best wishes wait upon all yr good family, including my Lord Egmont's.

214 TO GERVAIS

September 6, 1743

The book which you were so good as to procure for me (and which I shall not pay for till you come to receive the money in person) contains all that part of Dr. Pococke's travels for which I have any curiosity ; so I shall, with my thanks for this, give you no further trouble about any other volume.

I find by the letter put into my hands by your son (who was so kind as to call here yesterday, but not kind enough to stay a night with us), that you are taken up with great matters, and, like other great men, in danger of overlooking your friends. Prepare, however, for a world of abuse, both as a courtier and an architect, if you do not find means to wedge in a visit to Cloyne between those two grand concerns. Courtiers you will find none here, and but such virtuosi as the country affords ; I mean in the way of music, for that is at present the reigning passion at Cloyne. To be plain, we are musically mad. If you would know what that is, come and see.

215 TO GERVAIS

October 29, 1743

A bird of the air has told me that your reverence is to be dean of Tuam. No nightingale could have sung a more pleasing song, not even my wife, who, I am told, is this day inferior to no singer in the kingdom. I promise you we are preparing no contemptible chorus to celebrate your preferment : and if you do not believe me, come this Christmas, and believe your own ears. In good earnest, none of your friends will be better pleased to see you with your broad seal in your pocket than your friends at Cloyne. I wish I were able to wish you joy at Dublin ; but my health, though not a little mended, suffers me to make no excursions farther than a mile ot two.

What is this your favourite, the Queen of Hungary, has been doing by her emissaries at Petersburgh ? France is again upon her legs. I foresee no good. I wish all this may be vapours and spleen : but I write in sun-shine.

Cloyne, January 8, 1743/44

Rev. Sir,

You have obliged the ladies as well as myself by your candid judgment on the point submitted to your determination. I am glad this matter proved an amusement in your gout, by bringing you acquainted with several curious and select tryals ; which I should readily purchase, and accept your kind offer of procuring them, if I did not apprehend there might be some among them of too delicate a nature to be read by boys and girls, to whom my library, and particularly all French books, are open.

As to foreign affairs, we cannot descry or prognosticate any good event from this remote corner. The planets that seemed propitious are now retrograde : Russia, Sweden, and Prussia lost : and the Dutch a nominal ally at best. You may now admire the Queen of Hungary without a rival : her conduct with respect to the Czarina and the Marquis de Botta hath, I fear, rendered cold the hearts of her friends, and their hands feeble. To be plain, from this time forward I doubt we shall languish, and our enemies take heart. And while I am thus perplexed about foreign affairs, my private economy (I mean the animal economy) is disordered by the sciatica ; an evil which has attended me for some time past ; and I apprehend will not leave me till the return of the sun. Certainly the news that I want to hear at present is not from Rome, or Paris, or Vienna, but from Dublin ; viz., when the Dean of Tuam is declared, and when he receives the congratulations of his friends. I constantly read the news from Dublin ; but lest I should overlook this article, I take upon me to congratulate you at this moment ; that as my good wishes were not, so my compliments may not be behind those of your other friends.

You have entertained me with so many curious things that I would fain send something in return worth reading. But, as this quarter affords nothing from itself, I must be obliged to transcribe a bit of an English letter that I received last week. It relates to what is now the subject of public attention, viz. the Hanover troops, and is as follows :—' General Campbell (a thorough courtier) being called upon in the House of Commons to give an account whether he had not observed some instances of partiality, replied, he could not say he had : but this he would say, that he thought the forces of the two nations could never draw together again. This, coming from the mouth of a courtier, was looked on as an ample confession : however, it was carried against the address by a large majority. Had the question been whether the Hanover troops should be continued, it would not have been a debate : but, it being well known that the contrary had been resolved upon before the meeting of parliament, the moderate part of the opposition thought it was unnecessary, and might prove hurtful to address about it, and so voted with the court.' You see how I am forced to lengthen out my letter by adding a borrowed scrap of news, which yet probably is no news to you. But, though I should shew you nothing new, yet you must give me leave to shew my inclination at least to acquit myself of the debts I owe you, and to declare myself,

Rev. Sir,
Your most faithful and obedient Servt,
GEOR. CLOYNE.

My wife and family join their compliments and sincere wishes to behold the Dean of Tuam at Cloyne.

217 TO GERVAIS

Cloyne, March 16, 1744
I think myself a piece of a prophet when I foretold that the Pretender's Cardinal feigned to aim at your head, when he meant to strike you, like a skilful fencer, on the ribs. It is true, one would hardly think the French such bunglers : but this popish priest hath manifestly bungled so as to repair the breaches our own bunglers had made at home. This is the luckiest thing that could have happened, and will, I hope, confound all the measures of our enemies. I was much obliged and delighted with the good news you lately sent, which was yesterday confirmed by letters from Dublin. And though particulars are not yet known, I did not think fit to delay our public marks of joy, as a great bonfire before my gate, firing of guns, drinking of healths, &c. I was very glad of this opportunity to put a little spirit into our drooping Protestants of Cloyne, who have of late conceived no small fears on seeing themselves in such a defenceless condition among so great a number of Papists elated with the fame of these new

enterprises in their favour. It is indeed terrible to reflect, that we have neither arms nor militia in a province where the Papists are eight to one, and have an earlier intelligence than we have of what passes : by what means I know not ; but the fact is certainly true.

Good Mr. Dean (for Dean I will call you, resolving not to be behind your friends in Dublin), you must know that to us who live in this remote corner many things seem strange and unaccountable that may be solved by you who are near the fountain head. Why are draughts made from our forces when we most want them ? Why are not the militia arrayed ? How comes it to pass that arms are not put into the hands of Protestants, especially since they have been so long paid for ? Did not our ministers know for a long time past that a squadron was forming at Brest ? Why did they not then bruise the cockatrice in the egg ? Would not the French works at Dunkirk have justified this step ? Why was Sir John Norris called off from the chase when he had his enemies in full view, and was even at their heels with a superior force ? As we have two hundred and forty men-of-war, whereof one hundred and twenty are of the line, how comes it that we did not appoint a squadron to watch and intercept the Spanish Admiral with his thirty millions of pieces of eight ? In an age wherein articles of religious faith are canvassed with the utmost freedom, we think it lawful to propose these scruples in our political faith, which in many points wants to be enlightened and set right.

Your last was writ by the hand of a fair lady to whom both my wife and I send our compliments as well as to yourself : I wish you joy of being able to write yourself. My cholic is changed to gout and sciatica, the tar-water having drove it into my limbs, and, as I hope, carrying it off by those ailments, which are nothing to the cholic.

218   TO GERVAIS

Cloyne, May 30, 1744

Revd Sir

With my own I send you the sincere Congratulations of all here on your promotion to the Deanry of Tuam, which agreeable news was brought us by the last pacquets and without compliment gave us more pleasure than all the victories of this war put together. From what I had heard of courts and ministers I began to suspect their dilatory proceedings in your affair. But it seems they have turned out honest at last. I conclude you are in motion between Tuam Dublin and Lismore, so to direct a letter to you is the same thing as to shoot flying. I have therefore small hopes of this finding you, but could not dispense with doing my part on this occasion and assuring you that

I am Revd Sir,

Yr. most obedient & affectionate Servant,

G. CLOYNE.

Our rocks and groves & strands as well as my wife & brother & all this neighbourhood long to wish you joy in person.

219   TO PRIOR

To drink or not to drink ! that is the doubt,
With *pro* and *con* the learn'd would make it out.
Britons, drink on ! the jolly prelate cries :
What the prelate persuades the doctor denies.
But why need the parties so learnedly fight,
Or choleric *Jurin* so fiercely indite ?
Sure our senses can tell if the liquor be right.
What agrees with his stomach, and what with his head,
The drinker may feel, though he can't write or read.
Then authority's nothing : the doctors are men :
And *who drinks tar-water will drink it again.*

Cloyne, June 19, 1744

Dear Tom,

Last night being unable to sleep for the heat, I fell into a reverie on my pillow, which produced the foregoing lines ; and it is all the answer I intend for Dr. Jurin's letter, for that I am told is the writer's name of a pamphlet addressed to me, and which was sent me from London. When you cause these lines to be printed in the public papers, you will take care to have them transcribed, that the verses may not be known to be mine. Because you desire remarks on the affidavits (things very obvious to make), I send them back to you, who will remark yourself. I send you at the same time a Letter which I formerly wrote, before you sent the affidavits, as you will see by the date, but never sent, having changed my mind as to appearing myself in that affair, which can be better managed by a third hand. Let one of the Letters, cut and stitched in marble paper, be sent to every body in Dublin to whom a book was given ; and let one of the copies be sent Mr. Innys, to be printed in the same size in London ; also for the magazine, where you talk of getting it inserted.

I wish you to send the two volumes of *Universal History,* the six tomes of Wilkins's *Councils,* and the books from Innys, in a box together, to be left for me at Mr. Harper's in Cork. All here are yours. Adieu.

Yours affectionately
G. CLOYNE.

220   TO HANMER

Cloyne, August 21, 1744

Sir,

As I am with particular esteem and respect your humble servant, so I heartily wish your success in the use of tar-water may justify the kind things you say on that subject. But, since you are pleased to consult me about your taking it, I shall without further ceremony tell you what I think, how ill soever a physician's air may become one of my profession. Certainly, if I may conclude from parallel cases, there is room to entertain good hopes of yours : both giddiness and relaxed fibres having been, to my knowledge, much relieved by tar-water. The sooner you take it, so much the better. I could wish you saw it made yourself, and strongly stirred. While it stands to clarify, let it be close covered, and afterwards bottled and well corked. I find it agrees with most stomachs, when stirred even five or six minutes, provided it be skimmed before bottling. You may begin with a pint a day, and proceed to a pint and a half, or even a quart, as it shall agree with your stomach. And you may take this quantity either in half-pint or quarter-pint glasses, at proper intervals in the twenty-four hours. It may be drunk indifferently, at any season of the year. It lays under no restraint, nor obliges you to go out of your usual course of diet. Only, in general, I suppose light suppers, early hours, and gentle exercise (so as not to tire) good for all cases. With your tar-water I wish you may take no other medicines.

I have had much experience of it, and can honestly say I never knew it do harm. The ill effects of drugs shew themselves soonest on the weakest persons ; such are children ; and I assure you that my two youngest children (when they were one three, and the other not two years old) took it, as a preservative against the small-pox, constantly for six months together without any inconvenience. Upon the whole, I apprehend no harm and much benefit in your case, and shall be very glad to find my hopes confirmed by a line from yourself, which will always be received as a great favour by,

Sir, Your most obedient and most humble Servant,
GEORGE CLOYNE.

221   TO PRIOR

On SIRIS and its Enemies.   By a Drinker of Tar-Water.

How can devoted Siris stand
Such dire attacks ?   The licens'd band,
With upcast eyes and visage sad,
Proclaim, ' Alas ! the world's run mad.
' The prelate's book has turn'd their brains ;
' To set them right will cost us pains.
' His drug too makes our patients sick ;
' And this doth vex us to the quick.'
And, vex'd they must be, to be sure,
To find tar-water cannot cure,
But makes men sicker still and sicker,
And fees come thicker still and thicker.
　　Bursting with pity for mankind,
But to their own advantage blind,
Many a wight, with face of fun'ral,
From mortar, still, and urinal,
Hastes to throw in his scurvy mite
Of spleen, of dullness, and of spite,
To furnish the revolving moons
With pamphlets, epigrams, lampoons,
Against tar-water.   You'd know why—
Think who they are : you'll soon descry
What means each angry doleful ditty,
Whether themselves or us they pity.

Dear Tom,

The doctors, it seems, are grown very abusive. To silence them, I send you the above scrap of poetry, which I would by no means have known or suspected for mine. You will therefore burn the original, and send a copy to be printed in a newspaper, or the *Gentleman's Magazine*. I must desire you to get some bookseller in Dublin to procure me the *History of the Learned*, and the *Gentleman's Magazine*, two pamphlets that come out monthly. For the time past I would have the *History* or *Memoirs of the Learned* for the months of May, June, and July past, and the *Magazine* for last July. For the future, I would be supplied with them every month.

It is to be noted, that tar-water is best made in glazed earthen vessels. I would have the foregoing sentence inserted in the English edition, and next Irish edition of the *Letter*, at the end of the section that recites the manner of making tar-water. It is very lately I made this remark, that it is finer and clearer when so made than if in unglazed crocks.

Pray send the numbers of our tickets in this lottery. My sister wrote to Mrs. Hamilton, but has got no answer. Perhaps her niece might have been cured of her sore eye since she left Dublin.

I am, dear Tom,

Your affectionate humble Servant,

GEORGE CLOYNE.

Sept. 3, 1744

P.S. When you send the other books I desire you to put up with them two dissertations of Whiston's, upon our Saviour's miracles, and upon the Eternity of Hell Torments, if this can be got in town ; also half a guinea's worth (i.e. 25) *Gifts to Maid-Servants*, printed by Falkner.

September 3, 1744

222   TO LINDEN

December 3, 1744

En réponse aux questions que vous me faites touchant l'eau de goudron, voici ce que j'ai à vous dire.

Je n'ai jamais sçû qu'on en fît usage dans aucune des parties de l'Amérique où j'ai été, mais j'ai appris qu'on la prenoit en

Caroline comme un préservatif contre la petite vérole ; c'est ce qui me fit résoudre, lorsque cette maladie régnoit dans mon diocèse, d'en tenter l'expérience. Le succès fut admirable ; non seulement en qualité de préservatif, mais en qualité de remède. Ce qui m'engagea à tirer de là plusieurs conséquences, à faire divers raisonnemens et divers expériences, concernant l'usage de l'eau de goudron, dans l'autres maladies, aussi bien que dans la petite vérole, pour laquelle seule j'avois ouï dire qu'on s'en servît en Amérique. Mais au lieu que l'eau dont on use en Caroline est épaisse et dégoutante, je trouvai les moyens, après des essais réitérés, d'en faire d'une autre sorte, qui est claire et nullement désagréable. J'ai trouvé par quantité d'expériences que ses vertus sont d'une grande efficace dans la plupart des maladies, si ce n'est même dans toutes. Mais tout cela est exposé plus au long dans la seconde édition du Siris faite à Dublin, et spécialement dans une lettre à Mr. T. P. qu'on ajoute à cette édition, que j'ai donné ordre de vous envoyer de Dublin, à cause qu'elle contient divers changemens qui rendront votre traduction plus récommandable. Quant à ce que vous demandez si ce sont les Indiens ou les Blancs, qui se sont avisés les premiers de l'usage de l'eau de goudron, je ne puis rien en dire avec certitude, mais je crois que ce sont les Indiens.

Pour votre autre question, sçavoir, comment je suis parvenu à découvrir la grande étendue de la vertu de cette eau, et ses différentes propriétés, je ne puis que répéter que j'ai déjà touché ci-dessus, sçavoir, que c'a été en raisonnant, en faisant des obser-vations et des expériences. C'est ce qui est déduit plus amplement dans la lettre que j'ai déjà citée. Je finis en priant Dieu de bénir votre entreprise, afin qu'elle tourne à votre satisfaction et à l'avan-tage du genre humain. Je suis, Monsieur, votre, etc.

223 TO GERVAIS

June 3, 1745

I congratulate with you on the success of your late dose of physic. The gout, as Dr. Sydenham styles it, is *amarissimum naturæ pharmacum.* It throws off a sharp excrement from the blood to the limbs and extremities of the body, and is not less useful than painful. I think, Mr. Dean, you have paid for the gay excursion you made last winter to the metropolis and the court. And yet, such is the condition of mortals, I foresee you will forget the pain next winter, and return to the same course of life which brought it on.

As to our warlike achievements, if I were to rate our successes by our merits, I could forebode little good. But if we are sinners, our enemies are no saints. It is my opinion we shall heartily maul one another, without any signal advantage on either side. How the sullen English squires who pay the piper will like this dance, I cannot tell. For my own part, I cannot help thinking that land expeditions are but ill suited either to the force or interest of England ; and that our friends would do more if we did less on the continent.

Were I to send my son from home, I assure you there is no one to whose prudent care and good nature I would sooner trust him than yours. But, as I am his physician, I think myself obliged to keep him with me. Besides, as after so long an illness his constitution is very delicate, I imagine this warm vale of Cloyne is better suited to it than your lofty and exposed situation of Lismore. Nevertheless, my wife and I are extremely obliged by your kind offer, and concur in our hearty thanks for it.

224   TO CLARKE

[1745]

I would not suppose your affairs are at all the worse for my not being in towne ; for, to speak the truth, I would have been of no use with my Lord Lieutenant, unless he had given me a decent opportunity of speaking to the point, by consulting or advising with me about it, a thing which I had no right to expect. I have been told His Excellency expressed a particular esteem of you publickly at the Castle, on occasion of the compliment you made him on his first arrival. This personal prepossession in your favour, grounded on his own sense of your merit, is, in my opinion, worth twenty recommendations, even of those great men in power who alone have a right to make them. To conclude, I wish you all success in your undertakings, being with sincere regard, etc.

225   TO GERVAIS

Nov. 24, 1745

You are in for life.   Not all the philosophers have been saying these three thousand years on the vanity of riches, the cares of greatness, and the brevity of human life, will be able to reclaim you.   However, as it is observed that most men have patience enough to bear the misfortunes of others, I am resolved not to break my heart for my old friend, if you should prove so unfortunate as to be made a bishop.   The reception you met with from Lord Chesterfield was perfectly agreeable to his Excellency's character, who being so *clair-voyant* in everything else could not be supposed blind to your merit.

Your friends the Dutch have shewed themselves, what I always took them to be, selfish and ungenerous.   To crown all, we are now told the forces they sent us have private orders not to fight. I hope we shall not want them.

By the letter you favoured me with, I find the regents of our university have shewn their loyalty at the expense of their wit. The poor dead Dean, though no idolater of the Whigs, was no more a Jacobite than Dr. Baldwin.   And had he been even a Papist, what then ?   Wit is of no party.

We have been alarmed with a report that a great body of rapparees is up in the county of Kilkenny : these are looked on by some as the forerunners of an insurrection.   In opposition to this, our militia have been arrayed, that is, sworn : but alas ! we want not oaths, we want muskets.   I have bought up all I could get, and provided horses and arms for four-and-twenty of the Protestants of Cloyne, which, with a few more that can furnish themselves, make up a troop of thirty horse.   This seemed necessary to keep off rogues in these doubtful times.

May we hope to gain a sight of you in the recess ?   Were I as able to go to town, how readily should I wait on my Lord Lieutenant and the Dean of Tuam.   Your letters are so much tissue of gold and silver : in return I am forced to send you from this corner a patch-work of tailors' shreds, for which I entreat your compassion, and that you will believe me, &c.

226 IN THE *Dublin Journal*

17/21 December 1745

As several in this dangerous conjuncture have undertaken to advise the public, I am encouraged to hope that a hint concerning the dress of our soldiers may not be thought impertinent.

Whatever unnecessarily spends the force or strength of a man lessens its effect where it is necessary. The same force that carries one pound a hundred yards will carry two pounds but fifty yards ; and so in proportion. The body of a man is an engine. Its force should be managed to produce its full effect where it is most wanted ; and ought not, therefore, in time of action, to be dissipated on useless ornaments. There is a weight on our soldiers neither offensive nor defensive, but serving only for parade. This I would have removed ; and the loss will not be much, if the man's vigour grows as his pomp lessens, *spectemur agendo* being the proper motto and ambition of warriors.

Sleeves, facings, caps, flaps, tall caps, double breasts, laces, frogs, cockades, plaited shirts, shoulder-knots, belts, and buttons more than enough are so many drawbacks or obstacles to a soldier's exerting his strength in the proper way, in marching, fighting, and pursuing. Suppose two armies engage equal in strength, courage, and numbers, one clad in judges robes, the other in sailor's jackets ; I need not ask on which side the advantage lies. The same holds proportionably in other cases, where the difference is less notorious.

Our sailors seem the best dressed of all our forces ; and what is sufficient for a sailor may serve for a soldier. Their dress, therefore, I would recommend to the landmen, or if any other can be contrived yet more succinct and tight ; that so our men may march and fight with the least incumbrance, their strength being employed upon their arms and their enemes.

Soldiers thus clad will be more light, clever, and alert ; and, when the eye hath been a little used to them, will look much better than in more cumbersome apparel. I may add too, that something will be saved to the men in the article of clothing.

I am, Sir,

Your humble Servant,

EUBULUS.

4/7 January, 1746

To a Greek or Roman eye what was apt or fit seemed decent. Their military dress, though far more succinct and tight than the civil, was not thought the less becoming ; but our rude and Gothic eyes are taken with a great show. This false taste extends even to the men, who are chosen rather by measure than by fitness.

A soldier's end is fighting. This is best performed by strength and activity, neither of those can be rated by a man's stature. Many a tall body is heavy and ill made ; and many a little compact fellow, though he may not fetch so weighty a stroke, or so large a stride, may yet make amends by fetching two strokes, or two steps for one. The make of a man is more to be considered than his bulk in the estimation of strength and agility.

The Roman standard reduced to our measure was but five feet four inches, and the Roman sword had a broad, strong pointed blade, not above fourteen or fifteen inches long ; such were the men and such was the sword, that conquered the world.

But the modern discipline delighteth much in parade. This is a clog upon our levies and recruits, depriving the publick of the service of many a stout active fellow, who falls short of the present standard. And yet such a one hath his advantages. At a distance he is a less mark, and in close fight less embarrassed, more nimble either to avoid or give a blow, he is fitter for dispatch in marches and pursuits, in passing through bad roads, in clambering over rocks and mountains, and scaling of walls, he is a less burthen on a horse or carriage.

Regiments of little active men may be fit for many peculiar services, where large-bodied men might not do so well ; and those little men being formed into a distinct corps, the uniform appearance would be still preserved, and the eye pleased in a review.

And if such men are not so fit to fight with long swords or sabres, or clubbed muskets, yet they may succeed very well at other weapons. Long heavy sabres are not so easily managed as those short Roman swords—*habiles brevibus mucronibus enses.* It is more easy to ward off a stroke of the former, than a stroke or thrust of the latter, which being quickly redoubled, might be sped two or three for one.

A battalion of low, squat, well-set men, armed with Morrisons, targets, Roman swords, and blunderbusses, having made one fire, at a small distance, full in the face of the enemy, and instantly rushing on with their targets and short swords, would, if I mistake not, be found a match for any tall battalion.

I am, Sir,

Your humble Servant,
EUBULUS.

228   TO GERVAIS

Jan. 6, 1746

Two days ago I was favoured with a very agreeable visit from Baron Mountnay and Mr. Bristow. I hear they have taken Lismore in their way to Dublin. We want a little of your foreign fire to raise our Irish spirits in this heavy season. This makes your purpose of coming very agreeable news. We will chop politics together, sing *Io Pæan* to the Duke, revile the Dutch, admire the King of Sardinia, and applaud the Earl of Chesterfield, whose name is sacred all over this island except Lismore ; and what should put your citizens of Lismore out of humour with his Excellency I cannot comprehend. But the discussion of these points must be deferred to your wished-for arrival.

229   IN THE *Dublin Journal*

4/8 February 1746

Sir,

Pro aris et focis hath been always esteemed the strongest motive to fighting. Foreigners want this motive, and therefore should not be depended on. Its own proper Militia and soldiers raised at home, are the natural Defence of a country. Great evils have ensued from calling in foreigners ; History is full of such examples. Hence all wise nations have provided a domestic strength, by training up their youth to arms. The young Romans were betimes accustomed to military exercise ; therefore, their levies were not made from raw men. Among the Greeks, Gymnastic Sports were accounted a necessary part of education. Both the Roman and Grecian games were calculated to promote strength and activity, and to fit men for war. Public games are necessary to keep up the spirits and good humour of a people ; and if games, why not martial games ? To fence, race, wrestle, shoot at a mark, or go through military exercise would not be less diverting because useful. In former times, warlike sports, particularly shooting at buts, were the prevailing humour, encouraged also, and provided for by authority. The British youth were thus bred to arms. England was once a kingdom of warriors, and France felt the effects of it. We used indeed. . . . But that spirit is gone. Witness the late inroad of our Highland neighbours, who have taught us a lesson never to be forgot. They have shewed us what a change hath been wrought by the disuse of arms, and that albeit we breath the same air we are not the same men, which under our Edwards and Henrys followed their landlords into France. Notwithstanding the conduct and bravery of our leaders, it was impossible the regular troops could fly to every part. But a well-trained militia would have been ready in all places to oppose those invaders, and save the nation's honour, from being insulted by a handful of rebels. Would Swiss or Swedish peasants and burghers have tamely looked on such bold intruders ?

Some are apt to undervalue a militia. But in effect what difference is there, after a long peace, between regular troops and militia ? Did England ever make a greater figure than it hath done in former times by its militia ? In our own times have not the militia of Sweden shewn themselves an overmatch for a disciplined army of Danes ? and nearer home, have not the northern rebels played their part at Sheriffmuir and Preston Pans as well as regular troops ? and was not this solely owing to their having been accustomed to arms ? It is not the name, the apparel, or the ornaments that make a soldier, but the familiar use of arms, a body hardened by toil, an intrepid heart and a resolute mind ; talents to be found in labouring peasants, miners or tradesmen, if duly trained and exercised ; and nowhere more likely to be found than in Englishmen. The military art like all others is attained by practice, strength and courage grow by repeated acts. Novelty startles but frequency lessens surprize. The use of his own arms may be terrible as well as aukward to a novice. These are truths not unknown but overlooked ; if men asleep may be said to overlook.

I will not, nevertheless, presume to impute this neglect of cultivating the military virtue of these nations to the ignorance or indolence of our patriots, rather than to a fatality in the course of things, which hath changed the manners of our people. But

19

whatever be the cause, it is plain we are no more the same men, nor delighted with the same amusements. There is no danger that tilts and tournaments should come again in play ; on the other hand, it is to be hoped, (whatever the report may be) that our gentlemen will not chuse this juncture for introducing masquerades among us.

Non hoc ista sibi tempus spectacula poscit. Manly and military exercises befit the times, which may be performed on holidays or summer evenings, without neglect of business, and without expense of uniforms and treats, merely as a pastime ; which the genius of our people would readily take to, if encouraged by small premiums, or countenanced by the leading men of a parish.

I am, Sir,
Your humble Servant,
Eubulus.

230   TO PRIOR

Dear Tom,

The above letter contains a piece of advice which seems to me not unseasonable or useless. You may make use of Faulkner for conveying it to the public, without any intimation of the author. I send you this inclosed bill on Swift & Co., which you will tender to them, and see that I have credit for it in their books. There is handed about a lampoon against our troop, which hath caused great indignation in the warriors of Cloyne.

I am informed that Dean Gervais had been looking for the *Querist,* and could not find one in the shops, for my Lord Lieutenant at his desire. I wish you could get one handsomely bound for his Excellency ; or at least the last published relating to the Bank, which consisted of excerpta out of the Three Parts of the *Querist.* I wrote to you before to procure two copies of this for his Excellency and Mr. Liddel.

Adieu, dear Tom.
Your faithful humble Servant,
G. CLOYNE.

February, 1746

231 TO GERVAIS

Feb. 6, 1746

You say you carried away regret from Cloyne. I assure you that you did not carry it all away : there was a good share of it left with us : which was on the following news-day increased upon hearing the fate of your niece. My wife could not read this piece of news without tears, though her knowledge of that amiable young lady was no more than one day's acquaintance. Her mournful widower is beset with many temporal blessings : but the loss of such a wife must be long felt through them all. Complete happiness is not to be hoped for on this side Gascony. All those who are not Gascons must have a corner of woe to creep out at, and to comfort themselves with at parting from this world. Certainly if we had nothing to make us uneasy here, heaven itself would be less wished for. But I should remember I am writing to a philosopher and divine ; so shall turn my thoughts to politics, concluding with this sad reflection, that, happen what will, I see the Dutch are still to be favourites ; though I much apprehend the hearts of some warm friends may be lost at home, by endeavouring to gain the affection of those lukewarm neighbours.

232 TO GERVAIS

Feb. 24, 1746

I am heartily sensible of your loss, which yet admits of alleviation, not only from the common motives which have been repeated every day for upwards of five thousand years, but also from your own peculiar knowledge of the world and the variety of distresses which occur in all ranks from the highest to the lowest : I may add, too, from the peculiar times in which we live, which seem to threaten still more wretched and unhappy times to come.

' Ætas parentum, pejor avis, tulit
Nos nequiores, mox daturos
Progeniem vitiosiorem.'

Nor is it a small advantage that you have a peculiar resource against distress from the gaiety of your own temper. Such is the hypochondriac melancholy complexion of us islanders, that we seem made of butter, every accident makes such a deep impression upon us ; but those elastic spirits, which are your birthright, cause the strokes of fortune to rebound without leaving a trace behind them ; though, for a time, there is and will be a gloom, which, I agree with your friends, is best dispelled at the court and metropolis, amidst a variety of faces and amusements.

I wish I was able to go with you, and pay my duty to the Lord Lieutenant : but, alas ! the disorder I had this winter, and my long retreat, have disabled me for the road, and disqualified me for a court. But if I see you not in Dublin, which I wish I may be able to do, I shall hope to see you at Cloyne when you can be spared from better company. These sudden changings and tossings from side to side betoken a fever in the state. But whatever ails the body politic, take care of your own bodily health, and let no anxious cares break in upon it.

233   TO PRIOR

Dear Tom,
    I perceive the Earl of Chesterfield is, whether absent or present, a friend to Ireland ; and there could not have happened a luckier incident to this poor island than the friendship of such a man, when there are so few of her own great men who either care or know how to befriend her. As my own wishes and endeavours (howsoever weak and ineffectual) have had the same tendency, I flatter myself that on this score he honours me with his regard, which is an ample recompence for more public merit than I can pretend to. As you transcribed a line from his letter relating to me ; so, in return, I send you a line transcribed from a letter of the Bishop of Gloucester's relating to you. I formerly told you I had mentioned you to the Bishop when I sent your scheme. These are his words :—' I have had a great deal of discourse with your Lord Lieutenant. He expressed his good esteem of Mr. Prior and his character, and commended him as one who had no view in life but to do the utmost good he is capable of. As he has seen the scheme, he may have opportunity of mentioning it to as many of the cabinet as he pleases. But it will not be a fashionable doctrine at this time.' So far the Bishop. You are doubtless in the right, on all proper occasions, to cultivate a correspondence with Lord Chesterfield. When you write, you will perhaps let him know in the properest manner the thorough

sense I have of the honour he does me in his remembrance, and my concern at not having been able to wait on him.

Adieu, dear Tom,
G. CLOYNE.

June 23, 1746

May we hope to see you this summer ?

234   TO PRIOR

Cloyne, July 3, 1746

Dear Tom,

I send you back my *Letter*, with the new paragraph to be added at the end, where you see the ∧.

Lord Chesterfield's letter does great honour both to you and to his Excellency. The nation should not lose the opportunity of profiting by such a Viceroy, which indeed is a rarity not to be met with every season, which grows not on every tree. I hope your Society will find means of encouraging particularly the two points he recommends, glass and paper. For the former you would do well to get your workmen from Holland rather than from Bristol. You have heard of the trick the glassmen of Bristol were said to have played Dr. Helsham and Company.

My wife with her compliments sends you a present by the Cork carrier who set out yesterday. It is an offering of the first fruits of her painting. She began to draw in last November, and did not stick to it closely, but by way of amusement only at leisure hours. For my part, I think she shows a most uncommon genius ; but others may be supposed to judge more impartially than I. My two younger children are beginning to employ themselves the same way. In short, here are two or three families in Imokilly bent upon painting ; and I wish it was more general among ladies and idle people as a thing that may divert the spleen, improve the manufactures, and increase the wealth of the nation. We will endeavour to profit by your Lord Lieutenant's advice, and kindle up new arts with a spark of his public spirit.

Mr. Simon has wrote to me, desiring that I would become a member of the Historico-physical Society. I wish them well, but do not care to list myself among them : for in that case I should think myself obliged to do somewhat which might interrupt

my other studies. I must therefore depend on you for getting me
out of this scrape, and hinder Mr. Simon's proposing me, which
he inclines to do, at the request, it seems, of the Bishop of Meath.
And this, with my service, will be a sufficient answer to Mr.
Simon's letter.

235   TO PERCIVAL

Cloyne, Aug. 24, 1746

My Lord,
  This day I received your favour of the twelfth, and thank
your Lordship for your kind care in having got in my money.
If it was unlucky for me that it could not be got while the stocks
were lower, I do not in the least impute that to your Lordship.
  As there is no sending a deed of mortgage by post, and as I
have not the opportunity of a private hand, I must beg the favour
of you to remit the money to your bankers at Corke, and appoint
your Lordship's agent to receive the deed of mortgage and pay
the money thereupon, which I shall then remit back to purchase
annuities in London by Mr. Henry Hoare & Co. This will take
time and the stocks are daily rising. So your Lordship will be
so good as to consider, that the sooner it is done my loss will be
the less.
  My wife and I present our respects to your Lordship, good
Lady Egmont and all your family.
  I am my Lord,
    Yr Lordship's most obedient & most humble Servt,
     G. CLOYNE.

236   TO PRIOR

Cloyne, Sept. 12, 1746

Dear Tom,
  I am just returned from a tour through my diocese of
130 miles, almost shaken to pieces.
  What you write of Bishop Stone's preferment is highly probable.
For myself, though his Excellency the Lord Lieutenant might have
a better opinion of me than I deserved ; yet it was not likely that
he would make an Irishman Primate.
  The truth is, I have a scheme of my own for this long time past,

in which I propose more satisfaction and enjoyment of myself than I could in that high station, which I neither solicited, nor so much as wished for.

It is true, the Primacy or Archbishopric of Dublin, if offered, might have tempted me by a greater opportunity of doing good ; but there is no other preferment in the kingdom to be desired upon any other account than a greater income, which would not tempt me to remove from Cloyne, and set aside my Oxford scheme ; which, though delayed by the illness of my son, yet I am as intent upon it, and as much resolved as ever.

I am glad you have a prospect of disposing of my debentures soon.   Adieu.

Your affectionate humble Servant,
G. Cloyne.

237   TO PERCIVAL

My Lord,

I have the honour of your Lordship's long after its date occasioned by a stop of the pacquets by contrary winds. As I am at a loss for an attorney to receive my mony in London, I must repeat my request that you will please to order payment at Corke or, if you find it more convenient, at Dublin, the place mentioned in the bond.

What English money according to the exchange then current was paid by me to make up the sum of 3000ll Irish I do not now remember having no memorial thereof ; nor is it material, since Irish money alone is the subject of the bond, the obligation whereof is to pay 3000ll Irish whatever may be the value thereof on the present foot of exchange ; and this wheresoever the mony is paid, whether in Ireland or in England. Your Lordship therefore will be no loser by ordering payment to be made here or in Dublin, from whence I can have it remitted to London at three daies sight. All which will be evident to your Lordship upon perusing the enclosed copy of the bond. In which you will observe that the principal (3000ll) as well as the interest (150ll) is expressly limited to be paid in Irish money, whatsoever the current value thereof may be at the time of payment.

If your Lordship has any doubt about this matter, it may be referred to your agent or any other person whom you shall please to appoint to peruse the original deed and bond, and send your Lordship his opinion thereupon. I pray God preserve your life and recover your health, which will be a most acceptable blessing to all your friends and particularly to

My Lord,

Yr Lordship's most obedient humble Servant,

GEORGE CLOYNE.

P.S.—If the payment be made here, I doubt not Mr. Brereton and Mr. Purcel can easily attend and receive the deeds and see everything done that you direct.

My wife and all here concur in best respects to yr Lordship and good Lady Egmont.

Cloyne, 7ber 23, 1746

238   TO GERVAIS

Reverend Sir,

Your letter, with news from the Castle, found me in bed, confined by the gout. In answer to which news I can only say, that I neither expect nor wish for any dignity higher than I am incumbered with at present. That which more nearly concerns me is my credit which I am glad to find so well supported by Admiral Lestock. I had promised you that before the first of November he would take King Lewis by the beard. Now Quimpercorrentin, Quimperlay, and Quimperen, being certain extreme parts or excrescencies of his kingdom, may not improperly be styled the beard of France. In proof of his having been there, he has plundered the wardrobes of the peasants, and imported a great number of old petticoats, waistcoats, wooden shoes, and one shirt, all which are actually sold at Cove : the shirt was bought by a man of this town for a groat. And if you won't believe me, come and believe your own eyes. In case you doubt either the facts or the reasonings, I am ready to make them good, being now well on my feet, and longing to triumph over you at Cloyne, which I hope will be soon. Meantime I conclude

Revd Mr. Dean

from faithful & obedient Servt

All here salute you   G. Cloyne

Cloyne, Nov. 8, 1746

239   TO PERCIVAL

Cloyne, 1ober 23, 1746

My Lord,

I received the favour of your Lordship's letter and am glad to find that all things are transacted to your liking. You will give me leave to observe that for Miss Dering's further security I believe it will be proper that Mr. Purcell should get her mortgage registered.

Certainly if my money was to remain in this kingdom, there is no person in whose hands I should place it so willingly as in your Lordship's. But considering the uncertain fate and exposed condition of this island I was desirous of securing a provision for my family upon the credit of a British parliament.

If the war continues it is to be apprehended that our late weak and unsuccessful enterprise on the French coast may provoke them to make reprisals on our defenceless coast. In which case if Providence should not interpose by winds and weather we must, humanly speaking, become an easy prey.

I am glad to hear Lady Egmont takes to the drinking of tar-water believing she may receive great benefit by it. I wish she would take it in small doses not exceeding $\frac{1}{4}$ of a pint, and of these 2 or 4 in the day, as her stomach can bear. For cholic or any inward complaints in the viscera she will do well to drink it warm.

I hope your Lordship's health is better. I pray God long preserve her Ladyship and your self to the comfort of your friends among whom you will alwaies allow a place to
My Lord.
Yr Lordship's most obedient & obliged Servant,
GEORGE CLOYNE.

My wife sends her best respects.

240   TO PRIOR

Jan. 24, 1747

You asked me in your last letter, whether we had not provided a house in Cloyne for the reception and cure of sick persons. By your query it seems there is some such report : but what gave rise to it could be no more than this, viz. that we are used to lodge a few stroling sick with a poor tenant or two in

Cloyne, and employ a poor woman or two to tend them, and supply them with a few necessaries from our house. This may be magnified (as things gather in the telling) into an hospital : but the truth is merely what I tell you. I wish you would send a political pamphlet now and then, with what news you hear. Is there any apprehension of an invasion upon Ireland ?

241   TO PRIOR

Dear Tom,
      Your manner of accounting for the weather seems to have reason in it ; and yet there still remains something unaccountable, viz. why there should be no rain in the regions mentioned. If the bulk, figure, situation, and motion of the earth are given, and the luminaries remain the same, should there not be a certain cycle of the seasons ever returning at certain periods ? To me it seems, that the exhalations perpetually sent up from the bowels of the earth have no small share in the weather ; that nitrous exhalations produce cold and frost ; and that the same causes which produce earthquakes within the earth produce storms above it. Such are the variable causes of our weather ; which, if it proceeded only from fixed and given causes, the changes thereof would be as regular as the vicissitudes of the days, or the return of eclipses. I have writ this extempore, *Valeat quantum valere potest.*
      In my last I mentioned my cousin's death. My brothers and I are his heirs at law. I know nothing of his circumstances. He has been captain of a man of war for about twenty years, and must have left something. It is true he always commanded great ships, which have the fewest opportunities of getting, his very first having been a sixty gun ship : but still, as I said, there must be something probably worth looking after. I would therefore be advised by you what course to take. Would it not be right to employ your friend the solicitor, Mr. Levinge, to enquire at the late Captain George Berkeley's house in Lisle street, and see what is become of his effects ? Also to examine whether he has left a Will, and what it contains ? If this be the right way, pray lose no time. Adieu, dear Tom.

                    Your affectionate humble Servant,
                              G. CLOYNE.
      Cloyne, Feb. 6, 1746/47

Dear Tom, Desire your friend Mr. Levinge, without delay, to enter a caveat, in my name, in Doctors' Commons, against any one's taking out administration.

242   TO PRIOR

Cloyne, Feb. 9, 1746/47

Dear Tom,

You ask me if I had no hints from England about the Primacy. I can only say, that last week I had a letter from a person of no mean rank who seemed to wonder that he could not find I had entertained any thoughts of the Primacy, while so many others of our bench were so earnestly contending for it. He added, that he hoped I would not take it ill if my friends wished me in that station. My answer was, that I am so far from soliciting, that I do not even wish for it ; that I do not think myself the fittest man for that high post ; and that therefore I neither have, nor ever will, ask it.

I hear it reported that my cousin died worth about eighteen thousand pounds. He had spent the summer at the Earl of Berkeley's hunting-seat in Wiltshire. He came to town in an ill state of health, which he hoped Dr. Mead would have set right, but was mistaken. Had I known his illness, perhaps it might have been better for him. The Earl of Berkeley's agent, one Mr. Young, who was also my cousin's agent, pretends to be executor, with another gentleman, one Mr. Brome. By all means take the readiest method, that some person whom you know at London gets a sight of the original Will; and you will do a good service to,

Dear Tom,

Your faithful Servant,
G. CLOYNE.

I am unknowing in these matters ; but think that the best advice how to proceed.

Cloyne, Feb. 10, 1746/47

Dear Tom,

In my other letter that comes to you this post, I forgot to say what I now think very necessary, viz. that you must be so good as to get your friend by all means to send a copy of the Will, written in a close hand, by post, without loss of time.

In a letter from England, which I told you came a week ago, it was said that several of our Irish bishops were earnestly contending for the Primacy. Pray who are they? I thought Bishop Stone was only talked of at present. I ask this question merely out of curiosity, and not from any interest, I assure you; for I am no man's rival or competitor in this matter. I am not in love with feasts, and crowds, and visits, and late hours, and strange faces, and a hurry of affairs often insignificant. For my own private satisfaction, I had rather be master of my time than wear a diadem. I repeat these things to you, that I may not seem to have declined all steps to the Primacy out of singularity, or pride, or stupidity, but from solid motives. As for the argument from the opportunity of doing good, I observe that duty obliges men in high stations not to decline occasions of doing good; but duty doth not oblige men to solicit such high stations. Adieu.

Yours,

G. CLOYNE.

Cloyne, Feb. 19, 1746/47

Dear Tom,

It was very agreeable to hear you had taken proper measures to procure a copy of my cousin's Will, and to enter the caveat.

The ballad you sent has mirth in it, with a political sting in the tail; but the speech of Van Haaren is excellent. I believe it Lord Chesterfield's.

We have at present, and for these two days past had, frost and some snow. Our military-men are at length sailed from Cork harbour. We hear they are designed for Flanders.

I must desire you to make, at leisure, the most exact and distinct inquiry you can into the characters of the Senior Fellows, as to their behaviour, temper, piety, parts, and learning ; also to make a list of them, with each man's character annexed to his name. I think it of so great consequence to the public to have a good Provost that I would willingly look before hand, and stir a little, to prepare an interest, or at least to contribute my mite, where I properly may, in favour of a worthy man, to fill that post when it shall become vacant.

Dr. Hales, in a letter to me, has made very honourable mention of you. It would not be amiss if you should correspond with him, especially for the sake of granaries and prisons. Adieu.

Yours,

GEORGE CLOYNE.

245   TO PRIOR

Cloyne, Feb. 20, 1746/47

Dear Tom,

Though the situation of the earth with respect to the sun changes, yet the changes are fixed and regular : if therefore this were the cause of the variation of winds, the variation of the winds must be regular, i.e. regularly returning in a cycle. To me it seems that the variable cause of the variable winds are the subterraneous fires, which, constantly burning, but altering their operation according to the various quantity or kind of combustible materials they happen to meet with, send up exhalations more or less of this or that species ; which, diversely fermenting in the atmosphere, produce uncertain variable winds and tempests. This, if I mistake not, is the true solution of that crux.

As to the papers about petrifications which I sent to you and Mr. Simon, I do not well remember the contents. But be you so good as to look them over, and show them to some other of your Society ; and if, after this, you shall think them worth publishing in your collections, you may do as you please : otherwise I would not have things hastily and carelessly written thrust into public view.

As to your query, there were two mad women recovered, it seems, by a method we made use of, though not, as you have been told, by sweating. When you come, you shall know the particulars.

Yours,

GEORGE CLOYNE

Cloyne, March 5, 1746/47

My good Lord,

Your Lordship's letter with which I was favoured last post needed no apology. I wish it may have come time enough to be of use to the patient. Her distemper being of so long continuance arrived to so great a height, and nature spent and worn out by different courses of medicine, she cannot hope for a perfect recovery without length of time and a more attentive care than people commonly have of their health. I have nevertheless reason to hope she will find in a few months great relief from a constant drinking of tar water joined with a prudent regimen and abstinence from all other medicines.

I would advise that at first her tar water be made by stirring a gallon of water in a quart of tar strongly with a flat stick for the space only of two minutes ; and that she take of this daily a pint and a half in six glasses, a quarter of a pint in each glass. She may drink it cold or warm as she best likes upon tryal. But she may drink it first cold, and if this agrees with her, continue it so. It should be drunk night and morning and at an hour's distance at least from her meals. I verily think this course and a proper regimen of early hours, light nourishing food, and gentle exercise in good air will by the blessing of God give her great relief.

Her disorder is nervous in the highest degree, and nervous cases are slowest and most difficult to cure. However I do not think this case hopeless having known those symptoms of pain and stiffeness in the head and neck, terrours and agonies of mind, trembling and giddiness, and indeed all sorts of hysterical disorders to have been removed by tar water. I have also known that weakening wasting disorder peculiar to the female sex, which is often the cause and often the effect of low spirits to have been cured by the same medicine, which both supplies spirits and strengthens the tone of the vessels.

I cannot indeed say that I have known all the above named symptoms together in so high a degree in one and the same person. But I have known very high hypocondriac disorders that would yield to no other medicine removed by tar water. Some cures of this kind your Lordship may find in Mr. Prior's *Narrative*, particularly if you give yourself the trouble of looking into the case of John Ussher Esquire of Lismore. . . .

. . . . After her stomach is by custom reconciled a little to the tar water she will be able to take it a little stronger (made so by a minute or two longer stirring) and in greater quantity, perhaps so far as one quart per diem, which need not be exceeded. —If her stomach could bear it at first as strong as four minutes stirring would make it, it would be so much the better. I shall be glad to know what success the patient finds when she has continued this course for a month or six weeks. And on any occasion where your Lordship thinks I may be of use, you may freely command him who is with all respect

My Lord,
>   Yr Lordship's affectionate Brother & obedient Servant,
>   GEORGE CLOYNE.

P.S. Drams are often known to produce the most desperate & incurable hysterics, wch (if this should happen to be the patient's case) ought by all means to be laid aside, though not altogether at once, but gradually ; as soon as possible with safety. This may be whispered to her friend.

247   TO PERCIVAL

Cloyne, March 14, 1746/47

My Lord,
Nothing but the necessity I am under could tempt me to give your Lordship this trouble of employing you in so small a matter and so much beneath you, but to me and my family of no small concern. Last summer I wrote to Naples, and we have since ransacked all the music shops in Ireland, without being able to get one good string for the violincello : this is one bad effect of the present war which interrupts our commerce with Italy. The strings we get break as fast as they are put on, so that for several months past it has been impossible for my children to practice, and without practice they will be in danger of losing an art which has cost them much pains, and me a great deal of mony. It will therefore be a very seasonable and obliging benefaction if your Lordship will be so good as to send me by post one dozen of first and one dozen of second strings for the four stringed bass or violincello, enclosed in four covers, six in

each. I depend upon your Lordship's so often experienced goodness, that you will pardon the freedom of this address from
    My Lord,
            Yr most obedient & obliged humble Servant,
                G. CLOYNE.

P.S.—Being unwilling that the Princess Caroline should suffer
or tar water lose its credit I took the liberty in my last to desire
yr Lordship to give some hints to Mr. Schutz for the right way
of using it to which I must now add that as her stomach may
happen to be squeamish, it will not be amiss to begin with tar
water made by only two minute's stirring, and when she is
accustomed it may be given stronger i.e. made by stirring it
3 or 4 minutes.

248   TO PRIOR

Cloyne, March 22, 1746/47

Dear Tom,
        There is another query which arises on the Will, viz.
whether a mortgage be not a freehold, and whether it can be
bequeathed without three witnesses? This, and the two other
queries of the residue, &c., I would have stated to Mr. Kelly my
wife's cousin. He is a very sensible man, and would consider
the matter, as a friend, more attentively than those who, of greater
name, might offer their first thoughts. Pray give him the usual
fee for the best lawyer; and if he refuses to take it, tell him you
cannot take his advice if he does not take his fee.
        As to what you say, that the Primacy would have been a
glorious thing; for my part I do not see (all things considered)
the glory of wearing the name of Primate in these days, or of
getting so much money; a thing every tradesman in London
may get if he pleases. I should not choose to be Primate in pity
to my children; and for doing good to the world, I imagine
I may upon the whole do as much in a lower station.
                Adieu, Dear Tom.
                        Yours affectionately,
                            G. CLOYNE.

249   TO BEARCROFT

[before 10 April, 1747]

Revd. Sir
      Two hundred pounds of the money contributed towards
the College intended at Bermuda I have left many years lodged
in the Bank of Messrs. Hoare and Arnold in Fleet Street designing
to return it (as I had already done by other Sums) to the Donors
when known.   But as these continue still unknown, and there
is no likelyhood of my ever knowing them, I think the properest
use that can be made of that sum is to place it in the hands of
your Society for propagating the Gospel, to be employ'd by them
in the furtherance of their good work, in such manner as to them
shall seem most useful.   If the Society thinks fit, I believe fifty
pounds of it might be usefully employ'd in purchasing the most
approved writings of the Church of England, to which I would
have added the Earl of Clarendons History ofthe Civil wars, and
the whole sent as a benefaction to Harvard College at Cambridge
near Boston, new England, as a proper means to inform their
judgment and dispose them to think better of our church.
      I am Revd. Sir
                  Yr. faithful humble servant
                        G: CLOYNE

250   TO BEARCROFT

Cloyne [? 8 July 1747]
Revd Sir
      I begin to apprehend as you do that a present coming
from your Society may be regarded with some jealousy or dis-
trust.   But if the books come as a benefaction procured by me
for the Use of Harvard College I doubt not they will meet with
a good reception having formerly made that college a present
of some books of my own when I was in those parts, and since
my return having sent them others as a benefaction procured
20

from my friends all which were very thankfully received. The
books given from my self were ancient Greek Authors which I
found they wanted. Those sent afterwards were Latin books
of Literature. These make way for another benefaction which
they seemed to hope and wish for upon receiving the Last. And
I have reason to think the books undernamed (if the Society
approve thereof) may not improperly be admitted in such benefaction. I do not therefore think it necessary to trouble Governour
Shirley or to take any other steps in this matter. As to the method
of entering the benefaction in the books of the Society I leave
that to you having no objection to what you offer on that head.
I sincerely congratulate with you on the recovery of yr health
and wish you the continuance of it being very truly.

> Revd Sir
> Your most faithful and obedient Servant
> G: CLOYNE

P.S. As you intimated a desire that I should name some
more books I have ventured to set down the following, with due
submission nevertheless to the judgment of the venerable Society.
Hooker, Chillingworth, the Sermons of *Barrow*, *Tillotson* Sharp
& Clarke, Scot's Christian life, Pearson on the creed, Burnet on
the 39 Articles, Burnet's history of the Reformation, A: B: Spots-
wood's history of the church of Scotland, Clarendon's history,
Prideaux's connection, Cave's historia literaria eccles: Hammond's
annotations, Pool's Synopsis Critic:, the Patres Apostolici published by le Clerc with the dissertations of Pearson &c in the
epistles of S: Ignatius. These I guess will amount to about thirty
pounds ; if approved of, the Society will be pleased to add as
many more as will make up the fifty pounds, or otherwise they
will be pleased to name them all.

251   TO PERCIVAL

Cloyne, 1ober 3, 1747

My Lord,
       Ever since I was favoured with yr Lordship's letter I have
expected to see Mr. Purcell with the draught of the new conveyance
such as I agreed to sign, which I was ready to do when called on,

but he has not yet been with me.   I was much obliged for the hints
your Lordship gave me on the present state of our affairs, which
indeed are in a bad situation, but I doubt in no worse than we
deserve, but as our enemies do not seem to be better than we
are, it is to be hoped [Pr]ovidence will not suffer them to trample
upon us, and our late successes at sea are I think a proof of
this.   It should seem we are designed mutually to punish each
other.

It would give me great pleasure to hear of your and Lady
[Eg]mont's improvement in health.   But as this season is very
severe, I beg leave to observe that your Lordship cannot be too
[ca]reful to guard against the cold, which is very apt to increase
nervous disorders.

I cannot conclude my letter without returning my thanks for
the account you were pleased to send me of Mr. West.   Since
I read his excellent book, I have met with another very well writ
treatise of Mr. Lyttleton's, who (I understand) is one [of] the lords
of the treasury.   As these gentlemen cannot be supposed to write
out of interest, they are so much the fitter to draw their pens in
defence of Christianity, as they have done to very good
purpose.   Our best respects wait on yr Lordship and good Lady
Egmont.

I am yr Lordship's most obedient Servt,
G. CLOYNE.

252   TO PERCIVAL (*fils*)

My dear Lord,

I think my self obliged to condole with your Lordship on
the death of a father who honoured me with his friendship for
about forty years, and whose life adorned every part of that
private path he chose to walk in.   At the same time I console
myself with the share I hope I have in the good graces of the son,
and congratulate your Lordship on coming to an honour and
estate that may enable you to make a more conspicuous figure
in that active scene of life to which your genius leads with so
remarkable success.   The late Earl your father was a right honest
man and a good Christian.   Your Lordship by adding these
qualities to those of a Courtier and Politician will create a new
character, that will render you beloved by God and man, which

that you, your Lady and family may alwaies be is most sincerely
wished by
    My Lord,
        Your Lordship's most faithful and most obedient Servant,
            GEORGE CLOYNE.

    P.S.—I must beg your Lordship to present my best respects
and complements of condolance to the good Lady Dowager your
mother,
    Cloyne, May 14, 1748

253   TO PRIOR

                        Cloyne, Feb. 2, 1749
    Three days ago we received the box of pictures. The two
men's heads with ruffs are well done ; the third is a copy, and
ill-coloured : they are all Flemish : so is the woman, which is
also very well painted, though it hath not the beauty and freedom
of an Italian pencil. The two Dutch pictures, containing animals,
are well done as to the animals : but the human figures and sky
are ill done. The two pictures of ruins are very well done, and
are Italian. My son William had already copied two other
pictures of the same kind, and by the same hand. He and his sister
are both employed in copying pictures at present ; which shall be
dispatched as soon as possible ; after which they will set about
some of yours. Their stint, on account of health, is an hour and
half a day for painting. So I doubt two months will not suffice
for copying : but no time shall be lost, and great care taken of
your pictures, for which we hold ourselves much obliged.
    Our Round Tower stands where it did ; but a little stone
arched vault on the top was cracked, and must be repaired : the
bell also was thrown down, and broke its way through three
boarded stories, but remains entire. The door was shivered into
many small pieces, and dispersed ; and there was a stone forced
out of the wall. The whole damage, it is thought, will not amount
to twenty pounds. The thunder-clap was by far the greatest that
I ever heard in Ireland.

Cloyne, August 23, 1749

Reverend Sir,

I am obliged for the account you have sent me of the prosperous estate of learning in your College of Newhaven. I approve of the regulations made there, and am particularly pleased to find your sons have made such a progress as appears from their elegant address to me in the Latin tongue. It must indeed give me a very sensible satisfaction to hear that my weak endeavours have been of some use and service to that part of the world.

I have two letters of yours at once on my hands to answer, for which business of various kinds must be my apology.

As to the first, wherein you enclosed a small pamphlet relating to tar-water, I can only say in behalf of those points in which the ingenious author seems to differ from me, that I advance nothing which is not grounded on experience, as may be seen at large in Mr. Prior's *Narrative of the Effects of Tar-Water*, printed three or four years ago, and which may be supposed to have reached America.

For the rest, I am glad to find a spirit towards learning prevail in those parts, particularly New York where you say a College is projected which has my best wishes. At the same time I am sorry that the condition of Ireland containing such numbers of poor, uneducated people, for whose sake charity schools are erecting throughout the kingdom, obligeth us to draw charities from England so far are we from being able to extend our bounty to New York a country in proportion much richer than our own. But as you are pleased to desire my advice upon this undertaking, I send the following hints to be enlarged and improved by your own judgment.

I would not advise the applying to England for Charters or Statutes (which might cause great trouble expense and delay), but to do the business quietly within themselves.

I believe it may suffice to begin with a President and two Fellows. If they can procure but three fit persons, I doubt not the College from the smallest beginnings would soon grow considerable. I should conceive good hopes were you at the head of it.

Let them by all means supply themselves out of the seminarys in New England.   For I am very apprehensive none can be got in Old England (who are willing to go) worth sending.

Let the Greek and Latin classics be well taught.   Be this the first care as to learning.   But the principal care must be good life and morals to which (as well as to study) early hours and temperate meals will much conduce.

If the terms for Degrees are the same as in Oxford & Cambridge, this would give credit to the College, and pave the way for admitting their graduates *ad eundem* in the English Universities.

Small premiums in books, or distinctions in habit may prove useful encouragements to the students.

I would advise that the building be regular, plain and cheap, and that each student have a small room (about ten feet square) to himself.

I recommended this nascent seminary to an English bishop to try what might be done there.   But by his answer it seems the Colony is judged rich enough to educate its own youth.

Colleges from small beginnings grow great by subsequent bequests and benefactions.   A small matter will suffice to set one agoing.   And when this is once well done, there is no doubt it will go on and thrive.   The chief concern must be to set out in a good method, and introduce from the very first a good taste into the Society.   For this end its principal expense should be in making a handsome provision for the President and Fellows.

I have thrown together these few crude thoughts for you to ruminate upon and digest in your own judgment, and propose from yourself, as you see convenient.

My correspondence with patients who drink tar-water obliges me to be less punctual in corresponding with my friends.   But I shall be alwaies glad to hear from you.   My sincere good wishes and prayers attend you in all your laudable undertakings.

I am, your faithful, humble Servant,

G. CLOYNE.

255   TO JOHNSON

Cloyne, July 17, 1750

Rev. Sir,

A few months ago I had an opportunity of writing to you and Mr. Honyman by an inhabitant of Rhode Island government.

I would not nevertheless omit the present occasion of saluting you, and letting you know that it gave me great pleasure to hear from Mr. Bourk, a passenger from those parts, that a late sermon of yours at Newhaven hath had a very good effect in reconciling several to the church. I find also by a letter from Mr. Clap that learning continues to make notable advances in your College. This gives me great satisfaction. And that God may bless your worthy endeavours, and crown them with success, is the sincere prayer of,

   Rev. Sir,
     Your faithful Brother and humble Servant,
      G. CLOYNE.

P.S.—I hope your ingenious sons are still an ornament to Yale College, and tread in their father's steps.

256 TO CLAP

Revd. Sir,

  Mr. Bourk, a passenger from Newhaven, hath lately put into my hands the letter you favoured me with, and at the same time the agreeable pecimens of learning which it enclosed, for which you have my sincere thanks. By them I find a considerable progress made in astronomy and other academical studies in your College, in the welfare and prosperity whereof I sincerely interest myself, and recommending you to God's good providence I conclude with my prayers and best wishes for your Society,

   Revd. Sir,
     Your faithful, humble Servant,
      G. CLOYNE.

Cloyne, July 17th, 1750

257 TO BRACKSTONE

        Cloyne, Jan. 5th, 1750/51

Sir,

  In my opinion the acid extracted from tar hath no more vertue than any other common acid. The acid of tar being mixed with it's fine volatile oyle doth form a soap of a most subtil and penetrating nature fitted to remove obstructions and scour the smallest capillaries ; but being separated from the oyle, and left by it self it no longer retains it's saponaceous medicinal nature. If tar-water be nauseous it is less so than most other medicines ; moreover by use it becomes easy to take, and even agreeable to many. For your fuller satisfaction concerning the acid of tar I refer you to Doctor Linden's treatise on Selter water p. 302. Tar water taken copiously and constantly (i.e. a pint, or pint and half, or a quart per diem) is I am persuaded the best medicine in the world against the gout.

I am Sir,
Yr most humble Servt,
G. CLOYNE.

258   TO BENSON

Cloyne, March 8, 1751

My dear Lord,

I was a man retired from the amusement of politics, visits, and what the world calls pleasure. I had a little friend, educated always under mine own eye, whose painting delighted me, whose music ravished me, and whose lively, gay spirit was a continual feast. It has pleased God to take him hence. God, I say, in mercy hath deprived me of this pretty, gay plaything. His parts and person, his innocence and piety, his particularly uncommon affection for me, had gained too much upon me. Not content to be fond of him, I was vain of him. I had set my heart too much upon him—more perhaps than I ought to have done upon anything in this world.

Thus much suffer me, in the overflowings of my soul, to say to your Lordship, who, though distant in place, are much nearer my heart than any of my neighbours.

Adieu, my dear Lord, and believe me, with the utmost esteem and affection,

Your faithful, humble Servant,
G. CLOYNE.

Cloyne, 30th of March 1751

. . . They are going to print at Glasgow two editions at once, in quarto and in folio, of all Plato's works, in most magnificent types. This work should be encouraged. It would be right to mention it as you have opportunity. . . .

260　TO JOHNSON

Cloyne, July 25, 1751

Revd. Sir,

I would not let Mr. Hall depart without a line from me in acknowledgment of your letter which he put into my hands.

As for Mr. Hutchinson's writings, I am not acquainted with them. I live in a remote corner, where many modern things escape me. Only this I can say, that I have observed that author to be mentioned as an enthusiast, which gave me no prepossession in his favour.

I am glad to find by Mr. Clap's letter, and the specimens of literature inclosed in his pacquet, that learning continues to make a progress in Yale College ; and hope that virtue and Christian charity keep pace with it.

The letters which you and Mr. Clap say you had written, in answer to my last, never came into my hands. I am glad to hear, by Mr. Hall, of the good health and condition of yourself and family. I pray God to bless you and yours, and prosper your good endeavours.

I am, Rev. Sir,

Your faithful Friend and humble Servant,

GEORGE CLOYNE.

261 TO CLAP

Cloyne, July 25, 1751

Reverend Sir,

The daily increase of learning and religion in your seminary of Yale College give me very sensible pleasure and an ample recompense for my poor endeavours to further those good ends.

May God's Providence continue to prosper and cherish the rudiments of good education which have hitherto taken root and thrive so well, under your auspicious care and government.

I snatch this opportunity given me by Mr. Hall to acknowledge the receipt of your letter which he put into my hands together with the learned specimens that accompanied it, and to assure you that
I am very sincerely Revd. Sir,
                Yr faithful well wisher and humble Servant,
                        G. CLOYNE.

P.S. The letter wch you mention as written two months before your last never came to my hands.

262 TO PRIOR

Cloyne, August 6, 1751

Dear Tom,

Brother Will. in a few daies proposes being in Dublin. He brings with him two debentures of mine drawn some time ago, I think in 1749. I must desire you to receive their value at the treasury. He also carries with him a note of mine for fifteen pounds upon Gleadowe, which you will put into his bank to my credit. The enclosed sum of 846 pds. 15 shill. you may leave in Alderman Dawson's bank, as likewise the value of my two debentures, sending me his note for the whole, and seeing it placed in his books to my credit.

My intention was to have purchased ten debentures with this sum, but am at a loss in what banker's hands to leave them. Do you know any safe bank that would be at the trouble to keep my debentures and receive their produce, letting the whole lye in their hands till such time as I may hereafter have occasion to draw for it? Perhaps if you know Mr. Clements of the treasury you may get him to let my debentures lye in his bank and give his receipt for them ; in which case I would have them all ensured. Alderman Dawson, I doubt, is too wealthy to take such trouble on him. But if nothing of all this can be done, you will be so good as to place them in Gleadowe's bank, taking his receipt and directing him to receive the interest. It is the bank I have dealt with above thirty years, and if you think it as secure as another I should not desire to change it. There hath been some talk as if the late change in our cash (being mostly Spanish) might cause a run on some of our banks. If there be any likelyhood of this, you'll be so good as to act accordingly. Instead of the books I returned pray send the book called *L'esprit des lois* by the Baron Montesquieu.

Adieu dear Tom.

Yr affect. humble Servt,

G. CLOYNE.

263 TO ARCHDALE

[*c.* 1 November 1751]

For the particulars of your last favour I give you thanks. I send the above bill to clear what you have expended on my account, and also ten guineas beside ; which is my contribution towards the monument which I understand is intended for our deceased friend. Yesterday, though ill of the cholic, yet I could not forbear sketching out the inclosed. I wish it did justice to his character. Such as it is, I submit it to you and your friends.

Cloyne, Nov. 3, 1751

Revd Sir,

In the hurry in which I wrote the inscription sent in my last I forgot to mention the Dublin Society, which I have done in that I now enclose, and have added two or three punct[ums] to distinguish the periods.

I am yr faithful Servt,
G. CLOYNE.

I have chosen to do this in Latin as the universal and most lasting tongue.

Cloyne, November 22, 1751

Reverend Sir,

You will see by the inclosed paragraph, from *Faulkner's Journal* for Saturday, November the 16th, that the late Bishop of Clogher had left gold medals for encouraging the study of Greek in the College. Now I desire you will do me the favour to inquire what the value of those medals was, and in whose custody they were left, and let me know. Certainly if I had been informed of this, I should not have annually, for eighteen years past, have given two gold medals for the same purpose, through the hands of our friend Mr. Prior, who did constantly distribute them, and charge them to my account. I must entreat you to get the dye for those medals, which I left in Mr. Prior's hands, and secure it for me.

There is also an account between Mr. Prior and me, of which I must desire you to get a copy from the executor, and send it inclosed to myself.

I must further trouble you to secure for me two small books which I lent Mr. Prior, and cannot be had. One of them is a French translation of *Siris*; the other was a small tract relative to the same subject, printed in America. There are, I doubt not, many letters and memoirs relating to cures done by tar-water among Mr. Prior's papers, which I hope you will take care shall not be lost. What trouble you are at in these matters will oblige,

Reverend Sir,

Your faithful humble Servant,
G. CLOYNE.

P.S. All here send their compliments. The pictures borrowed from Mr. Prior are this day boxed up, and shall be sent on Monday to Corke, to the Dublin carrier.

266   TO ARCHDALE

Cloyne, Dec. 8, 1751

Rev. Sir,

This is to desire you may publish the inscription I sent you in Faulkner's paper. But say nothing of the author.

I must desire you to cause the letters G. B., being the initial letters of my name, to be engraved on the dye of the gold medal, at the bottom beneath the race-horse ; whereby mine will be distinguished from medals given by others.

I am, Reverend Sir,

Your faithful humble Servant,
G. CLOYNE.

267   TO ARCHDALE

Cloyne, Dec. 22, 1751

I thank you for the care you have taken in publishing the inscription so correctly, as likewise for your trouble in getting G. B. engraved on the plain, at the bottom of the medal. When that is done, you may order two medals to be made, and given as usual. I would have only two made by my dye : the multi-plying of premiums lessens their value.

If my inscription is to take place, let me know before it is engraved ; I may perhaps make some trifling alteration.

Cloyne, Jan. 7, 1752

I here send you enclosed the inscription, with my last amendments. In the printed copy *si quis* was one word ; it had better be two, divided, as in this. There are some other small changes which you will observe. The bishop of Meath was for having somewhat in English : accordingly, I subjoin an English addition, to be engraved in a different character, and in continued lines (as it is written) beneath the Latin. The bishop writes that contributions come in slowly, but that near one hundred guineas are got. Now, it should seem that if the first plan, rated at two hundred guineas, was reduced or altered, there might be a plain, neat, monument erected for one hundred guineas, and so (as the proverb directs) the coat be cut according to the cloth.

269   TO GERVAIS

Cloyne, April 6, 1752

Good Mr. Dean,

Your letter by last post was very agreeable : but the trembling hand with which it was written is a drawback from the satisfaction I should otherwise have had in hearing from you. If my advice had been taken, you would have escaped so many miserable months in the gout, and the bad air of Dublin. But advice against inclination is seldom successful. Mine was very sincere, though I must own a little interested : for we often wanted your enlivening company to dissipate the gloom of Cloyne. This I look on as enjoying France at second hand. I wish any thing but the gout could fix you among us. But bustle and intrigue and great affairs have and will, as long as you exist on this globe, fix your attention. For my own part, I submit to years and infirmities. My views in this world are mean and narrow : it is a thing in which I have small share, and which ought to give me small concern. I abhor business, and especially to have to do with great persons and great affairs, which I leave to such as you who delight in them and are fit for them. The evening of life I choose to pass in a quiet retreat. Ambitious projects, intrigues and quarrels of statesmen, are things I have formerly been amused with ; but they now seem to me a vain, fugitive dream. If you thought as I do, we should have more of your company, and you less of the gout. We have not those transports of you Castle-hunters ; but our lives are more calm and serene. We do, however, long to see you open your budget of politics by our fireside. My wife and all here salute you, and send you, instead of compliments, their best sincere wishes for your health and safe return. The part you take in my son's recovery is very obliging to us all, and particularly to, &c.,

Your Reverence's most faithful Brother and obedient Servant,
G. CLOYNE.

270   TO FAULKNER

[1752]
There is, at present, while I am writing, a most remarkable case here at Cloyne of a poor soldier in a dropsy, whose belly was swoln to a most immoderate size. He said he had been five months in a hospital at Dublin, and having tried other methods in vain, left it to avoid being tapped. It is a fortnight since he came to Cloyne, during which time he hath drank two quarts of tar-water every day. His belly is now quite reduced ; his appetite and sleep, which were gone, are restored ; he gathered strength every moment ; and he who was despaired of, seems to be quite out of danger, both to himself and to all who see him. It is remarkable that upon drinking the tar-water, he voided several worms of a very extraordinary size. This medicine which is observed to make some persons costive is but one of several instances, wherein the dropsy hath been cured by tar-water, which I never knew to fail in any species of that malady.

NOTE

A communication from Berkeley to Dr. Hans Sloane, at that time Secretary of the Royal Society, has been discovered recently by Dr. E. St. J. Brooks among the Sloane MSS. (No. 4040, f. 176) in the British Museum. It is in the form of a letter, in Latin, and is addressed ' Clarissime Vir ' and signed ' Tui observantissimus G. B.' It is dated ' e Musaeo in Trin. Coll. Dub. Junii 11. 1706,' and is thus the earliest extant Berkeley letter. Hitherto it has been attributed to Provost George Brown who died in 1699, and it was identified as Berkeley's by Dr. Brooks. The greater part of it is, in substance, Berkeley's paper ' De Aestu Aeris,' in criticism of Dr. R. Mead's *De imperio solis ac lunae in corpora humana* (1704). Berkeley invites Sloane to publish it in the *Transactions* of the Royal Society. He did not do so, and Berkeley published it in his *Miscellanea Mathematica* (1707). See Vol. IV, pp. 209–12. A fuller account of the letter will be included in Vol. IX.

Printed in Great Britain by
Thomas Nelson (Printers) Ltd, London and Edinburgh